Sociology
a
Post

D0370726

SOCIOLOGY
AFTER
POSTMODERNISM

edited by
David Owen

SAGE Publications
London • Thousand Oaks • New Delhi

Introduction and editorial selection © David Owen 1997
Chapter 1 © Malcolm Waters 1997
Chapter 2 © Samantha Ashenden 1997
Chapter 3 © Paul Connolly 1997
Chapter 4 © Nigel South 1997
Chapter 5 © Alan Hunt 1997
Chapter 6 © Ralph Schroeder 1997
Chapter 7 © Douglas Kellner 1997
Chapter 8 © Arlene Stein 1997
Chapter 9 © Sean Watson and Peter Jowers 1997
Chapter 10 © Thomas Osborne 1997
Chapter 11 © Mitchell Dean 1997

First published 1997

SAGE Publications Ltd
6 Bonhill Street
London EC2A 4PU

SAGE Publications Inc.
2455 Teller Road
Thousand Oaks, California 91320

SAGE Publications India Pvt Ltd
32, M-Block Market
Greater Kailash – I
New Delhi 110 048

British Library Cataloguing in Publication data

A catalogue record for this book is available
from the British Library.

ISBN 0 8039 7514 7
ISBN 0 8039 7515 5 (pbk)

Library of Congress catalog record available

Typeset by Mayhew Typesetting, Rhayader, Powys
Printed in Great Britain by Redwood Books,
Trowbridge, Wiltshire

Contents

Notes on Contributors vii

INTRODUCTION

The Postmodern Challenge to Sociology 1
David Owen

CLASS

1 Inequality after Class 23
 Malcolm Waters

GENDER

2 Feminism, Postmodernism and the Sociology of Gender 40
 Samantha Ashenden

RACE AND ETHNICITY

3 Racism and Postmodernism: Towards a Theory of Practice 65
 Paul Connolly

CRIMINOLOGY AND DEVIANCE

4 Late-Modern Criminology: 'Late' as in 'Dead' or 'Modern' as
 in 'New'? 81
 Nigel South

LAW

5 Law, Politics and the Social Sciences 103
 Alan Hunt

SCIENCE AND TECHNOLOGY

6 The Sociology of Science and Technology after Relativism 124
 Ralph Schroeder

CULTURE AND MEDIA

7 Social Theory and Cultural Studies 138
 Douglas Kellner

SEXUALITY

8   Sex after 'Sexuality': From Sexology to Post-Structuralism   158
    Arlene Stein

AFFECTIVITY

9   Somatology: Sociology and the Visceral   173
    Sean Watson and Peter Jowers

MEDICINE AND THE BODY

10 Body Amnesia – Comments on Corporeality   188
    Thomas Osborne

HISTORY AND POLITICS

11 Sociology after Society   205
    Mitchell Dean

Notes on Contributors

Samantha Ashenden teaches in the Department of Politics and Sociology, Birkbeck College, University of London. She is currently working on questions of law, science and democracy and on the relationship between the critical theory of the Frankfurt School and genealogical modes of criticism. She has published on issues of governmentality and child sexual abuse, and is currently co-editing *Foucault Contra Habermas* (with David Owen) and authoring *Child Abuse and the State: Social Knowledges and the Ambivalence of Liberal Reason.*

Paul Connolly is a Lecturer in Sociology at the University of Ulster. His current research interests lie in understanding the articulation of discourses on 'race', gender, class and sexuality in young children's lives. He has written a number of articles and is the author of two forthcoming books: *Racism, Gender Identities and Young Children* and (with Barry Troyna) *Researching Racism in Education: Politics, Theory and Practice.*

Mitchell Dean is Senior Lecturer in Sociology at Macquarie University in Sydney. He has contributed to English, Australian and North American social science journals on theoretical, historical and applied perspectives on governmental and ethical practices. He is the author of *Governmentality* (forthcoming, Sage), *Critical and Effective Histories* (1994) and *The Constitution of Poverty* (1991). He is also editing a volume with Barry Hindess called *Governing Australia.*

Alan Hunt holds Professorships in the Departments of Law and Sociology at the Carleton University in Ottawa, having previously lectured in England. He has written widely on sociological and legal themes. He is the author of *Governance of the Consuming Passions: A History of Sumptuary Regulation* (1996); *Foucault and Law* (with Gary Wickham, 1994), *Explorations in Law and Society* (1993), *Reading Dworkin Critically* (1992), *Marx and Engels on Law* (with Maureen Cain, 1979) and *The Sociological Movement in Law* (1978).

Peter Jowers is Senior Lecturer in Politics at the University of the West of England. He has published several articles in the areas of philosophy and contemporary music including a forthcoming article 'Festival Culture and the New Cycle of Political Protest in Britain'.

Douglas Kellner is Professor of Philosophy at the University of Texas at Austin and is author of many books on social theory, politics, history, and culture, including *Camera Politica: The Politics and Ideology of*

Contemporary Hollywood Film (with Michael Ryan), *Critical Theory, Marxism, and Modernity, Jean Baudrillard: From Marxism to Postmodernism and Beyond,* (with Steven Best), *Postmodern Theory: Critical Interrogations, Television and the Crisis of Democracy, The Persian Gulf TV War, Media Culture,* and *The Postmodern Adventure* (with Steven Best). He is currently working on the impact of new informational and entertainment technologies on society and culture.

Thomas Osborne is a Lecturer in Sociology at the University of Bristol. Most of his published work to date has focused on the history of medical rationalities in Britain, and on questions of 'governmentality'. He is co-editor of *Foucault and Political Reason* (1996) and is currently writing a book on social theory and the ethics of enlightenment.

Ralph Schroeder is a Lecturer in Sociology at the Royal Holloway University of London. He is the author of *Max Weber and the Sociology of Culture* (1992) and *Possible Worlds: The Social Dynamic of Virtual Reality Technology* (1996).

Nigel South is a Reader in Sociology at the University of Essex, England. His current research interests include comparative criminology, crimes against the environment, and drug cultures. Recent books include *Eurodrugs* (with V. Ruggiero, 1995), *Drugs, Crime and Criminal Justice* (edited, 1995) and *The Social Construction of Social Policy* (edited with C. Samson, 1996).

Arlene Stein is an Assistant Professor of Sociology at the University of Oregon. She is the author of *Sex and Sensibility: Stories of a Lesbian Generation* (1997) and numerous essays on gender/sexuality, cultural sociology and social movements.

Malcolm Waters is Professor of Sociology at the University of Tasmania. He has published widely on issues of class and contemporary societal transformation. He is the author or co-author of *Postmodernization, Modern Sociological Theory, Globalization, The Death of Class* and *Daniel Bell*. He is working on a new book for Sage with Stephen Crook and Jan Pakulski provisionally titled *Orderings: Solidarity and Stability in a Postmodernizing World*.

Sean Watson is Lecturer in Sociology at the University of the West England. He has published on policing and social theory and in particular the sociology of emotion. He is the author of the forthcoming book *The Emotions of Social Control: A Study and Theory of Police Paranoia*.

INTRODUCTION

The Postmodern Challenge to Sociology

David Owen

This is not an apocalyptic text. It does not seek to proclaim the death of sociology. Rather, it assembles an overview of current transformations in, and of, sociology by attending to several of its main domains in the light of the 'postmodern' challenge to contemporary sociology. The question posed to the contributors to this collection with respect to their specific areas of interest is straightforward: in what ways, given the 'postmodern' challenge, can the practice of sociology best go on? Consequently, this volume can be approached as an ensemble of distinct voices engaged in an ongoing set of arguments which cross, entangle and fold into each other concerning, on the one hand, the character of sociology and, on the other hand, the nature of the postmodern challenge to sociology. These arguments give rise to a plurality of positions in contemporary sociological discourse and this volume is no exception to this condition; it is these arguments, however, which provide a central site for reflection on the state of the discipline.

In this context, this introduction takes up two tasks. First, it seeks to provide some reflective distance on this double debate concerning the character of sociology and the postmodern challenge to sociology by offering some brief historical and theoretical reflections on the emergence and the development of sociology and its relationship to the themes of 'the social' and the 'modern'. Secondly, it attempts to deploy this reflective distance in specifying the diverse understandings of the postmodern challenge to sociology manifest in contemporary sociological discourse and, more particularly, in this collection of chapters on the future of sociology. Readers familiar with, or uninterested in, the historical conditions of emergence of sociology may wish to skip straight to the second, more contemporary, section.

Sociology, the social and the 'modern'

The historical conditions of possibility of sociology as an intellectual enterprise can be traced to the reconceptualization of society which emerges alongside the development of the modern theory of the state in European political thought during the late seventeenth and eighteenth centuries in terms of 'the erosion of the distinctively political': 'The basic concept pitted

against the political was "society"' (Wolin, 1960: 290). The lines of emergence that result in the modern understanding of society in its general sense
as 'the sum of bonds and relations between individual and events – economic, moral, political – within a more or less bounded territory governed
by its own laws' (Rose, 1996: 1) and in its abstract sense as the condition
out of which such bonds and relations develop, can be traced through a
variety of interwoven problematics central to seventeenth and eighteenth
century thought. These problematics include, amongst others:

1   the relationship of state and society within moral, political and econ-
    omic discourses of governance;
2   the relationship between the ideas of the unity and diversity of humanity,
    and the development of the modern concepts of history and historical
    progress, in the context of the quarrel between the ancients and moderns
    – and in the context of Europe's colonial relationship to the non-
    European other.

In this section I will offer some brief remarks on both these related
problematics before attempting to draw together their implications for
the emergence of sociology and the relationship between sociology and the
themes of the social and the modern.

The relationship of state and society

In Europe, the modern sense of the state emerges by the end of the
sixteenth century and it is the delineation of this object which provides the
foundations for the development of a modern theory of the state in the
seventeenth and eighteenth centuries (Skinner, 1978). In an early instance
of such a theory – Johannes Althusius' *Politica Methodice Digesta* (1603,
expanded version 1610) – the relationship between politics and society is
specified in terms of an understanding of politics as 'the art of associating
men for the purpose of establishing, cultivating, and conserving social life
amongst them' (Althusius, 1990: 27). Here 'social' relates to *consociato*
(association) and, thereby, to society in its primary meaning of fellowship
as well as to the emerging sense of society as commonwealth and to the
idea of man as a social/sociable being: 'it is evident that the commonwealth
or civil society exists by nature, and that man is by nature a civil animal
who strives eagerly for association' (Althusius, 1990: 30). This mixture of
specific and general senses of society is linked to a mixture of specific
(relating, for example, to 'status' and 'estate') and general senses of 'state'.
It is the gradual separating of these senses and the emergence of a distinction between state and civil society, that is, a conception of society 'as an
entity distinct from political arrangements and as the shorthand symbol of
all worthwhile human endeavor' (Wolin, 1960: 291), which is crucial for the
emergence of the modern general and abstract sense of society requisite to
the development of sociology.

This is the juncture at which Wolin identifies the influence of Locke's political thought as central:

> Instead of asking the traditional question: what type of political order is required if society is to be maintained? Locke turned the question around to read, what social arrangements will ensure the continuity of government? (1960: 308)

By introducing 'a conception of society as a self-activating unity capable of generating a common will' (1960: 308) and identifying property as a social institution which is pre-political (1960: 309–11) – both points which will be appropriated and transformed by Rousseau – Locke provided the initial articulation of the opposition of state and civil society. It is this opposition which acts as the ground of the French and Scottish Enlightenment attacks on 'the identity of state reason and governmental reason characteristic of the conjunction of reason of state and police within European absolutism' (Dean, Chapter 11) – an attack which is radicalized by Tom Paine and William Godwin and that is decisive for the development of the general and abstract senses of society.

To contextualize the significance of the French and Scottish Enlightenment, it may be useful to note a few features of the identification of state reason and governmental reason at which their attacks are directed. The doctrines of *raison d'état* and of police are themselves aspects of a particular trajectory within the project of providing a theory of the modern state which runs between the end of the sixteenth and the end of the eighteenth centuries (Foucault, 1988). The doctrine of reason of state was concerned with 'a rationality specific to the art of governing states' (Foucault, 1988: 75) which aims at strengthening the state. In this context, government of the state – which is not distinguished from society in its general sense – requires knowledge of, and intervention on, those things which make up the state. The doctrine of reason of state in its German cameralist and English and French mercantilist forms is bound up with the development of *stat*istics or political arithmetic and *polizeiwissenschaft* (administrative/policy science) which come, in the eighteenth century, to delineate the internal object of state-government as the 'population' – a term derived from primary sixteenth century use of 'popular' as a legal and political term denoting 'belonging to the people' (Williams, 1976: 236) – and applying in this context to the totality of individuals as living elements of the state. The centrality of the doctrine of police to the absolutist theory of the state lies in its articulation of government in terms of the identity of state and society in which the idea of an utterly detailed determination by the state of all its own elements and mechanisms is combined with an equally rigorous regulation of these elements and mechanisms. It is against this background that the French Physiocrats' and the Scottish Liberals' contributions to the delineation of the modern concept of society can be grasped.

While these eighteenth century liberal thinkers share a concern with the external security of the state with the theorists of absolutism, the central themes which emerge from the French and the Scottish Enlightenment concern, first, the Physiocrats' announcement of the quasi-natural character of society and, secondly, the demonstration by the Scottish Liberals, contra the Physiocrats, of the opacity of the totality of the interactions which constitute the self-regulating natural processes of society. The first of these 'sets limits to the sovereign's capacity to direct things at will', while the second 'disqualifies the sovereign's capacity either to know or direct them' (Burchell, 1991: 134). In stressing the complex natural relationships of the domains of economy (Smith), population (Malthus) and civil society (Ferguson) as the more or less spontaneous and relatively opaque products of 'society' in the abstract sense of the natural condition of human existence out of which institutions (such as the state) and relationships develop, the Scottish Enlightenment combines a concern with security which is oriented to maintaining society as an association of free individuals who are subjects of interests, desire, opinions and sentiments with an emerging juxtaposition of the right to govern and knowledge with which to govern well that emphasizes restraint against unnecessary intervention – and, thereby, requires the production of forms of knowledge (and expertise) capable of determining the proper place and occasions of intervention. The significance of this point emerges if we reflect that the Scottish Enlightenment ends the eighteenth century by effectively articulating both the general idea of society as a system of common life characterized by institutions, customs and relationships *and* the abstract idea of society as a natural condition out of which institutions (including the state), customs and relationships develop which form the modern concept of society – and that these thinkers, simultaneously, locate society as an object of knowledge and articulate the necessity of such knowledge. Thus, by the beginning of the nineteenth century, the concept of society has become sufficiently delineated as an object 'to allow such formations as *social reformer*' and 'to define the relationship between *man and society* or *the individual and society* as a problem' (Williams, 1976: 294; original emphasis).

Ancients and moderns

Interwoven with the debate on governance is another set of topics central to eighteenth century thought which revolves around issues concerning the nature of man and the idea of human history. The first aspect of this topic is marked by a series of conceptual shifts in relation to the terms 'human(e)' and 'humanity' which emerge in the early eighteenth century in terms of, firstly, the establishment of a distinction between 'humane' as a set of qualities and 'human' as general term, and secondly, the emergence of a general sense of 'humanity' as a neutral, descriptive reference to human characteristics (Williams, 1976: 148–9). The second aspect under discussion concerns the changing conceptual character of 'history' which is indicated by the emergence of a sense of history as human self-development in the early eighteenth century which leads to a general sense of history revealed in the project of universal history and, eventually (for example, in

Hegel), to an abstract sense of history as the process in which the self-development of humanity unfolds (Williams, 1976: 146–7). The significance of these conceptual shifts for our concerns relates to the eighteenth century problem of reconciling the unity and diversity of mankind in the context of the quarrel between the ancients and moderns, and the relationship of Europe to 'native' peoples in its colonial territories – and the relationship of this problem to transformation of the concept of history.

In the seventeenth century, the quarrel between the ancients and the moderns may be understood as a reaction against the Renaissance and the 'authority of the dead' as well as against a doctrine of degeneration which applied equally to man and nature (Bury, 1920). While Tassoni in Italy, Boisrobert in France and Hakewill in England were engaged in arguing the modern case prior to the publication of Descartes' *Discourse on Method* (1637), there is no doubt that the influence of Cartesian thought, alongside the already important role of Bodin's and Bacon's ideas, play a major role in the development of this debate – most noticeably through figures such as Perrault (*Paralleles des Anciens et des Modernes*, 1688–96), Glanvill (*Plus Ultra*, 1668) and Fontanelle (*Dialogues of the Dead*, 1683 and *Digression on the Ancients and Moderns*, 1688). Of these participants, Fontanelle is the most significant in so far as he bases his case on the Cartesian commitment to the immutability of the laws of nature in order to argue for the natural equality of ancient and modern man – and, thus, claims that any differences which do exist can be accounted for in terms of, on the one hand, time and, on the other hand, political institutions and general states of affairs (Bock, 1978; Bury, 1920). With respect to knowledge, at least, this argument gives rise to the idea of the continual intellectual progress of mankind; yet this idea of continuous and inevitable human progress was not taken as central at this juncture, rather, it is not until the second half of the eighteenth century that this idea is fully articulated.

While the focus of the seventeenth century debate on establishing the natural equality of ancients and moderns is integral to the development of the idea of the essential sameness of humanity across time and space (and, thus, to the conceptual shift in the terms 'human(e)' and 'humanity') which the eighteenth century adopts as part and parcel of the general idea of the uniformity of nature, it is the opening up of the space for accounting for the diversity of mankind across space and time which becomes significant for two related eighteenth century developments: on the one hand, the emergence of the idea of man as a *social* animal in a relatively general and abstract sense; on the other hand, the emergence of the modern idea of history and the idea of universal history which eventually develops into the understanding of man as a *historical* being.

The first of these developments emerges clearly in Montesquieu's *Persian Letters* (1721) and, even more so, in his *The Spirit of the Laws* (1748) which attempts to account for human diversity in terms of the diversity of forms of 'spirit' (culture) with the latter being related to the influence of natural (e.g., climatic) conditions and social (e.g., religious) factors. Indeed,

Montesquieu's remark in his *Persian Letters* that 'Man is born in society and there he remains' becomes a central motif of both French and Scottish Enlightenment thinking in which it is taken in the general and abstract sense of referring to society as the natural state of man. In France, this idea is developed by Rousseau in the *Discourse on Inequality* (1750) and *The Social Contract* (1762) as well as by Voltaire in his *Lettres sur l'Anglais* (1733) and *Essai sur les moeurs* (1765) in which he remarks 'There are two empires, the Empire of Nature, which unites all men on the basis of certain common principles; the Empire of Custom, which . . . spread variety through the world' (cited in Bierstedt, 1978: 13). In Scotland, the idea of man as a social animal is most directly developed by Ferguson's *An Essay on the History of Civil Society* (1767) and Millar's *The Origin of the Distinction of Ranks* (1771) which highlighted the need to study man through society. This theme is also developed in the more anthropological work of Lord Kames (Henry Home) and Lord Monboddo (James Burnet) which stressed the need 'to sift the sensationalized accounts of exotic cultures for the real gold: the common features of humankind' (Gordon, 1991: 116).

The second development, that of the modern concept of history, emerges contemporaneously in Voltaire's *Age of Louis XIV* (1751), which attempts to sketch the '*l'esprit des hommes*' in what he takes to be the most enlightened age thus far, and in his critique of Brousset's *Discours sur l'historie universalle*, which Voltaire takes to task for only touching on four or five peoples and for appealing to Providence rather than providing an entirely naturalistic account. This modern sense of history as the naturalistic study of history as human self-development is closely tied to the articulation of the claim of historical progress which is made by the Abbé de Saint-Pierre in his *Observations on the Continuous Progress of Universal Reason* (1737) and by Turgot in a series of essays and plans written in 1751–2 that present a view of history in terms of developmental stages. Whereas the quarrel between the ancients and moderns in its seventeenth century form had focused on two periods in European history, the multiplication of the periods of this history and the need to accommodate non-European history within the same universal framework involved the production by Turgot of a linear view of history conceptualized in terms of a single path of development. In this context, 'the task became one of detecting among the varieties of human experience the true or natural condition and course of history and depicting them by an arrangement of selected types' (Bock, 1978: 51).

The connection of the modern concept of history to the emphasis on man as a social animal entails that this universal developmental account of history focuses on the development of society. The French Enlightenment thinkers (with the exception of Rousseau) placed an emphatic stress on the inevitability of progress, of which Condorçet's *Sketch of a Historical Picture of the Progress of the Human Mind* (1793) is the best example. This linkage of man–society–history within an account of progress opens up the possibility of envisaging the perfectability of man within a rational society in which humanity controls its own historical development through an understanding of the laws of history (a theme which will later be taken up by Marx). At the same time, the thinkers of the Scottish Enlightenment also adopted a 'stages' view of history while remaining far more equivocal about the inevitability of progress, far more ambivalent about the costs of progress and deeply sceptical of the possibility of its control. Thus, Ferguson's *An Essay on the History of Civil Society* not only attempted to account for instances of decline or regression (which were also recognized by the French thinkers) but also to cast scepticism on the claims that progress entails happiness and that the state can govern the process of progress. However, the main issue relevant to our immediate concerns is the general establishment of the view of history as developing through stages in which grasping these stages required examining societies on the premise that man is fundamentally a social animal. At this juncture, let us return to another aspect of the debate between the ancients and moderns within the context of Europe's relationship to the non-European other.

Although the distinction between the 'savage' and 'civilized' portions of mankind is already present in the seventeenth century, for example, in Locke's *Two Treatises of Government* (1689), the idea that contemporary 'savages' could be taken as representative of early stages in the development of human society by contrast with Europeans as representatives of the highest stage reached thus far emerges fully in the eighteenth century with figures such as the Abbé de Saint-Pierre (Bock, 1978: 51). In its developed form, this idea played a crucial role in the debate on ancient and modern constitutions in the context of colonialism in so far as theorists of modern constitutionalism such as Hume, Smith, Sieyes, Paine, Kant and Constant 'took as their starting point the premise that a modern constitution must recognize the institutional and sociological conditions of a modern society and the type of liberty and equality that corresponds to them' (Tully, 1995: 64). We can flesh this point out by noting that one of the main features of modern constitutionalism was the definition of a modern constitution through a contrast with an ancient or historically earlier constitution which

> refers to pre-modern European constitutions . . . and, secondly, to the customs of non-European societies at 'earlier' and 'lower' stages of historical development. These two contrasts ground the imperial character of modern constitutionalism. The contrast is made in reference to two aspects of pre-modern European and non-European constitutions: their stage of development and their irregularity. (Tully, 1995: 64)

Now my concern with this debate is not that it provides a justification for colonization, although it certainly does perform this role (and consider, in this context, Marx's remarks on British colonialism in India), but rather with two related issues. First, this debate is a central site on which the concept of *modern society* develops, such that by the time Constant publishes *The liberty of the ancients compared with that of the moderns* (1819) there is a clearly defined sense of modern society which is interwoven with a developmental account of history with global application. Secondly, the concern with matching constitutional arrangements to the form and stage of societal development acts as a demand for appropriate forms of knowledge of the social processes that act as the real indicators of the stage of development – and, increasingly, as sites of active intervention on the part of governments. Thus, through various routes, the end of the eighteenth century demarcates 'modern society' as an object and calls for what will come to be known as 'sociological' knowledge of this object.

Sociology, the social and the 'modern'

What is the significance of these brief historical reflections? I want to suggest that three related points emerge from this all too rapid survey.

1 The emergence of the *modern* concept of society is contemporaneous with the emergence of the concept of *modern society*.
2 The emergence of these concepts is interwoven with, on the one hand, the formation of 'man', in the general and abstract sense of humanity, as a social and historical being, and, on the other hand, a conceptualization of history in terms of a developmental account of human societies.
3 The trajectory of these conceptual developments is tied into a series of practical problematics concerning the self-understandings and forms of governance of eighteenth century Europe. Thus, by 1830 when Comte gives the name 'sociology' to this specifically *modern* form of knowledge, a term which passed into English in 1843 (Williams, 1976: 295), the relationship between a self-understanding predicated on the term 'modern' and the articulation of governance through the concept of society is established.

In this section, I will conclude these historical reflections by briefly attending to the relations of sociology to the themes of the social and the modern as these develop in the nineteenth and twentieth centuries. In discussing each of these themes, I will introduce my remarks by offering some observations on the transformation and extension of the concepts involved.

We have already noted the development of the term 'social' to include an abstract and general use which is manifest in the description of man as a social animal. However, at least from the mid-eighteenth century and, in particular, in the confessional writings of Rousseau, we also find a sense of 'social' as a term describing a realm distinct from that of intimacy (Arendt, 1958: 35) which manifests itself in, for example, the contrast between the phrases 'social life' and 'family life'. This use of the concept 'social' is related to one of the seventeenth century uses of the term to refer to 'sociable' which is connected to the use of 'society' to refer to personal company or fellowship (Williams, 1976: 294). It is with respect to the eighteenth century development of this sense of 'social' that the distinction between public and private realms takes on two distinct meanings: on the one hand, the distinction between the political (public) and non-political (private) spheres in which social activity is generally located as private (unless it is *also*, separately and additionally, specified as political activity) and, on the other hand, the distinction between the social (public) and the intimate (private) in which social activity is, by definition, public in character. Now, while this use of the term 'social' remains with us, the central development with which I am concerned relates to the transformation of the concept of 'the social' which is concomitant with the general and abstract uses of 'society' which have become prevalent by the early nineteenth century.

This transformation is indicated by Hannah Arendt in *The Human Condition* when she comments: 'Since the rise of society, . . . an irresistible tendency to grow, to devour the older realms of the political and private as well as the more recently established sphere of intimacy, has been one of the outstanding characteristics of the new realm' (1958: 42). The initial phenomenon to which I take Arendt to be pointing in this remark is the transformation of the concept of 'the social' which attends the *general* use of the concept of society to refer to 'the sum of bonds and relations between individuals and events – economic, moral, political – within a more or less bounded territory governed by its own laws' (Rose, 1996: 1) and which is specified by Deleuze, in his introduction to Donzelot's *The Policing of Families*: '*the* social refers to a *particular sector* in which quite diverse problems and special cases can be brought together, a sector comprising specific institutions and an entire body of qualified personnel' (cited in Rose, 1996: 3). Thus, in his chapter in this volume, Mitchell Dean refers to the formation from the mid-nineteenth century into the twentieth century of policy assemblages such as 'the social question', 'social promotion', 'social defence', 'social security' and 'social insurance' which involve institutions such as 'schools, juvenile courts, government departments, police stations, unemployment exchanges, wage-fixing tribunals, borstals, baby health and family planning clinics, and so on' and qualified personnel such as 'the general practitioner, the social worker, the professional police officer, the child psychologist, the career public servant, and so on'. In other words, as Nikolas Rose remarks:

> 'The social' was certainly a hybrid domain, emerging out of a whole lot of little lines of mutation that occurred in most European nations and in North America over the course of the nineteenth century and the first half of the twentieth. But it formed as the plane upon which all these little lines came to intersect, a way of problematising all manner of ills, speaking about them, analysing them and intervening upon them. (1996: 3)

As Rose points out, 'the social' is a plane upon which 'human intellectual, political and moral authorities, within a limited geographical territory, thought about and acted upon their collective experience' and which, thereby, acts as a site of intersection such that the 'political rationalities that have played so great a part in our own century – socialism, social democracy, social liberalism – may have differed on many things, but on this they agreed – one must pose the question of how to govern from "the social point of view"' (1996: 3). In this respect, the emergence of the social sciences and, in particular, sociology can be grasped as the forms of knowledge which develop on the plane of 'the social', and the institutionalization and professionalization of these forms of knowledge as disciplines can be understood in terms of the development of the hegemony of 'the social' as a way of thinking about, and acting on, our collective experience which is elaborated through categories such as 'social relations' (Marx), 'social facts' (Durkheim) and 'social action' (Weber) – and revealed in Marx's comment contra Feuerbach that 'The standpoint of the old materialism is civil society; the standpoint of the new is human society, or social humanity' (1975 [1845]: 423).

However, this development of the category of 'the social' is not simply related to the general use of the concept of society but also to its *abstract* use to refer to the human conditions out of which bonds and relations, institutions and activities, develop. While the initial use of the concept of 'social' in an abstract sense in the eighteenth century typically refers to the fact that human beings need to live in society to flourish and are, thus, by nature social creatures, the increasing abstraction of the concept of society is concomitant with an increasing abstract use of 'social' to refer to the *essence* of human being. It is in this respect of this abstraction that the category of 'the social' becomes foundational; not simply a plane on which, or an aspect under which, human experience can be grasped but *the* plane, *the* aspect, which is *proper* to knowledge of human beings. Historically, while the conditions of possibility of this development are more or less present from the beginning of the nineteenth century, the actual development of this abstract sense of 'the social' is tied to the development of the hegemony of the category of 'the social' (in its general sense) in thinking about, and acting on, human experience, that is, the increasing *totalization* of 'the social' as a way of reflecting and acting on ourselves. This production of the category of 'the social' as a *simultaneously* general and abstract concept is revealed in Durkheim's injunction to '*consider social facts as things*' (1964 [1895]: 14), Weber's ascription of ontological status to 'social action' (1968 [1921]: 4), and, perhaps, most clearly in Marx's ontologizing of 'social relations' *qua* human being which is exhibited in thesis six of his 'Theses on Feuerbach': 'Feuerbach resolves the religious essence into the *human* essence. But the human essence is no abstraction inherent in each individual. In its reality it is the ensemble of social relations' (1975 [1845]: 423).

The significance of this doubling of the category of 'the social' and, concomitantly, that of 'society' is twofold. *Firstly*, it entails that sociology as the form of knowledge which takes 'the social' or 'society' as its object assumes the *foundationalist* mantle of philosophy: Kant's philosophical question 'What is Man?' is transposed into the equally fundamental sociological question 'What is Society?'. In this respect, the task of sociology becomes that of developing the categories and methods appropriate to the disclosure of 'the social' as 'the real'. *Secondly*, the double status of 'the social' or 'society' as both the transcendental condition of possibility, the foundation or ground, of sociological knowledge and the empirical object of sociological knowledge opens up a problem space with respect to the status of sociological knowledge which entails that philosophical and methodological debates on this topic become an integral element of the disciplinary development of sociology. As the title of Ahmed Gurnah and Alan Scott's recent book on this topic puts it, sociology emerges as, and remains, 'The Uncertain Science' (1992).

At this juncture, let us turn from sociology's relationship to the concept of 'the social' to its relations with the family of concepts that emerge from the concept 'modern'. We can open this discussion by recalling the point that the modern concept of society and the concept of modern society are contemporaneous and by asking how this relationship is interwoven with conceptual shifts in related terms such as 'modernize', 'modernization', 'modernism', 'modernist' and 'modernity'. Raymond Williams places the emergence of these terms in the seventeenth and eighteenth centuries and notes that their usage prior to the nineteenth century was both largely pejorative and generally restricted to issues of architecture, fashion and spelling (1976: 208). However, from the early nineteenth century, as 'modern' comes to be virtually synonymous with concepts such as 'improved', 'progressive', 'highest' and 'best' – a development which is integrally related to the stages view of history which generates the concept of modern society – these related concepts also take on positive hues as well as undergoing general shifts. Firstly, the concept 'modernize' has become general by the mid-nineteenth century, being used to refer to 'making modern', and this provides the route whereby 'modernization' takes on its general twentieth century sense as a deliberate process of making modern (Williams, 1976: 208–9). Secondly, modernism and modernist take on specialist senses at the end of the nineteenth century (c. 1890–1940) in referring to an artistic and literary movement (Williams, 1976: 208), before 'modernism' becomes generalized in reference to both a social and political ideology and a sociocultural formation of beliefs, values and self-understandings in the mid-twentieth century. The former development is bound up with the concepts 'modernize' and 'moderniza-tion', that is, the practical production of 'modernity' (for example, in the 1950s and 1960s programmes of modernization with respect to the Third World). Furthermore, both 'modernism' and 'modernist' become general-ized in the late twentieth century in reference to intellectual activity in terms of the theoretical articulation and defence of 'modernity' as an epoch and/or project (for example, in Habermas' *The Philosophical Discourse of Modernity*, 1987). Thirdly, the concept 'modernity' develops in two related but distinct ways from the first half of the nineteenth century: 'at some point during the first half of the 19th century an irreversible split occurred between modernity as a stage in the history of Western civilization . . . and modernity as an aesthetic concept' (Calinescu, 1987: 41). On the one hand, 'modernity' refers to 'modern society' and, thus, to a historical epoch whose salient features can be specified in relations of contrast to previous epochs. On the other hand, 'modernity' develops a distinct aesthetic use, manifest in Baudelaire's essays on modern life, which refers to our experience of our relationship to the present as modern and, in a connected development (which will be taken up by Foucault), to a particular mode of relating to the present which is modern. How are these developments related to sociology?

The central relationship between sociology and this family of terms related to 'modern' is that articulated through the concept of 'modernity' as epoch which is integral to sociology's understanding of its own identity as a distinctively modern form of knowledge. To put it in terms of a distinction developed by Blumenberg (1983), we can say that from the mid-nineteenth century onwards, sociology's *assertion* of itself as a modern form of knowledge, that is, as a feature of modernity, is predicated on its *foundation* of itself in a determination of modernity. Thus,· the concern with determining the character of modernity is integral to the emergence and development of sociology as discipline. In this context, it is perhaps unsurprising that, alongside *and related to* the philosophical and methodological debates on the character and status of sociological knowledge, the question of modernity becomes a central problematic for sociological discourse. Thus, we find a series of conflicting determinations of modernity as capitalism (Marx), organic solidarity (Durkheim), disenchantment (Weber), and so on, which are each tied to a developmental account of the history of human society articulated in terms of a *social* dynamic – the mode of production (Marx), the division of labour (Durkheim), diverse processes of rationalization (Weber) – and involving a set of methodological categories – social relations (Marx), 'social facts' (Durkheim), 'social action' (Weber) – and modes of analysis. Moreover, although Weber's work presents a more complex case in all of these respects, for both Marx and Durkheim, the project of generating a determination of modernity within a universal developmental history are tied to political programmes, namely, revolutionary socialism and *solidarisme*.

The continuation of this sociological endeavour of linking self-assertion and self-foundation in contemporary sociological practice can be seen in the 'modernization' debates in which social modernism deploys modernist sociology to replace Locke's assertion that 'in the beginning all the world was America' (1993 [1689]: 285) with the programme of making all the world America (where America is straightforwardly identified with modernity), an eschatological positivism which recalls the utopias of the French Enlightenment and is echoed in Fukyama's recent declaration of 'the end of history' (1992). Today, the continuing resonance of the topic of modernity for sociology's assertion and foundation of itself is exhibited in the accounts offered in Habermas' *The Theory of Communicative Action* (1984), Giddens' *The Consequences of Modernity* (1990) and Beck's *Risk Society: Towards a New Modernity* (1992). In the case of Habermas, in particular, the articulation and defence of this relationship between self-assertion and self-foundation is taken as a defining feature of 'modernist' positions in the current plurality of debates between modern and postmodern arguments, and this use of modernist and, relatedly, modernism (Pippin, 1991) – which is also related to a general commitment to the rationalism and universalism of 'the unfinished project of Enlightenment' – has passed into general use within these debates. Thus, in its emergence and development, sociology has been thoroughly interwoven with the themes of modernity, modernization and modernism.

At this point, having all too briefly sketched some aspects of the emergence and development of sociology and its relations to the concepts of 'the social' and 'modern' in order to demonstrate the centrality of these concepts to sociology and to indicate certain of the difficulties to which these concepts give rise, let me conclude this set of historical reflections. The purpose of these observations has been to generate some distance from the fury of contemporary debates in order to provide a context in which we grasp the different, and often contradictory, ways in which the postmodern challenge to sociology has been presented. It is to the delineation of these diverse conceptions of the postmodern challenge that I now turn.

Postmodern challenges to sociology

Before taking up the main task of this section, a few comments on the rationale behind the selection of topics for inclusion may be appropriate. The criteria involved were basically twofold. First, to address those topics which are almost defining features of contemporary sociology such as class, gender, race and ethnicity, criminology and deviance, law, culture and media, science and technology, sexuality, the emotions, medicine and the body, and historical and political sociology. If the postmodern challenge to sociology in any of its forms is to have salience, it must exhibit its power on this terrain. Secondly, to leave aside other significant topics such as industrial or economic sociology, leisure, tourism, ecology, etc., on the grounds that these have been dealt with at considerable length elsewhere, most notably in the journal *Theory, Culture and Society* and the book series attached to this journal which has seen a number of significant publications on these topics. Thus, although an element of arbitrariness almost necessarily enters into selective processes of this kind, it is hoped that this selection covers a significant range of the sociological concerns of importance to contemporary students and practitioners. With this point clarified, let us turn to explore the types of arguments for renewing sociology offered in this text in the context of a discussion of the postmodern challenge to sociology.

The use of the term 'postmodern' as a periodizing concept can be traced back to the mid-twentieth century, while the concept 'postmodernism' – as an internal conservative reaction to aesthetic modernism – emerges even earlier (Smart, 1990: 26–7). However, it is not until the 1960s that the concept of postmodernism emerges in architecture and literature to refer to a radical gesture beyond the modernist avant-garde, and it is not until the 1970s that the general use of 'postmodern' and its cognate terms begins to become prevalent. Consequently, it may be useful to begin by simply listing a number of different ways in which the postmodern challenge to sociology has been articulated and relating these uses to the 'modern' counterparts in respect of which these concepts draw their rhetorical force.

1 Postmodernity as an epoch or social formation (distinct from, and succeeding, modernity).
2 Postmodernization as the social processes leading from modernity to postmodernity (contrasted with modernization as the processes leading from traditional society to modernity).
3 Postmodernism as the social and political ideology which corresponds to the process of postmodernization and is directed towards the achievement of the condition of postmodernity (contrasted with social and political modernism as the ideology of modernization directed to the achievement of global modernity).
4 Postmodernism as a set of social and cultural beliefs, values and forms of behaviour which express living under postmodernization or in postmodernity (contrasted with modernism as a set of social and cultural beliefs, values and modes of behaviour).
5 Postmodernism as the critique of foundationalism (contrasted with modernism as committed to the foundationalism which characterizes Enlightenment rationalism and universalism).

The response of sociology to the development of these concepts and claims has been various, but two general and distinct debates which indicate the main lines of this response can be indicated, namely, (i) whether or not we are moving into a new postmodern form of social condition and (ii) whether or not sociology as a modernist enterprise needs to be displaced by a postmodern form of sociology. Let us consider each of these debates, the positions to which they have given rise, and the ways in which they are featured in the chapters which make up this book

Reflexive modernization or postmodernization?

This is a debate concerning whether or not we are subject to processes of postmodernization and the emergence of a new type of social formation which can be named 'postmodernity'. This debate highlights a contrast between the features of socioeconomic modernism and our contemporary social condition. The former is specified in terms of the structural stability of capitalism, the centrality of class and class-based politics, the primacy of nation-states, and sustainable growth through material production. The latter involves features such as the increasingly disorganized character of capitalism (Lash and Urry, 1987, 1993; Offe, 1985), the fragmentation of class allegiances (Pakulski and Waters, 1996), the growth of a culture of consumerism (Featherstone, 1990, 1995), the development of lifestyle politics (Giddens, 1991), the increasing role of mass media and information technologies (Baudrillard, 1983, 1993), shifts in the social production and circulation of knowledge (Stehr, 1994) and the impact of globalization on nation-states and national economies (Featherstone et al., 1995; Robertson, 1992).

The central question at issue in this debate concerns whether these contemporary developments mark a movement to a new, distinct form of social condition, that is to say postmodernity, characterized by a complex (non-mechanical) system which 'appears as a space of chaos and chronic *indeterminacy*, a territory subjected to rival and contradictory meaning-bestowing claims and hence perpetually *ambivalent*' (Bauman, 1992: 193; cf. also Harvey, 1989; Crook et al., 1992) *or* whether they are better grasped as processes internal to the development of a global and reflexive modernity and can thus be specified in terms of 'reflexive modernization' (Beck, 1992; Beck et al., 1994). Notably the proponents of postmodernization locate the emergence of postmodernism in its sociocultural and sociopolitical forms as part and parcel of the process of emergence of postmodernity and, in this respect, external to modernity; whereas the theorists of reflexive modernization situate postmodernism in these senses as internal to late-modernity.

One site of considerable significance for this debate concerns social stratification, that is, the structuring of patterns of inequality in contemporary society, and this is the topic taken up by Malcolm Waters in his chapter 'Inequality after Class'. Presenting the case for postmodernization, Waters offers a detailed critique of class-grounded theories of inequality and presents a revisionist history of class which provides the basis for a theory of social inequality in postmodernity. Highlighting four central principles of class analysis (namely, economism, groupness, behavioural and cultural linkage, and transformational capacity), Waters demonstrates the incapacity of class-based theory to account for the role of political domination, conventional status and ascribed status (e.g., ethnicity and gender) in effecting the structuring of social inequality in contemporary society. His suggestion is that an understanding of the history of stratification in terms of the movement from economic-class society (in which industrial class acts as the main structuring principle of social inequality) to organized-class society (in which national-political classes play a predominant role) to status-conventional societies (in which patterns of inequality are primarily sourced in the cultural sphere) provides a starting point for theorizing postmodern forms of stratification. Such a theory, Waters argues, shifts from the principles of class-analysis to the following principles: culturalism, fragmentation, autonomization and resignification. It is notable here that while Waters recognizes the continuities between his account of postmodernization and recent accounts of reflexive modernization, he resists the latter label in so far as class ceases to play a dominant role in structuring inequality; recalling Marx's seminal distinction between feudal estates and capitalist classes, Waters urges us to cease thinking in terms of class and to open our imaginations to the development of new concepts for a distinct social formation.

Against this position, Ralph Schroeder's chapter 'The Sociology of Science and Technology after Relativism' presents a case for the continuing salience of the category of modernity, grasped in its distinctively Weberian sense as *disenchantment*. Schroeder's argument is that an adequate socio-logical understanding of scientific and technological development requires a recognition of the way in which scientific knowledge involves an extension of instrumental rationality throughout the social world. On this account, the linkage of science and technology in contemporary society is a modern development in which increasing mastery over natural and social worlds is tied to the increasing impersonality of the external conditions of life. This Weberian picture presents an account of modernity as essentially ambiva-lent – empowering and impersonalizing at the same time. Thus, far from signifying the emergence of postmodernity, Schroeder's arguments have an affinity with recent work on reflexive modernization in which the risk and ambivalence are represented as modernity's increasing consciousness of itself.

Nigel South's chapter on late-modern criminology explores a position between the arguments of Waters and Schroeder in attempting to negotiate the significance of the social developments claimed by theorists of postmodernity and of reflexive modernity for criminology and the sociology of deviance. Sceptical of the more apocalyptic accounts of postmodernity, South acknowledges the force of developments of such as the growth of 'social control districts', of an urban underclass and of possibilities for an authoritarian populism in the context of the changing nature of state-society relations as well as the potentially positive aspects of postmodern-ism as a social and political ideology oriented to issues of ecology, pluralism and individual liberty. He also highlights the increasing signifi-cance of globalization with respect to civil, criminal and security aspects of inter-state and intra-state relations. However, as his title reference to 'late-modern criminology' indicates, South adopts a cautious approach which recognizes the significance of contemporary developments for sociology and the corresponding need for sociology to develop the conceptual apparatus requisite for accounting for these changes, but he is not (yet) prepared to ascribe *fundamental* significance to these social developments by situating them as aspects of a distinctively postmodern social formation.

No doubt this debate between the theorists of postmodernity and of reflexive modernization, and the advocates of cultural modernism and postmodernism, will continue for some time to come. It is, after all, a question concerned with the fundamental character of contemporary society – the structuring of the plane of the social. However, there is a second debate which also requires our attention, namely, that between modernist and postmodernist accounts of sociology as a discipline.

Modern or postmodern sociology?

This second debate, perhaps, offers a greater challenge to the disciplinary identity of sociology in so far as it requires not simply a rethinking of the conceptual apparatus of sociology to cope with changing conditions but a rethinking of the character of sociology as an intellectual enterprise and the status of its claims. Thus, as Gurnah and Scott (1992: 144–5) note, the postmodern critique of foundationalism involves the following theses which are deeply unsettling for sociology in the form in which it has emerged and developed:

1 The rejection of grand narratives.
2 Anti-foundationalism.
3 The critique of attempts to adjudicate between competing cognitive claims from a position of assumed, or usurped, privilege.
4 Anti-Eurocentrism.
5 In place of grounded positions, postmodernism embraces what its critics would consider 'relativism', and in particular a relativism of 'discourse'.

If we recall the sketch of the emergence and development of sociology developed in the opening pages of this introduction, it is immediately apparent that all of these features of postmodernism run counter to what have been taken to be central features of sociology as a project. It is, no doubt, for this reason that one finds that it is a fairly standard feature of the first debate on modernity and postmodernity that its participants are generally united around a commitment to a *modernist* form of sociology. Thus, Zygmunt Bauman – perhaps the major theorist of postmodernity – offers the injunction that,

> rather than seeking a new form of a postmodernist sociology . . . sociologists should be engaged in developing a sociology of postmodernity (i.e., deploying the strategy of systematic, rational discourse to the task of constructing a theoretical model of postmodern society as a system in its own right, rather than a distorted form, or an aberration from another system). (Bauman, 1992: 61)

This general feature is exhibited explicitly by South and Schroeder. South acknowledges the liberatory character of some aspects of postmodernism such as the critique of meta-narratives but is disturbed by, and sceptical of, the 'deconstructive' implications of postmodernism for sociological thinking; while Schroeder condemns postmodernism as relativism. Schroeder's argument situates postmodernist sociology as a form of culture-centered and anti-scientific theorizing which has developed significant social bases in academic institutions but which offers little to meeting the challenge of constructing sociological theories which satisfy scientific criteria.

At the level of culture, a related ambivalence to that expressed by South is articulated by Peter Jowers and Sean Watson in their chapter on affectivity and by Doug Kellner in his contribution on culture and the media. Contrasting the modernist attempts to theorize affect exhibited in the work of Adorno and Horkheimer with the postmodern positions articulated by Deleuze and Guattari, Burroughs, Lyotard and Zizek, Jowers and Watson highlight the need for a sociology of the body which does not simply focus on its semiotics but on issues of affective intensity and viscerality in order to understand human violence. Yet Jowers and Watson are concerned to resist a postmodernist embrace of hybridity and creativity which does not also affirm the modernist commitment to trust, tolerance and the capacity to live with ambivalence. In this respect, while they adopt an approach to the sociology of affect which stresses features of neomaterialism exhibited by these postmodernist cultural critics, they are concerned to distance themselves from certain cultural aspects of post-modernism in its more apocalyptic moments. Doug Kellner's chapter on culture is also concerned with negotiating the modern/postmodern debate, however, Kellner's proposed route through this debate is the adoption of a multi-perspectival approach which avoids a penchant for the a priori privileging of a given perspective and stresses the need for synoptic pluralism in sociological investigations. In a critical review of the development of the sociology of culture and the media, Kellner highlights the different purposes which are played by distinct theoretical accounts ranging from the Frankfurt School to the Birmingham School to postmodern theory in developing a synoptic sociology of culture which will be informed by a concern with human freedom. Thus, while Kellner remains significantly committed to the modernist vision on sociology as ideology-critique, his chapter is characterized by an openness to the aspects of culture disclosed by postmodern theories.

By contrast with South's sympathetic yet wary response and Schroeder's utterly sceptical account, both Samantha Ashenden in her chapter on gender and Paul Connolly in his on race and ethnicity argue for explicitly postmodern forms of sociological enquiry. Ashenden, in the more philosophical of these two essays, approaches the question of the relationship of sociology to the category of gender in terms of the feminist commitment to thinking through the relations of the political and the epistemic. Her argument develops through a critique of the sociology of gender which highlights the *supplementary* role assigned to gender in stratification theory and a critique of attempts to develop a feminist sociology as a form of epistemic *separatism*. Focusing on the claims of feminist standpoint epistemology, Ashenden demonstrates how the presumption of the categories of 'woman' and 'experience' are problematic both in terms of the philosophical assumption of a fundamental, constitutive subject and in relation to the role of this epistemological position in legislating a politics of identity. Yet while Ashenden adopts an anti-foundationalist perspectivism at the philosophical level, she is also deeply critical of the tendency to try to articulate politics at this level and, thereby, to bypass the sociological and historical work of accounting for the diverse ways in which gendered modes of subjectivity are constituted within power relations. For Ashenden, in other words, it is precisely because of the deconstruction of the category of 'woman' that the political project of feminism requires sociological accounts. A similar position emerges in the chapter by Paul Connolly, but whereas Ashenden offers a more abstract argument, Connolly attempts to indicate how such a postmodern sociology would practically proceed by drawing on the work of Bourdieu and his own investigations of the construction of racialized identities. Deploying the concepts of 'habitus', 'capital' and 'field', Connolly seeks to show how an anti-foundational sociology can develop middle-range theories which unite the micro and macro level of sociological analysis. This is also a feature of Arlene Stein's chapter on sexuality, which seeks to argue for a combination of psycho-analysis, symbolic interactionism and discourse analysis which highlights the relations and interactions of intrapsychic scripts, interpersonal scripts and cultural scenarios. Examining the development of accounts of sexuality from sexology to post-structuralism, Stein frames her argument in terms of a need to resist both sociological voluntarism and determinism without slipping into psychological reductionism. While she is less sure of the consequences of the postmodernist critique of the subject than Ashenden and Connolly, she shares an awareness of the political character of sociological accounts of sexuality and a commitment to the 'messiness' of empirical work.

It is in notable contrast with Schroeder's emphasis on the scientific character of sociology that Ashenden, Connolly and Stein all locate their work as embedded in political contexts – feminism, anti-racism, gay and lesbian struggles – and a related, although distinctly expressed, concern is exhibited in Mitchell Dean's chapter 'Sociology after Society' and also in Alan Hunt's chapter on law, politics and the social sciences, which both draw on the work of Michel Foucault. Both Dean and Hunt are concerned to acknowledge a form of sociology which is concerned with our ability to identify and subject to judgement the limits imposed on us. This theme is developed by Hunt in terms of a critical review of the sociology of law and a critical appropriation and development of Foucault's work on governmentality. Avoiding the dualisms of law vs. regulation and law vs. politics, Hunt argues that a focus on modes of governance and on the shifting role and character of law in articulating the relations of modes of governance provides a route beyond the increasingly sterile debates set up in terms of being 'for' or 'against' law. This is achieved through the opening up of the question of how it is best to govern a given object of enquiry without presupposing law as a foundational category. This emphasis on governance is also developed by Dean, who focuses on sociology as a form of diagnostics. Illustrating his case through an analysis of the changing character of modes of governance from those that operate through 'society' (e.g., social democracy, socialism etc.) to those that operate through neo-liberal rationalities of rule and technologies of risk, Dean argues for sociology to act as a form of *parrhesia* or truth-telling which opens up the possibilities of being otherwise than we are for public debate.

One of the central figures of both Hunt's and Dean's chapters which is also exhibited by Ashenden and Connolly is a certain commitment to

irrealism, that is, the anti-foundational recognition that we constitute ourselves as particular kinds of subjects with various features, capacities, etc.,
in the course of the ongoing practical construction of the social, cultural,
economic, political and other worlds in which we engage. This position
does not imply that there are not natural limits on this practical construction of our worlds but it does entail that the treatment of 'society' or
'the social' as foundational categories is mistaken. This position is strongly
expressed in Tom Osborne's contribution on medicine and the body, 'Body
Amnesia', in which he develops both a critique of the surreptitious attempt
to reintroduce the body as a foundational subject for sociology and an
approach to the sociology of the body which highlights the ways in which
bodily techniques act to produce a forgetting of our embodiment.
Assembling a series of reminders through examples of bodily techniques,
Osborne's ethological approach demonstrates how the practical construction of worlds is limited through the capacities which bodies exhibit and,
relatedly, the techniques for the fusion of bodies developed in a way that
recalls Wittgenstein's location of our ways of being in the world as features
of the natural history of humanity. In this respect, Osborne's deployment of
Deleuze in seeking to show how the forgetting of the body is integral to
such techniques may be grasped as the bodily correlate of Wittgenstein's
(and Heidegger's) point that the self-understandings exhibited in our
everyday practices or modes of being are taken-for-granted, background
conditions which appear to consciousness only in their becoming problematic. As such, while Osborne sees little of use in the term 'postmodern',
his chapter serves as a site on which many of the philosophical and
sociological themes of postmodernism (whether the label is retained or not)
can be brought together productively.

No doubt, the arguments offered with respect to the formulation of an
irrealist, anti-foundational sociology will seem otiose to some practitioners
of the discipline. However, although the challenge posed by these arguments is a serious one, it is noteworthy that all of the advocates of what I
have been calling 'postmodern sociology' are committed to the discipline,
even as they call for a more transdisciplinary approach and offer a more
modest set of claims for the status of sociological knowledge.

The final point I would like to make in this section is this: by contrast
with theorists of postmodernity for whom the category 'postmodern' is of
central significance, many of those authors whom I have placed under the
title of postmodern sociology would reject the term. It is, I think, no
accident that only Ashenden and Connolly, who are involved in the most
explicitly political forms of sociological work, explicitly affirm the term
itself in order to distance themselves from a modernist politics of identity.
For Dean, Hunt and Osborne, in particular, the contrast between modern
and postmodern forms of sociology is subordinate to the general theme of
anti-foundationalism and irrealism. This may suggest that the periodizing
use of the term postmodern is becoming dominant and, perhaps following
Foucault's late adoption of the term 'modern', that this second usage will

drop out of general currency. Indeed, at least for the sake of conceptual clarity this move might be welcome. The challenge of this form of sociology, however, will remain.

Conclusion

In this introduction I have tried to situate sociology's relationship to the themes of the modern and the postmodern in order to provide a context for the contributions to this volume. I have indicated the two main axes along which the postmodern challenge to sociology has developed and, at this point, leave you to engage with the arguments and judge for yourselves.

Bibliography

Althusius, J. (1990) 'Human association and politics', in M. Lessnoff (ed.), *Social Contract Theory*. Oxford: Basil Blackwell.

Arendt, H. (1958) *The Human Condition*. New York: Doubleday.

Baudrillard, J. (1983) *Simulations*. New York: Semiotext(e).

Baudrillard, J. (1993) *Symbolic Exchange and Death*. London: Sage.

Bauman, Z. (1992) *Intimations of Postmodernity*. London: Routledge.

Beck, U. (1992) *Risk Society: Towards a New Modernity*. London: Sage.

Beck, U., Giddens, A. and Lash, S. (1994) *Reflexive Modernization*. Cambridge: Polity Press.

Bierstedt, R. (1978) 'Sociological thought in the eighteenth century', in T. Bottomore and R. Nisbet (eds), *A History of Sociological Analysis*. London: Heinemann.

Blumenberg, H. (1983) *The Legitimacy of the Modern Age*. Cambridge, MA: MIT Press.

Bock, G. (1978) 'Theories of progress, development, evolution', in T. Bottomore and R. Nisbet (eds), *A History of Sociological Analysis*. London: Heinemann.

Burchell, G. (1991) 'Peculiar interests: civil society and governing "The System of Natural Liberty"', in G. Burchell, C. Gordon and P. Miller (eds), *The Foucault Effect*. Brighton: Harvester Wheatsheaf.

Bury, J. (1920) *The Idea of Progress*. London: Macmillan.

Calinescu, M. (1987) *Five Faces of Modernity*. Durham, NC: Duke University Press.

Crook, S., Pakulski, J. and Waters, M. (1992) *Postmodernization*. London: Sage.

Dean, M. (1994) *Critical and Effective Histories*. London: Routledge.

Deleuze, G. (1979) 'Introduction' to Jacques Donzelot, *The Policing of Families*. London: Hutchinson.

Durkheim, E. (1964) *The Rules of Sociological Method*. London: Routledge.

Featherstone, M. (ed.) (1990) *Global Culture*. London: Sage.

Featherstone, M. (1995) *Undoing Culture*. London: Sage.

Featherstone, M., Lash, S. and Robertson, R. (1995) *Global Modernities*. London: Sage.

Foster, H. (1983) *Postmodern Culture*. London: Pluto Press.

Foucault, M. (1977) *Discipline and Punish*. Harmondsworth: Penguin.

Foucault, M. (1979) *The History of Sexuality*, vol. 1. Harmondsworth: Penguin.

Foucault, M. (1984) *The Foucault Reader* (ed. P. Rabinow). Harmondsworth: Penguin.

Foucault, M. (1988) 'Politics and reason', in *Politics, Philosophy, Culture*, ed. L. Kritzman. New York: Routledge.

Fukyama, F. (1992) *The End of History and the Last Man*. New York: The Free Press.

Giddens, A. (1990) *The Consequences of Modernity*. Cambridge: Polity Press.

Giddens, A. (1991) *Modernity and Self-Identity*. Cambridge: Polity.

Gordon, S. (1991) *The History and Philosophy of Social Science*. London: Routledge.

Gurnah, A. and Scott, A. (1992) *The Uncertain Science*. London: Routledge.

Habermas, J. (1984) *The Theory of Communicative Action*, vol. 1. Cambridge: Polity Press.
Habermas, J. (1987) *The Philosophical Discourse of Modernity*. Cambridge: Polity Press.
Harvey, D. (1989) *The Condition of Postmodernity*. Cambridge: Basil Blackwell.
Lash, S. and Urry, J. (1987) *The End of Organised Capitalism*. Cambridge: Polity Press.
Lash, S. and Urry, J. (1993) *Economies of Signs and Space*. London: Sage.
Locke, J. (1993) *Political Writings*. Harmondsworth: Penguin.
Lyotard, J-F. (1984) *The Postmodern Condition*. Manchester: Manchester University Press.
Marx, K. (1975) *Early Writings*. Harmondsworth: Penguin.
Offe, C. (1985) *Disorganised Capitalism*. Cambridge: Polity Press.
Owen, D. (1994) *Maturity and Modernity: Nietzsche, Weber, Foucault and the Ambivalence of Reason*. London: Routledge.
Pakulski, J. and Waters, M. (1996) *The Death of Class*. London: Sage.
Pippin, R. (1991) *Modernism as a Philosophical Problem*. Oxford: Basil Blackwell.
Robertson, R. (1992) *Globalisation*. London: Sage.
Rorty, R. (1979) *Philosophy and the Mirror of Nature*. Princeton, NJ: Princeton University Press.
Rose, N. (1996) 'The death of the social? Re-figuring the territory of government', *Economy and Society*, 25(3).
Skinner, Q. (1978) *The Foundations of Modern Political Thought*, vol. 2. Cambridge: Cambridge University Press.
Smart, B. (1990) 'Modernity, postmodernity and the present', in B. Turner (ed.), *Theories of Modernity and Postmodernity*. London: Sage.
Stehr, N. (1994) *Knowledge Societies*. London: Sage.
Tully, J. (1995) *Strange Multiplicity: Constitutionalism in an Age of Diversity*. Cambridge: Cambridge University Press.
Weber, M. (1968) *Economy and Society*. New York: The Free Press.
Williams, R. (1976) *Keywords*. London: Fontana.
Wolin, S. (1960) *Politics and Vision*. Boston: Little, Brown and Company.

1 Inequality after Class

Malcolm Waters

The debate about the salience of class is back on the sociological agenda. At least five journals of international scope and repute have recently hosted debates on the issue.[1] These debates have introduced a body of new evidence and new arguments on the declining social and political relevance of class and on the increasingly problematic nature of class-based explanations of social inequalities and conflicts. Even such pioneers of class analysis as Lipset (Clark and Lipset, 1991; Clark et al., 1993) and contemporary sympathizers (e.g. Crompton, 1993; Emmison and Western, 1990) admit to problems and inadequacies that can no longer be glossed over. Two major new books have been published that canvass and take positions in the debate (Lee and Turner, 1996; Pakulski and Waters, 1996). This chapter therefore seeks to provide an alternative to what might be called the class manifesto.[2] It outlines the patterns of inequality that sociology needs to theorize, assuming that class is dead. However, it does not call for the class tradition to be ditched but rather seeks to apply the general methodological approach of class theory and analysis to the contemporary formation.

Class theory has arguably always been central to sociological analysis. One of the discipline's main claims has been to an expertise in demonstrating the ways in which the underlying realities of class can structure behaviour, opportunities, attitudes, living conditions and lifestyles. In an important sense sociology has been about the relationship between class structure and the Lebenswelt. Given this success it is appropriate to take class theory as the template for theorizing about whatever might succeed it. The class-theoretic template, of which Marxist class theory is the best known example, embraces the following four propositions.

1 The proposition of *economism*. It views class as a fundamentally socio-economic phenomenon. Class refers often to differential ownership of property, especially of productive or capital property with an accumulation potential. It can also refer to differential market capacity, especially labour-market capacity. Such economic phenomena as property or markets are held to be fundamental structuring or organizing principles in societal arrangements.

2 The proposition of *groupness*. Classes are held to be more than statistical aggregates or taxonomic categories. They are real features of social structure having detectable boundaries that set up the main lines of

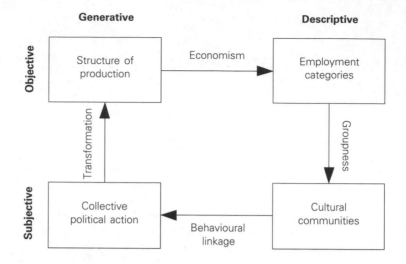

Figure 1.1   *Aspects of the sociology of class*

cleavage in society. So deep and fundamental are these cleavages that they are the enduring bases for conflict, struggle, possible exploitation and distributional contestation.

3   The proposition of *behavioural and cultural linkage*. Class membership is also claimed causally to be connected to consciousness, identity and action outside the arena of economic production. It determines values and norms, political preferences, lifestyle choices, child-rearing practices, opportunities for physical and mental health, access to educational opportunity, patterns of marriage, occupational inheritance, income, and so on. This linkage legitimizes the continuing salience of class analysis.

4   The proposition of *transformational capacity*. Classes are important collective actors in the economic and political fields. They have latent access to resources that can hold entire societies in thrall and, in so far as they consciously struggle against other classes, they can transform the general set of social arrangements of which they are a part. Class struggle therefore generates the dynamic thrust that energizes society – classes are collective actors that can make history.

Figure 1.1 summarizes these propositions. It draws two distinctions about the ways in which sociologists use the concept of class: first, between class as a generative or determining factor in social life and class as a set of categories for describing society; and secondly, between class as an objective condition of human existence and class as a subjective component of experience and consciousness. Intersecting these distinctions gives us the four aspects of class on which sociological debates focus. Sociologists variously identify class as an abstract structure of positions, as a formation that sets up a hierarchy of economic categories, as communities of common interest and culture, and as collective political actors. The propositions establish theoretical linkages between these four: economism specifies that the main divisions in society are aspects of the economic structure; groupness specifies that these economic categories will develop into identifiable social entities; behavioural linkage specifies that this will determine their norms, attitudes and political behaviour; and transformation argues that class-based political action will lead to reform of the fundamental underlying structure.

Emergent features of the stratification system

Economically determined class has typically been regarded as the predominant feature of the capitalist system since it emerged to disrupt the feudal order of estates. However, many observers now identify as salient three emergent features of the stratification system that previously could be regarded as either reducible to or repressed by class. These three features are: power and domination; conventional status as expressed in lifestyles and value-commitments; and ascribed status memberships, particularly those specified by structures of gender, race and ethnicity.

Domination

A key feature of the development of industrial societies in the twentieth century has been an expansion of state activity. This development impacts radically on the stratification system. First, the state provides access to social resources and rewards that are autonomous relative to processes of production. Whatever social strata are generated by state employment and state benefits, they are not economic classes in the sense of being sourced in processes of production. Secondly, state action can modify social arrangements built around production processes so that economic areas previously defined as private and autonomous become subject to state control and regulation. States can regulate labour and commodities markets; they can intervene to provide capital infrastructure; and they can sponsor corporatist relations between employers and employees (Offe, 1984).

Where state activity intrudes into the economic sphere it provides the basis for a political restructuring of stratification arrangements. A bureaucratic-political elite controls the distribution of state resources and establishes consumption privileges on this basis – improved access to salaries, travel, working conditions, pension schemes, and so on. Below this a less autonomous and less privileged public service category of workers nevertheless enjoys a relatively high level of material security. The receipt of socioeconomic protection creates membership of a third and lower stratum of dependent citizens whose social location is entirely contingent on state activity. These are the recipients of welfare benefits, unemployment insurance, pensions, and so on. They include the structurally unemployed and underemployed, the physically and mentally disabled, female heads of households, and the aged. Membership in the dependent underclass is stable and reproducing. This is especially true where membership intersects with age, gender, race or ethnicity.

It is also possible to mount an argument that even in the private sector, the critical stratifying feature is rather more to do with the distribution of domination than the distribution of ownership. The principal issue here is the 'separation of ownership from control' in which the functions of capital are increasingly performed by managers while stockholders merely own the corporation in a legal sense. Actual capitalists thus disappear from the production process and therefore, it might be argued, class relations cannot be understood merely in terms of property ownership (Berle and Means, [1932] 1967; Burnham, 1941). Below the senior managerial level, increases in the scale and specialization of organizations can generate imperatives for coordination. A key characteristic of contemporary capitalism is its hierarchical and bureaucratic organization. In other words, organized capitalism offers a stable basis for the formation of intermediate strata defined by their access to domination. Dahrendorf (1959) offers what is perhaps the most influential account of contemporary stratification in terms of domination, although, like many others, he insists on continuing to use the term 'class' for the groups that he identifies. He observes that capitalist societies are composed of a wide range of complex organizations, not only production enterprises but also distribution enterprises, state bureaucracies, political parties, churches, voluntary associations and trade unions (1959: 157–209). Each of these organizations is made up of specialized activities that must be coordinated in the direction of organizational goals. This is a functional imperative for complex organizations, so that each will include people who give commands and people who respond to them. These authority groups are the basis for 'class' formation. But the 'classes' are intra-organizational rather than societal. This allows Dahrendorf to conceive of multiple lines of authority-based divisions intersecting with one another and thereby to mount a conflict-based theory of social cohesion.

Conventional status

Conventional status is another possible contender in the contest to be at the centre of stratification arrangements. Here status must be understood in Weberian terms, that is as a coherent and shared lifestyle that consists of consumption patterns, forms of social intercourse, marital practices, associational memberships and shared value-commitments. Status differentiation can therefore be based on formal education, hereditary prestige, or occupational prestige. An argument in favour of conventional status would suggest that status groups can form across class divisions. Status groups can prevent the formation of classes because they monopolize privilege and thus prevent the mobilization of property or skills in order to gain access to it.

If one accepts that occupations are ranked by processes specified neither by production nor by a legal order, then they must be ranked or evaluated in terms of negotiation between human beings. Indeed, on such an argument, power-groups and classes can be reduced to conventional 'socio-economic status':

> The occupational structure in modern industrial society not only constitutes an important foundation for the main dimensions of social stratification but also serves as the connecting link between different institutions and spheres of inequality . . . The hierarchy of prestige strata and the hierarchy of economic classes have their roots in the occupational structure; so does the hierarchy of political power and authority, for political authority in modern society is largely exercised as a full-time occupation. (Blau and Duncan, 1967: 6–7)

Educational credentials are an important component in formulations of socioeconomic status. Larson (1977) shows that the original basis for credentialism was the establishment of medicine, and later law and academia, formally as professions as a response to the burgeoning specialization and monetarization of the market and to the growth of state bureaucracies engaged in its reproduction. Here, credentials found an important function in commodifying service provision by standardizing professional practices as well as by arranging pricing structures in relation to them in a fee-for-service system. However, the rise of credentialism in the twentieth century is the outcome of efforts by employed occupational groups, seeking to imitate the success of free professionals in monopolizing closure in the market. A similar argument, developed by Perkin (1989), shows how the professional principle progressively evicts the class principle.

On a reading of twentieth century developments that emphasizes status and credentials, the middle occupations can be seen as highly successful in their monopolizing activities. Indeed one of the central problems for recent class theory has been how to explain the emergence of the 'new middle class' (Abercrombie and Urry, 1983). The post-war rise in numbers of professional and technical workers has been little short of spectacular, so that in most industrial societies they constitute about 20 per cent of the labour force. They have been variously interpreted by class theorists as a new ruling class (Bell, 1973), a 'service class' (Goldthorpe, 1982), a 'new petty bourgeoisie' (Poulantzas, 1974), a 'new working class' (Mallet, 1975), a contradictory class (Wright, 1982), 'expert classes' (Wright, 1985), a 'new middle class' (Johnson, 1972), a 'professional-managerial class' (Ehrenreich and Ehrenreich, 1979), or simply as a 'new class' (Konrad and Szelenyi, 1979).

Class theory and class analysis have always found difficulty in specifying a class location for professional and technical workers. This is because, in class terms, their locations are highly diverse. They exhibit a wide range of relationships to the state, for example, from state employment through state-authorized monopoly and state licensing to formal independence. Their organizational location is also diverse, encompassing participation in both large-scale state or private sector bureaucratic systems and small-scale partnerships, and incorporating various relationships to the system of authority including hierarchical, specialist-staff, collegial and consultancy relationships. Finally, particular individual workers have differential locations in authority and reward systems.

Ascribed status: ethnicity and patriarchy

The class paradigm has also found difficulty in accommodating the ascribed statuses of ethnicity, race and gender. Its principal coping strategy has been to assert that they are unimportant, irrelevant, irrational or non-existent and that economic class is the only significant structuring principle for society. In so far as it has done so it has constituted an ideology of white male supremacism. Historically, gender has exhibited far more pronounced inequalities of power and material rewards as well as offering more extreme examples of exploitation and brutal coercion than those occurring between classes. It is also arguable that in the public sphere the extremes of discrimination that have occurred between races as well as the passionate and bloody conflicts that continue to take place between ethnic groups far outweigh any supposed division and struggle between classes.

In treating ethnicity and race the class paradigm has always taken its lead from its intellectual ancestors. Marx viewed ethnic groups as 'national left-overs' and 'fanatic partisans of the counter-revolution' that threatened to divide the working class and thwart its historical mission (Parkin, 1979: 31). Equally, Weber theorized ethnic group formation as a form of irrational action that ran counter to the technical rationalization of modern bureaucracies and markets. In a sense, the development of the state that is outlined above conspired in this view. Originally an expression of nationality, the nation-state operated to suppress national minorities and sought to assimilate the entire population it controlled to the project of a national cultural community. Because sub-state nationalities were rendered invisible, sociologists often treated them as if they were unreal, as if they were only 'imagined communities' (Anderson, 1983) relative to the structural realities of class.

Such a view is increasingly difficult to maintain. Three historical developments mean that race and ethnicity are now prominent features of the social topography. First, the previously colonized societies of the 'South' have managed to re-establish self-government, albeit in a form shaped by the Northern colonizers. Part of the ideology that supported this shift was an attempt to establish that racism was an unethical and irrational form of behaviour by claiming that inequalities of race far outweighed those of class. Secondly, one of the emerging features of the contemporary world is mass migration motivated by relative economic disadvantage. Flows from ex-colonies into colonizing societies and from Eastern and Southern Europe into Western Europe have radically altered the ethnic mix in societies previously claimed to be ethnically homogeneous and these ethnic cleavages are now too apparent to be ignored. Thirdly, during the past quarter of a century the state has gone through a series of crises that have weakened its powers allowing the re-emergence of previously repressed national minorities. Nowhere is this more apparent than in the ex-socialist states of Eastern Europe and the ex-USSR where ethnic resurgence now threatens fragile political and economic arrangements but is also apparent in Western capitalist societies.

If sociology turned a blind eye to ethnicity then it must have turned two to gender. Gender inequalities and exploitations were obscured by the 'naturalism' of sex-role theory and the triumphalism of a modernization theory that stressed the adaptive superiority of the nuclear family. In one sense the class paradigm can be regarded as less than culpable because one of its claims was that class processes transpired largely in the public sphere, and because women were excluded from employment and politics they were irrelevant to class processes. This was a widespread view found, for example, in Parsons: 'The separation of the sex roles in our society is such as . . . to remove women from the kind of occupational status which is important for the determination of the status of the family' (1954: 80); in Giddens: 'Given that women still have to await their liberation from the family, it remains the case in the capitalist societies that female workers are largely peripheral to the class system' (1973: 288); and Parkin: 'for the majority of women . . . the allocation of social and economic rewards is determined primarily by the position of their families – and, in particular, that of the male head' (1979: 14–15). In a famous article, Goldthorpe (1983) asserted that he would continue to measure the class of any woman by classifying the occupation of her conjugal partner because household income was largely determined by the male partner, because women's labour force participation was intermittent, and because women's socio-political attitudes could be predicted more accurately by their partner's occupation than by their own, even if they were themselves employed.

Such a position is certainly no longer tenable. Female participation in the employment sphere is now at a higher level, is more stable and more influential than it has ever been. Patriarchy has been transformed into a 'public patriarchy' (Walby, 1990) or 'extended viriarchy' (Waters, 1989). This development raises a fundamental problem. It suggests that the class paradigm might have been wrong in claiming pre-eminence as a structuring principle. The development of a class structure was only possible in so far as it was based on a domestic division of labour that allowed men exclusively to construct a public sphere. In these terms we must consider the possibility that gender is primordial as *the* structural principle and that class is merely contingent. Certainly one could make a more convincing case that gender has always structured society than one could for class.

A revisionist history of class

The continuing salience and the return to prominence of political domination, conventional status and ascribed status as principles of stratification suggest that an undifferentiated history of capitalism as the extended reproduction of class might have less to offer than a periodized framework. Within such a framework each period can be conceptualized as reflecting the predominance of one or more stratificational principles. Nineteenth century Britain, for example, might be viewed as a close approximation to the class-theoretic template set out in the early part of this chapter. This section rehearses an alternative history (built on Waters, 1994, 1995a; Pakulski and Waters, 1996) in which stratification can be conceptualized as exhibiting radically different features from those outlined in the class model.

On this argument, the term 'class society' must be restricted to the particular configuration in which collective actors determined by production relations struggle within that arena for control of the system of property ownership. Employment relations or labour market position may continue to have salience in determining social rewards in periods during which this configuration is not central. However, in many, if not most instances these will be mediated by factors other than property ownership, including organizational position, skills and credentials, the social worth of value-commitments, the social construction of ascribed statuses, and patterns of political domination (see e.g. Mann, 1993).

In summary, the stratification order of capitalist societies might be traced as a succession of three periods roughly periodized into the nineteenth century, the first three-quarters of the twentieth century, and the contemporary period. In highly formalized and abstracted terms they may be described as economic-class society, organized-class society and status-conventional society.

Economic class society is arranged into patterns of domination and struggle between interest groups that emerge from the economic realm. In the familiar terms of Marx, the classes will be property owners and sellers of labour power but they could be conceptualized as employers and employees. The dominant class can control the state and maintain itself as a ruling class either by capturing its apparatuses or by rendering them weak. In so far as the subordinate class undertakes collective action it will be rebellious or revolutionary in character, aimed at dislodging this ruling class by the abolition of private property. Culture is divided to match class divisions, into dominant and subordinate ideologies and into high and low cultures.

In terms of the four cells identified in Figure 1.1, class society exhibits the following characteristics.

1 The social structure consists in a radically unequal distribution of property between capitalists and workers that enables the former to exploit the latter. Capital property is largely owned privately and familially rather than by the state and is inherited dynastically.

2 The social formation consists of a series of closed communities operating within the confines of a weak or liberal state that are divided by a central rift marked by antagonism, exploitation, struggle and conflict. Classes stand in a functional relationship with patriarchy in which each

serves to reproduce the other. The family is the main site for class reproduction.

3   Class societies are characterized by bounded subcultures. Capitalist class families legitimate their capital accumulation and its inheritance by reference to such dominant ideologies as Protestant thrift, divine election and puritan temperament. These show that the ruling class is entitled to its privileges because it has earned them and God recognizes the fact. Working-class cultures typically absorb such cultural imposts in expressions of deference, although radicalization is also possible especially where an alternative religious ideology can promote it.

4   Working-class political action is militant, ideological and occasionally revolutionary. It involves a close association between industrial organization and action and political organization and action. It expresses a deep sense of injury, pain and exploitation in an active hostility to 'the bosses'. Ruling-class political action involves the suppression and repression of working-class organizational vehicles and attempts to seduce working-class commitments within the rubrics of patriotism and paternalism.

Organized-class society is defined by a political or state sphere. The state is typically dominated by a single unified bloc, a political-bureaucratic elite, that exercises power over one or more subordinated masses. These blocs may be factionalized horizontally into formally opposed parties. The elite will comprise either a party leadership or a corporatized leadership integrating party leaders with the leaders of other organized interest groups, including economic and cultural ones. The elite uses the coercive power of the state to regulate economics and culture. The state can dominate the economy by redistribution or by the conversion of private into public property, although this need not be a complete accomplishment. Classes, in turn, reorganize themselves in national-political rather than industrial terms by establishing links with milieu parties. Meanwhile, the cultural realm can be unified under the state umbrella or under the aegis of state-sponsored monopolies. It can thus be turned into an industrialized or mass culture.[3]

Again, we can examine the contents of the four cells provided by the model given in Figure 1.1 for organized-class systems.

1   In organized-class society property is still distributed unequally but the sharp break between ownership and non-ownership disappears in favour of a gradient that, over time, progressively becomes less steep. An important element in this redistribution is the intervention of states in property ownership. Under the aegis of socialist, communist or fascist ideologies states can appropriate the means of production on behalf of the working class. In other societies property ownership can be reorganized by the formation of shareholder corporations that tend to separate ownership from control and to facilitate the dispersal of the former. The key role in market participation is the occupation. What many sociologists now call classes are in fact groups of similar occupations effecting an unreliable closure against external recruitment and battling to climb the ladder of consumption privileges. The critical contexts for occupational advancement

are the hierarchies of authority and responsibility established in state agencies and corporations. It is here that mobility barriers are erected and that participants strive for sufficient income to reproduce their standing by providing adequate educations for their offspring.

2   In organized-class society, the nation-state orchestrates national class formation by incorporating its organizational forms into national compacts. Here 'organized classes' are the political expression of occupational groupings but they are far more unstable than their predecessors. This is because education has become a critical vehicle for socioeconomic reproduction. Positions expand to a much wider variety and diversity especially in what is often called the 'new middle class' and the allocation of persons to positions occurs at least as much in terms of individual ability and good fortune and the capacity of schools to develop talent as it does on family background. Patriarchy experiences some reorganization as women re-enter the public sphere if only in stereotypical roles and subordinated positions.

3   Organized-class societies, especially in their corporatized and welfare versions, transform cultural orientations. Class cultures become more differentiated, profligate and indulgent at the top and the bottom although regulative and privatized in the middle. Nationally organized political ideologies match this development: social democracy favours a redistribution of consumption possibilities to the bottom; liberalism favours rewards for hard work in the middle; and conservatism the maintenance of privilege at the top. However, these political-ideological meta-narratives do not penetrate everyday meaning systems, social norms, consumption patterns and images very deeply. Their impact on lifeworlds is limited to a handful of committed and ideologically conscious activists and intellectuals. Such class ideologies function mainly as elite political formulae.

4   Social classes take a new lease on life despite market fragmentation and a progressing division of labour. The political-organizational superstructures of class, trade unions and parties take over the dominant social-structuring role. Within the political programmes and platforms of these self-declared class bodies, class issues and interests are articulated, elaborated and disseminated. So class ideologies are constructed as totalizing packages combining specific social values with general strategies of implementation. Socialism, liberalism and conservatism became associated with broad class interests because of their deployment as the political formulae of the major parties. Popular identifications, outlooks and interests are increasingly organized by the political activism and ideological appeals of these national class bodies. They reflect these packages rather than people's work and life experiences. The working classes are closely identified with support for social democratic parties; the 'middle classes' are defined in terms of political programmes of the liberal-conservative parties and allegiances to liberal-conservative ideological packages. Even rightist extremism acquires class overtones as fascist parties appeal to petit bourgeois, anti-modernist, anti-industrial sentiments. Modern industrial classes are thus reconstituted as 'imagined communities', powerful abstractions occupying a central place

in individual and collective identifications. This re-constitution of classes involves not only an organizational articulation of class, where the organizations become the real class actors, but also the development of uniform class symbolism, iconography and the dissemination of class identities and discourses.

In **status-conventional society** stratification is sourced in the cultural sphere. The strata are lifestyle and/or value-based status configurations. They can form around differentiated patterns of value-commitment, identity, belief, symbolic meaning, taste, opinion or consumption. Because of the ephemeral and fragile nature of these resources, a stratification system based on conventional status communities appears as a shifting mosaic that can destabilize economics and politics. The state is weakened because it cannot rely on mass support, and the economy is weakened (in its societal effectivity) because of the critical importance of symbolic values. Each order is deconcentrated by a prevailing orientation to values and utilities that are established conventionally rather than by reference to collective interests.

1   In status-conventional society the redistribution of property that begins in organized-class society continues, especially in the context of privatization. More importantly the character of property changes so that it is much less easy to accumulate and monopolize. Intellectual property becomes more important relative to material property and the economy of intellectual and aesthetic signs is highly fluid and competitive (Lash and Urry, 1994). Education becomes a chancey mediator of socioeconomic reproduction. Under these conditions markets become casinos. Each individual is his or her own market player, needing to make educational and occupational career decisions in contexts that defy parental advance planning. Social rewards depend on performance, although the markets will not necessarily evaluate performance on a just calculus.

2   The reproductive lineaments of class disappear. In a globalized world of symbolic currents the nation-state can no longer orchestrate class groupings because it has been beaten into submission by irresolvable problems and besieged by entitlement claimants who stand outside the old organized classes. The central site for reproduction is now the mobile, biographically self-composing individual. Moreover the stress on individual performance and capacity and on individual selection of lifestyle and value-commitment means that patriarchy becomes susceptible to feminist opposition.

3   Status-conventional societies experience simultaneous cultural homogenization and fragmentation. They homogenize at the level of material culture and milieu emphasizing consumption, especially symbolic consumption, but fragment at the level of lifestyles and value-commitments as these issues become redefined as matters of election and choice. Each of these developments spells the dissolution of class subcultures.

4   At the political level, status-conventional society is marked by class and partisan disalignment, declining partisanship and party trust, the

appearance of 'third parties', especially of the left-libertarian type and a growing tide of 'new politics', 'issue politics' and 'life politics' (Dalton, 1988; Giddens, 1991; Kitchelt, 1989). With the decline of class organizations and the ideological packages that these organizations promote, the organized quasi-communities of class fade. The new political configurations promote the elaboration of new value-commitments that themselves become the focuses of differentiation and inequality.

Postclass society

This historical-phase model suggests that the stratification system might be moving into a culturalist or **status-conventional** phase. Figure 1.2 is a rejigging of Figure 1.1 that outlines a status-theoretic template to replace the class-theoretic one. It shows that a historical transformation from class society to organized-class society to status-conventional society is not only an issue of socioeconomic stratification but one of wide-ranging societal transformation. The argument offered here is therefore a development of the general theoretical effort that focuses on postindustrialization (Bell, 1973), detraditionalization and reflexive modernization (Beck, 1992; Beck et al., 1994; Giddens, 1991), postmodernization (Crook et al., 1992; Harvey, 1989; Lyotard, 1984), societal disorganization (Lash and Urry, 1987, 1994; Offe, 1985) and globalization (Featherstone, 1990; Robertson, 1992; Waters, 1995b).

We can now theorize this transformation more formally. The early part of this chapter disaggregates class theory into four propositions that can be used to explain the substantive aspects of class. We can follow a similar procedure in theorizing status-conventional society. The four propositions that class theory makes are: economism; groupness; behavioural linkage; and transformative capacity. A status-conventional theory would offer the following parallel propositions.

- The proposition of **culturalism**. Status-conventional stratification is primarily a cultural phenomenon. It is based on subscription to lifestyles that form around consumption patterns, information flows, cognitive agreements, aesthetic preferences and value-commitments. Material and power phenomena are reducible to these symbolically manifested lifestyle phenomena.
- The proposition of **fragmentation**. Conventional statuses, like classes, are real phenomena. However they consist of a virtually infinite overlap of associations and identifications that are shifting and unstable. Status-conventional society is a fluid matrix of fragile formations that cycle and multiply within a globalized field.
- The proposition of **autonomization**. The subjective orientation and behaviour of any individual or aggregate of individuals is very difficult to predict by virtue of stratificational location. There is no central cleavage or single dimension along which preferences can be ordered.

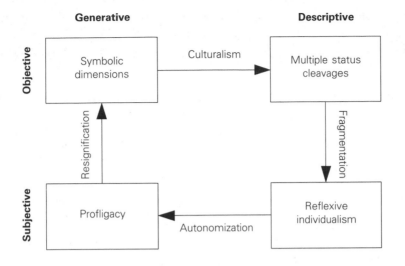

Figure 1.2 *Aspects of a sociology of status-conventional society*

Such attributes as political preference, access to educational opportunity, patterns of marriage and income are self-referential rather than externally constrained.

- The proposition of **resignification** based on subjective interests. The stratification process is continuously fluid. Its openness allows a constant respecification and invention of preferences and symbolic dimensions that provides for continuous regeneration. The source of novelty is a process of restless subjective choice that seeks to gratify churning and unrepressed emotions that include anxiety and aggression as well as desire.

Figure 1.2 also outlines the substantive status-conventional parallels to Figure 1.1. It shows that the propositions can specify the possible phenomena that sociologists might seek to theorize and analyse. The starting point is the top left cell which indicates that the objective-generative phenomena in which we should be interested are 'symbolic dimensions'. These are socially subscribed scales or networks of symbols that can provide focuses for identification and preference. They are broadly similar to the phenomena that Appadurai (1990) refers to as 'scapes' (ethnoscapes, theoscapes, financescescapes etc.) in his analysis of cultural globalization. These symbolic dimensions include some of the 'economic' phenomena traditionally associated with class, including socioeconomic status, but in a symbolized form. So 'occupation' is now critical not in terms of its capacity to put one in a relationship of exploitation but because it is a badge of status, an indicator of one's importance and of one's capacity to consume. Alongside these we can place ascribed-status membership dimensions that have now become value-infused, symbolized and reflexive (ethnicity, religion, education, race, gender and sexual preference) plus consumption statuses (yuppie, trekkie, hacker, clothes-horse, punk, gothic, jogger, opera buff etc.) and value-commitment statuses (feminist, environmentalist, Zionist, redneck, right-to-lifer etc.). Identity is thus not linked either to property or to organizational position. Under conditions of advanced affluence, styles of consumption and commitment become socially salient as markers and delimitators.

The proposition of culturalism specifies that these symbolic dimensions will compete with each other in the field of social structure. This will produce the phenomenon of multiple status cleavages. The stratificational categories of status-conventional society are a complex mosaic of taste subcultures, 'new associations', civic initiatives, ethnic and religious revolutionary groups, generational cohorts, community action groups, new social movements, gangs, alternative lifestyle colonies, alternative production organizations, educational alumni, racial brotherhoods, gender sisterhoods, tax rebels, fundamentalist and revivalist religious movements, internet discussion groups, purchasing co-ops, professional associations, and so on. Many are ephemeral, some are continuous and stable.

A key feature of these multiple status cleavages is that because they are specialized and intersecting, membership in any one does not necessarily contradict membership in any other. From the subjective point of view the proposition of fragmentation ensures that individuals apprehend the stratification system as a status bazaar. Individuals stand simultaneously as members of several status-groups and have the potential to be members of any others. Their identities are reflexively self-composed as they move between status groups. However, the fact of a status market does not imply an absolute voluntarism, and indeed the freedoms in most cases are relevant to exit from status groups rather than entry. Closure processes remain effective in status-conventional society.

The proposition of autonomization nevertheless allows individuals to be profligate in their behaviour. They will tend to spend their resources of time, energy, money, influence and power in the pursuit of symbolic attachments that tend to advance the interests, identities, values and commitments to which they subscribe and aspire. The very act of doing this will, by the proposition of resignification, tend to redefine and re-order the symbolic dimensions that reference the system. Indeed, a particular effect is the redefinition of some traditional status-membership dimensions, especially education, religion and ethnicity into a more ephemeral and conventional regime. So education becomes a marketplace for credentials, religion becomes a vehicle for handling this week's anxieties, and ethnicity is something one rediscovers through community action and involvement.

Conclusion

Postclass societies will remain internally differentiated in terms of access to economic resources, political power and prestige. Indeed it is possible to argue that an organized-class society in its late corporatist form can have the greatest potential to achieve a historically unique degree of egalitarianism and that postclass society will bring about an increase in inequality. Nor will the emergence of postclass society imply the end of social division and conflict. Non-class social divisions and non-class conflicts have survived class, even if overshadowed by it under conditions of industrial capitalism. The new divisions and conflicts that might emerge in postclass society may prove even more crippling and destabilizing than the old ones. Unlike many postindustrial visions of social change, this argument then, does not imply progressive equalization and social harmony.

The sociology of class is already adjusting to these changing social conditions. Marxist class theory has all but disappeared and is influential only in the empiricist form developed by Wright and his associates (1982, 1985, 1989) that both accepts that class can be sourced in authority and credentials as much as in property and that the stratificational map can identify up to 12 different class locations. The other mainstream approach, what is often called 'class analysis', is even more diffident in its defence of a sociology of class. It claims only to be a research programme within which different theories can be assessed empirically (Goldthorpe and Marshall, 1992: 382–3). Interestingly, it also insists, 'that specific consideration should also be given to theories holding that class relations are in fact of diminishing importance for life-chances and social action or that other relations and attributes – defined, for example, by income or consumption, status, lifestyle, ethnicity or gender – are or are becoming, of greater consequence' (1992: 382). Class analysis appears to be adjusting to the fact that class can empirically explain very little, a mere 17 per cent of income (Halaby and Weakliem, 1993) and perhaps 10 per cent of voting behaviour (Clark et al., 1993; Franklin et al., 1992), and even here class is operationalized as occupation. People may identify with classes but only when prompted and only after they have identified with occupation, family role, national citizenship, gender, ethnicity, age, region of residence, and supporting a sports team, so that 'the discursive salience of class is almost minimal' (Emmison and Western, 1990: 241).

If class then is a traditionalistic remnant in a postmodernizing world, the question remains of whether sociology can continue to make a central theoretical contribution if it abandons the concept of 'class' on which it relied for a hundred years. The answer is that it indeed must abandon its insistence on the centrality of class if it is to survive. The most instructive recent sociological studies are those that emphasize the intersection of multiple status cleavages within a single local context. These tend to the view that patterns of oppression and exploitation can become extreme where the status cleavages reinforce one another or can be moderated where they run counter to one another. Phizacklea's study (1990) of gender and ethnicity in the British fashion industry is an example of the former while Kornblum's study (1974) of Chicago steelworkers represents the latter. As the above quotation from Goldthorpe and Marshall shows, empirical 'class analysis' equally can accommodate stratificational multi-dimensionality so long as it does not continue to privilege class. However, the key task that remains is the development of a macro-theoretical paradigm that can match the brilliant capacity of Marx and Weber to theorize a new principle of social stratification. They managed to avoid the dangers of retrospection, to avoid theorizing classes as 'new estates' and we too must seek likewise to seek to avoid theorizing emergent status-conventional arrangements as 'new classes'.

Notes

1 *American Sociological Review*, 58 (1); *British Journal of Sociology*, 44(2,3); *International Journal of Urban and Regional Research*, 15(1); *International Sociology*, 8(3), 9(2–3); *Sociology*, 24(2), 26(2–3), 28(2–4).

2 This chapter is based on work done in the 'Impact of Class' project being carried out at the University of Tasmania and the Research School of Social Sciences, Australian National University in conjunction with Jan Pakulski and Gary Marks. It draws on material co-authored with Pakulski and published as *The Death of Class* (London: Sage, 1996). Some of the ideas and a few of the words belong to him and I am grateful for his permission to publish this chapter under sole authorship.

3 This argument about organized-class society is similar to that taken by early Frankfurt School theorists (see, for example, the contributions in Arato and Gebhardt, 1978, Part 1).

References

Abercrombie, N. and Urry, J. (1983) *Capital, Labour and the Middle Classes*. London: Allen & Unwin.

Anderson, B. (1983) *Imagined Communities*. London: Verso.

Appadurai, A. (1990) 'Disjuncture and difference in the global cultural economy', in M. Featherstone (ed.), *Global Culture*. London: Sage. pp. 295–310.

Arato, A. and Gebhardt, E. (1978) *The Essential Frankfurt School Reader*. New York: Urizon.

Beck, U. (1992) *Risk Society: Towards a New Modernity*. London: Sage.

Beck, U., Giddens, A. and Lash, S. (1994) *Reflexive Modernization*. Cambridge: Polity Press.

Bell, D. (1973) *The Coming of Post-Industrial Society*. New York: Basic Books.

Berle, A. and Means, G. ([1932] 1967) *The Modern Corporation and Private Property*. New York: Harcourt.

Blau, P. and Duncan, O. (1967) *The American Occupational Structure*. New York: Wiley.

Burnham, J. (1941) *The Managerial Revolution*. New York: Doubleday.

Clark, T. and Lipset, S. (1991) 'Are social classes dying?', *International Sociology*, 6(4): 397–410.

Clark, T., Lipset, S. and Rempel, M. (1993) 'The declining political significance of social class', *International Sociology*, 8(3): 279–93.

Crompton, R. (1993) *Class and Stratification*. Cambridge: Polity Press.

Crook, S., Pakulski, J. and Waters, M. (1992) *Postmodernization*. London: Sage.

Dahrendorf, R. (1959) *Class and Class Conflict in Industrial Society*. London: Routledge.

Dalton, R. (1988) *Citizen Politics in Western Democracies*. Chatham: Chatham Publishers.

Ehrenreich, B. and Ehrenreich, J. (1979) 'The professional-managerial class', in P. Walker (ed.), *Between Labour and Capital*. Boston: South End. pp. 5–45.

Emmison, M. and Western, M. (1990) 'Social class and social identity: a comment on Marshall et al.', *Sociology*, 24(2): 241–53.

Featherstone, M. (ed.) (1990) *Global Culture*. London: Sage.

Franklin, M., Mackie, T. and Valen, H. (1992) *Electoral Change: Responses to Evolving Social and Attitudinal Structures in Western Countries*. Cambridge: Cambridge University Press.

Giddens, A. (1973) *The Class Structure of Advanced Societies*. London: Hutchinson.

Giddens, A. (1991) *Modernity and Self-Identity*. Cambridge: Polity Press.

Goldthorpe, J. (1982) 'On the service class, its formation and future', in A. Giddens and G. Mackenzie (eds), *Social Class and the Division of Labour*. Cambridge: Cambridge University Press. pp. 162–85.

Goldthorpe, J. (1983) 'Women and class analysis', *Sociology*, 17(4): 465–88.

Goldthorpe, J. and Marshall, G. (1992) 'The promising future of class analysis: a response to recent critiques', *Sociology*, 26(3): 381–400.

Halaby, C. and Weakliem, D. (1993) 'Ownership and authority in the earnings function', *American Sociological Review*, 58(1): 16–30.

Harvey, D. (1989) *The Condition of Postmodernity*. Oxford: Basil Blackwell.

Johnson, T. (1972) *Professions and Power*. London: Macmillan.

Kitchelt, H. (1989) *The Logics of Party Formation*. Ithaca, NY: Cornell University Press.

Konrad, G. and Szelenyi, I. (1979) *Intellectuals on the Road to Class Power*. Brighton: Harvester Press.

Kornblum, W. (1974) *Blue Collar Community*. Chicago: University of Chicago Press.

Larson, M. (1977) *The Rise of Professionalism*. Berkeley, CA: California University Press.

Lash, S. and Urry, J. (1987) *The End of Organised Capitalism*. Cambridge: Polity Press.

Lash, S. and Urry, J. (1994) *Economies of Signs and Space*. London: Sage.

Lee, D. and Turner, B. (eds) (1996) *Conflicts about Class*. London: Longman.

Lyotard, J. (1984) *The Postmodern Condition*. Manchester: Manchester University Press.

Mallet, S. (1975) *The New Working Class*. Nottingham: Spokesman.

Mann, M. (1993) *The Sources of Social Power*, vol. 2. Cambridge: Cambridge University Press.

Offe, C. (1984) *Contradictions of the Welfare State*. London: Hutchinson.

Offe, C. (1985) *Disorganised Capitalism*. Cambridge/Cambridge, MA: Polity/MITP.

Pakulski, J. and Waters, M. (1996) *The Death of Class*. London: Sage.

Parkin, F. (1979) *Marxism and Class Theory*. London: Tavistock.

Parsons, T. (1954) *Essays in Sociological Theory*. Glencoe, IL: Free Press.

Perkin, H. (1989) *The Rise of Professional Society*. London: Routledge.

Phizacklea, A. (1990) *Unpacking the Fashion Industry: Gender, Racism and Class in Production*. London: Routledge.

Poulantzas, N. (1974) *Classes in Contemporary Capitalism*. London: Verso.

Robertson, R. (1992) *Globalization*. London: Sage.

Walby, S. (1990) *Theorizing Patriarchy*. Oxford: Basil Blackwell.

Waters, M. (1989) 'Patriarchy and viriarchy', *Sociology*, 32(2): 193–211.

Waters, M. (1994) 'Succession in the stratification order: a contribution to the "death of class" debate', *International Sociology*, 9(3): 295–312.

Waters, M. (1995a) 'The thesis of the loss of the perfect market', *British Journal of Sociology*, 46(3): 409–28.

Waters, M. (1995b) *Globalization*. London: Routledge.

Wright, E. (1982) 'Class boundaries in advanced capitalist societies', in A. Giddens and D. Held (eds), *Classes, Power and Conflict*. Berkeley, CA: California University Press. pp. 112–29.

Wright, E. (1985) *Classes*. London: Verso.

Wright, E. (ed.) (1989) *The Debate on Classes*. London: Verso.

GENDER

2 Feminism, Postmodernism and the Sociology of Gender

Samantha Ashenden

The uneasy relationship between sociological knowledge and feminist politics has been mediated through the category 'gender' as a central site of personal, social and political analyses over the past three decades. This chapter explores the implications of the emergence of gender as a category of sociological analysis and traces a number of stages of thinking in this area, focusing on the transformation of the relations between 'sociology' and 'gender' under the impact of 'postmodernism'.[1]

Beginning with the challenge posed by the full recognition of gender to the sociological mainstream, this chapter examines the empirical sociology of gender, feminist epistemology, and recent attempts to think through the question of gender from within postmodern modes of analysis.[2] These three ways of engaging with the sociology of gender are addressed by taking up two themes: the understandings of identity and the models of self involved in different accounts, and the conceptions of knowledge underpinning these notions of self together with the relation of sociological thinking to political practice. Each of these accounts has implications for the politics of theory; disentangling these distinctions is central to understanding what is at stake in the relationship between sociological and feminist theorizing and political practice.

This is significant because, for feminism, the sociological theorizing of gender has always been tied to the question of political change: knowledge of the world and the possibility of its social and political transformation are linked. Thus, a central question raised by the relation of feminism and sociology is how we can best open space in which to imagine the future differently. Thus, a guiding question will be the relation of different forms of sociological thinking to social and political practice.

Postmodernism has called into question the bases of sociological knowledge and the boundaries of sociology as a discipline, and has problematized the emancipatory politics of a feminist movement based on women's identity. Consequently, this chapter will work with the nexus of terms sociology–gender–feminism, examining the challenges occasioned by the conjunction of these ideas in the context of postmodernism. By tracing the emergence of the relation between gender and sociology, this chapter argues that while the sociology of gender operates by assimilating gender into the dominant terms of sociological discourse, and feminist standpoint epistemology produces a form of epistemological separatism, the productivity of the postmodern challenge, both for sociological theorizing and for feminist politics, lies in transforming the terms of debate. This conjuncture, rather than suggesting an epochal 'after sociology' and 'post-feminism', instead makes a refigured project of sociology central to the analysis of gender relations and gender a central focus in refiguring the project of sociology. In this context, the challenge presented by the conjunction of gender and sociology under postmodernism is for sociology to make itself properly historical and political and for issues of gender to be rethought in terms of the forms of identity and practice they make possible and foreclose; through this process it is possible to envisage a reconnection of theoretical work and practice in a manner productive for gender struggles.

The sociology of gender

The gendered character of social relations that was brought into focus by late 1960s consciousness-raising and liberation movements became a site of sociological investigation from the 1970s. This took two directions: the analysis of social movements (as part of a wave of concern about the changing character of social protest following 1968) and the emergence of the sociology of gender, that is of the description and explanation of the gendering of social relations. It is this redescription of the social produced by a focus on the sociology of gender relations which will provide the focus of this section.[3]

Within sociological theorizing, a dominant manifestation of the recognition and mobilization of 'gender' as a category has been to add 'gender', along with categories such as 'race/ethnicity', to a list of descriptive dimensions of social existence. This has centred on revealing aspects of social life previously overlooked by mainstream sociology. An early example of such work is Oakley's *Housewife* (1974), a detailed analysis of the work done by women and the ways in which this is part of a gendered division of emotional and physical labour both within and outside of families. This initial work was followed by a plethora of sociological studies, demonstrating a gendered dimension to many aspects of social life.[4]

The redescription of the social produced through including gender dynamics within sociological analysis precipitated a debate about the concepts and theories used within sociology, provoking a challenge to some of the central categories of mainstream sociological thought. A clear example of this is the discussion of the relationship between class and gender in the context of theories of social stratification.

Since its beginnings in the nineteenth century, sociology has been centrally concerned to document and explain structures of social inequality. A major focus of sociological research has therefore been the stratification of societies, that is, the analysis and explanation of enduring divisions between groups.[5] Within sociology, standard conceptual frameworks for understanding inequality have failed to recognize or de-emphasized gender as a dimension of stratification. Thus, a central site of contestation for feminists working within 'mainstream' sociology has been to focus on the gendering of power relations and on the reconceptualization and redescription of the social structures in order more adequately to describe relations of inequality.

In the contemporary dispute over stratification theory Lockwood (1986) maintains that 'class' should remain the central indicator in research and that this should be based on the family unit. Where the family is headed by a male, the class position of a wife or partner should be derived from that of the head of household. Women are seen to lack a coherent class position as they do not form a cohesive group, being divided by status. Lockwood's method is therefore to derive women's class position from that of male heads of household. In contrast, others, such as Walby (1989, 1990) and Mann (1986), have argued that while women's social position cannot necessarily be derived directly from their labour market position, this is a problem generated by the presuppositions of class analysis and that to adequately account for stratification in modern societies there is a need to theorize gender as an independent dimension which intersects with that of class (along with race/ethnicity, sexuality, disability, age, and so on) to produce a complex account of patterns of social stratification. This set of criticisms is made convincing by the entry of increasing numbers of women into paid employment during this century, so that today women form half of the labour force in the UK (Game and Pringle, 1984). Neither does this development mean that there can simply be a 'disaggregation' of the family unit and treatment of all 'individuals' according to their 'class' position, since there is evidence of occupational segregation with women being concentrated in traditionally female areas of employment and in low paid and part-time work (Glendinning and Millar, 1987; Scott, 1984). That is, there continues to be a 'gendering' of inequality.[6]

Perceived inadequacies in the framework of stratification theory have pointed to the limitations of traditional class analysis and the need to consider both gender and class as central concepts in understanding social inequality. This debate has focused on the relationship between 'capitalism' and 'patriarchy',[7] with some arguing that traditional stratification theory has represented a 'malestream' emphasis on the public world to the exclusion of the private, and that there is a need to understand how these intersect if we are properly to account for the structures and dynamics of social stratification.[8]

Attempts to develop complex analyses of patterns of inequality have been conducted by Walby (1989, 1990) and by Mann (1986). These analyses take up the question of the relation between capitalism and patriarchy and attempt to respond to some of the criticisms of earlier formulations of the concept 'patriarchy' as ahistorical (Rowbotham, 1981) and essentialist (Segal, 1987), by producing accounts that recognize social and historical specificity. In this context, Walby theorizes patriarchy as a system of structures involving a number of patriarchal practices. She posits six patriarchal structures whose relative importance is context-specific: the patriarchal mode of production, patriarchal relations in paid work, patriarchal state, male violence, patriarchal relations in sexuality and patriarchal culture. Her aims are to develop a complex account of relationships involving patriarchy as a form of male dominance over women and to account for different and interrelated forms of such relations. This provides an account of patriarchy as socially and historically embedded, with no one causal base but multiple forms of possibility which must be specified contextually.

Walby suggests that in the recent history of western societies two major forms of patriarchal relation are discernible: public and private. Private patriarchy is based on the exclusion of women from areas of social life, with individual men expropriating the labour of individual women in the home. Public patriarchy is a form of domination which does not exclude women from public life but which subordinates them within it. She suggests a movement from nineteenth-century private patriarchy expressed within, for example, the ideal of domesticity, to increasingly public forms of patriarchy, where women have equal political, civil and social rights but face continued inequality. In this latter context women are included and subordinated.[9] Mann (1986) suggests a similar approach, arguing that we have moved from a situation of two separate systems of patriarchal and class stratification, involving a division of public and private life in which patriarchal relations were private and class relations were public, stratification theory being concerned with the latter, to a point where, with women entering the public world of work and citizenship, we now have a gendering of stratification. Both analyses point to the need to theorize complexity.

We have examined a number of attempts to rethink sociological concepts to include gender. However, full recognition of the gendering of social existence problematizes traditional sociological theorizing more thoroughly than much of this literature recognizes, threatening the attempt of sociology to provide disinterested and totalizing explanations. The next section explores the development of an explicitly *feminist* sociology as a challenge to the idea that gender can simply be added, as another dimension, to existing sociological description. Before developing this discussion, we can reflect upon the character of the accounts of the sociology of gender just discussed, relating their productivity and limitations to the way in which the self is figured in these accounts and to the conception of knowledge which lies behind this work.

We have seen how, as feminism began to inform sociology, this effected a redescription of social life and a reworking of the categories of sociological understanding and explanation in which, for example, 'patriarchy' was a term brought into relation with the dominant terms of capitalism and class in stratification theory. This work affirmed the importance of gender as a dimension of experience and as a sociological category, thus transforming the shape of sociological knowledge by providing both a thicker description of the social world and descriptions of previously untheorized dimensions of social existence.

The sociology of gender operates by assuming gender categories and attempting to redescribe social existence by foregrounding this set of relations for analysis. In this, the central task of the sociology of gender is conceived as one of supplementing previous accounts, rectifying absences and distortions in sociology's description of social life with the aim of producing increasingly objective knowledge, better and more complete description. This form of engagement with the relation of sociology–gender–feminism can therefore be regarded as resting within a conventional social scientific project in which the social scientist is cast as a neutral cipher.[10]

Feminist sociology

The aims of the sociology of gender have centred on providing more adequate description; in this, the engagement of sociology–gender–feminism remains within and supplements the worldview of previous sociological knowledge. The sociology of gender thus lends itself to assimilation within the dominant terms of sociological discourse. An alternative, 'separatist' strategy is pursued by feminist standpoint epistemology. This challenges the parameters of previous sociological thought and contributes to a set of criticisms of the supposed objectivity and completeness of sociological description by demonstrating the partiality of previous and existing sociology and providing the impetus for a set of criticisms of the methods and epistemological status of sociological knowledge.[11]

Feminist standpoint epistemology draws out the implications of the sociology of gender for discussions of methodology and epistemology. It focuses on the questions which feminism has presented to 'malestream' knowledge, providing a challenge to the knowledge base of traditional sociology as falsely universalizing 'masculine' knowledge. Instead, feminist standpoint epistemology suggests a mode of sociological theorizing that is by women[12] for women. The challenge to sociology which this provides is expressed clearly by Dorothy Smith: 'Women's perspective . . . discredits sociology's claim to constitute an objective knowledge independent of the sociologists' situation. Its conceptual procedures, methods and relevances are seen to organise its subject matter from a determinate position in society' (1987: 91). This challenges the status of sociological knowledge as disinterested science and suggests starting from women's experience. Smith again: 'start thought from marginalised lives [and] take everyday life as problematic' (1987, in Harding, 1993: 50). In this, therefore, feminist standpoint epistemology operates as an epistemological corollary of the production of knowledge by and for women which has been central to the second wave of the women's liberation movement; this has been both its strength and the source of a number of problems.

Harding and Hartsock

Feminist standpoint epistemology has been developed in a number of ways by a range of feminist theorists in recent years.[13] Here we will focus on the work of Sandra Harding and Nancy Hartsock, as these accounts provide two of the clearest expressions of this development and of the character of its challenge to sociology. We will examine the challenge presented by feminist epistemology to the sociological mainstream, develop an account of what this challenge consists in and raise a number of problems and limitations with this approach, ending the section by reflecting on the character of the self and knowledge thus produced and the problems of this for feminist politics.

In her first essay in *Feminism and Methodology* (1987), Harding begins with the question of whether there is a unique method of feminist enquiry. If so, what? If not, how are we to explain what the challenge of feminism consists in? She then argues the need to differentiate method, methodology and epistemology, claiming that the contribution of feminism is not in producing unique methods for social scientific research but in the area of methodology, that is in theories of how analysis should proceed, and in epistemology, the justificatory strategies advanced for knowledge produced.[14] She recognizes that 'adding women' to traditional analyses, as in the sociology of gender, is a valuable but limited endeavour, suggesting that feminist sociology needs to move beyond this supplementary frame of reference to challenge 'male accounts of reality' (Harding, 1987: 5). This is because full recognition of the challenge posed by feminism to traditional social science requires a deep transformation in our understanding of the character of social scientific knowledge.

In order to differentiate feminist sociology from traditional knowledge and to ground the claim that feminist knowledge is more objective than its forerunners in traditional theory, Harding (1993) has developed an account of 'strong objectivity'. This consists not in the elimination of bias through more rigorous research, but rather in the recognition of situated knowledge as more capable of objectivity than that which assumes a 'God's eye view'. She suggests using the inevitably situated character of knowledge as a resource rather than regarding it as an obstacle to be overcome in the production of an objective account. Harding suggests that we reconceptualize objectivity:

> standpoint approaches have had to learn to use the social situatedness of subjects of knowledge systematically as a resource for maximizing objectivity. They have made the move from declaiming as a problem or acknowledging as an inevitable fact to theorizing as a *systematically accessible* resource for maximizing objectivity the inescapable social situatedness of knowledge claims (1993: 69, emphasis in original)

According to Harding, feminist work provides 'stronger standards for maximizing objectivity' (1993: 69) as a result of a number of distinct aspects of feminist work. Harding (1987) outlines three such aspects. First, feminist work uses new empirical and theoretical resources by focusing on 'women's experiences' and by recognizing that all knowledge is situated in relation to a problematic or perspective, challenging the division between contexts of discovery and of justification. Women's experiences therefore provide the distinct ground or starting point for feminist research.[15] Secondly, and related to the first point, feminist analyses should be *for* women; that is, they should begin with what is problematic for women (not, for example, bureaucratic organizations). Thirdly, feminism brings a new subject matter of enquiry, locating the researcher in the same critical plane as the overt subject matter by recognizing that the researcher is a situated individual with specific interests. Thus the aim is seen as that of studying women from the perspective of their own experiences. This provides Harding with an account of 'strong objectivity' as distinctive of feminist research and allows her to combine the idea of the inevitably situated character of knowledge with the claim to advance objectivity in social scientific research, thus maintaining the aim of producing 'less distorted accounts' (1987: 181).[16] She talks of 'operationalizing objectivity' in this way as making a stronger claim to objectivity than the 'weak objectivity' claimed by 'feminist empiricism' (Harding, 1993: 52).

Harding's attempt to retain the idea of a scientifically better under-standing and at the same time to recognize the importance and inevitability of perspective is underpinned by an appeal to the standpoint epistemology developed by Nancy Hartsock. This is tied to Harding's concern to reject epistemological relativism (1993: 61). By briefly examining Hartsock's account of a specifically feminist standpoint epistemology, we can draw out the distinctiveness and tensions involved in this approach to the social, political and epistemic significance of gender.

Beginning from the concern to provide theoretical work to aid the feminist movement, Hartsock's standpoint epistemology sets out to 'develop . . . an important epistemological tool for understanding and opposing all forms of domination – a feminist standpoint' (1983: 283). In this, women's experience is taken as the ground of the account and the concern is to sketch the 'epistemological consequences' (Hartsock, 1983: 284) of women's life activity (see also Harding, 1987, 1993).

Hartsock's account of a feminist standpoint is developed through a critical appropriation of Marx's theory of knowledge. This posits that socially mediated interaction shapes human consciousness; that is, determinate social position structures a person's experience and possibilities of knowing. Knowledge is only possible from a determinate social location. Hartsock adopts the Marxist distinction between appearance and essence and the idea of a number of levels of reality revealed from different social locations, developing out of this claim her theory of a feminist standpoint. She argues that, in modern societies, the position of women is structurally distinct from that of men due to the sexual division of labour. This division of labour produces a different lived reality for men and for women and therefore different access to knowledge. 'A standpoint, however, carries with it the contention that there are some perspectives on society from which, however well-intentioned one may be, the real relations of humans with each other and with the natural world are not visible' (Hartsock, 1983: 285).

Thus, Hartsock's argument moves from asserting the distinctiveness of women's structural position in modern societies, due to responsibilities for reproduction, childcare, and so on, to arguing that this provides the ground for a distinct epistemology because this experience gives women the possibility of privileged access to reality, one not available from the position of men as the dominant group. This second move, within Marx's theory of knowledge and within feminist epistemology, draws on Hegel's account of the master/slave dialectic in which the slave's position offers the possibility of a less distorted account of reality due to the slave's need to understand both his/her own position and that of the master in order to survive. It is on this basis that Marx argued for the standpoint of a potentially universal knowledge rooted in a universal class (the proletariat due to their specific social and historical location in the context of capitalism). It is also on this basis that Harding argues for the increased objectivity of observation from the contexts of women's lives.

> The logic of the standpoint epistemologies depends on the understanding that the 'master's position' in any set of dominating social relations tends to produce distorted visions of the real regularities and underlying causal tendencies in social relations – including human interactions with nature. The feminist standpoint epistemologies argue that because men are in the master's position *vis à vis* women, women's social experience – conceptualized through the lens of feminist theory – can provide the grounds for a less distorted understanding of the world around us. (1986: 191)

Feminist standpoint epistemology has been enabling for women and for feminist theory. It has provided a foundation and academic justification for recovering and revaluing women's accounts and life histories and activities. This work has played an important role in making methodological and political questions raised by feminist work central to contemporary debates within sociology and the philosophy of social science. It is important to recognize the role played by the development of feminist epistemology in underscoring the significance of feminist work within sociology. However, the strategy of attempting to build feminist epistemological foundations is problematic for feminism in a number of ways. These difficulties can be specified by examining the theoretical and political implications of the commitment to a distinction between appearance and reality, science and ideology, truth and power engaged by the production of a feminist standpoint as an epistemological mode of criticism, and by critically evaluating the commitment to grounding criticism in the theorized 'experiences of women'. The rest of this section will address the theoretical and methodological questions raised by feminist standpoint epistemology, the next section drawing out the ethical and political implications of this approach and the stakes raised for the future of sociology–gender–feminism.

Standpoint epistemology foregrounds two fundamental issues for social theory and methodology: first, the possibility of distinguishing between science and ideology, appearance and reality, truth and power, and of whether epistemology is an appropriate vehicle for this and, secondly, the idea and meaning of 'experience' and specifically 'women's experiences' as the ground of and basis for a liberatory knowledge to be revealed through critique. These presuppositions are woven together in the work of Harding and Hartsock.

Science and ideology

Within feminist standpoint epistemology, it is argued that the distinction between science and ideology can be grounded in women's lives because material life structures our understanding of social relations, this is different for the groups involved and the dominant groups' views prevail. Therefore, the vision of the oppressed group represents an *achievement* which must be struggled for through revealing the truth of women's experiences behind masculinist ideology:

> I use the term 'feminist' rather than 'female' here to indicate both the achieved character of a standpoint and that a standpoint by *definition* carries liberatory potential. (Hartsock, 1983: 289, emphasis added)

The concept of a standpoint thus provides feminism with a position from which to distinguish between appearance and essence on the basis of the theorized experiences of subjects. Hartsock bases this in women's experiences of motherhood, using the object relations school of psychoanalysis to provide an account of the distinctness of a 'relational' mode of being to women, derived from 'women's life activity' (1983: 283). In this way, she argues that a 'feminist standpoint could allow for a much more profound critique of phallocentric ideologies and institutions than has yet been achieved' (Hartsock, 1983: 288). This is tied to the aim of producing more universal knowledge – the aim of theorists like Harding and Hartsock has been to produce new knowledge from the point of view of women's lives, new grand theories and claims to truth, to out-universalize the universalism (assumed) of Marxism:

> A specifically feminist historical materialism might enable us to lay bare the laws of tendency which constitute the structure of patriarchy over time and to follow its development in and through the Western class societies on which Marx's interest centred. A feminist materialism might in addition enable us to expand the Marxian account to include *all human activity* rather than focusing on activity more characteristic of males in capitalism. (Hartsock, 1983: 283, emphasis added)

A feminist standpoint is thus conceived as a *privileged position*, implying that feminism can reveal the truth of women's experiences (this is the import of Harding's desire to hold on to a notion of objectivity). Indeed Harding (1991: 123) draws a distinction between women's experiences as 'unscientific' and women's lives as a good starting point for research. The problem is how she can maintain her position as distinct from the feminist empiricism she criticizes without assuming the privileged position of the theorist in explaining the meaning of 'women's experiences'. Harding's position here appears to imply that women are not capable of understanding themselves and their 'real' interests without the help of feminist academics, assuming a hierarchy in which some have greater or privileged access to knowledge of 'the real' sources of women's subordination. This replicates a fundamental source of tension within Marxist and other radical social and political thought (Benton, 1981). Let us follow this line of argument as it opens a series of problems with the science/ideology distinction occurring within feminist standpoint epistemology.

The distinction made between women's experiences and women's lives reveals a tension in feminist standpoint epistemology between privileging the immediate experiences of women as the essential subjects of the account(s) and the feminist theorist as a privileged knower in relation to the import of these experiences within feminist theory (just what does being on the same critical plane as the subject of enquiry mean here?). Further, the appeal to and privileging of women's daily lives suggests that women are the bearers of authentic knowledge *due to* their subordination. This knowledge is then revealed through feminist standpoint epistemology. This line of argument has two peculiar consequences. First, it places women as the bearers of truth *through* their subjugation and leads to the idea that the greatest truths about our social world will emerge from the most oppressed positions.[17] Secondly, the idea of a feminist standpoint as a privileged position implies that feminist knowledge contains the *truth* of women's experience(s). It posits an *authentic identity* of and for women: feminist standpoint epistemology is politically for women and is based on an idea of what women really are. Yet this belies fundamental differences between women (or at least makes it impossible really to theorize these, see below) and makes a claim at the level of epistemology that there is a common authentic relation with oneself and others as a woman: 'I propose to lay aside the important differences among women across race and class boundaries and instead search for central commonalities' (Hartsock, 1983: 290).

This leaves feminist standpoint epistemology unable to theorize differences between women. If we do attempt to think through the question of how to theorize differences amongst women from within this approach this produces a multiplication of standpoints (see, for example, Hill-Collins, 1990), additions of new and varied positions but not theoretical development, a limitation which is especially important given the original concern not simply to 'add' gender to the previous concerns of sociology.[18]

In sum, we can note a series of problems with the attempt to divide science and ideology which underpins feminist standpoint epistemology as a mode of criticism: the assumption of a privileged truth, the assumption of commonality, the attempt to universalize theory and a residual essentialism. I wish to suggest that these dilemmas are produced by reading from feminist discussions of women's experiences to epistemology as providing an innocent and secure ground of criticism. This will be the focus of the next section.

We can conclude our reflection on the effects of the science/ideology distinction and the role it plays within feminist standpoint epistemology by noting that standpoint theory aims to make connections and discover hidden relationships through assuming that with the right methods, methodology and epistemological 'toolkit' we can produce 'more objective' knowledge, but in doing so it raises problems concerning the production of a 'feminist knowledge'. These problems emerge when the attempt is made to assert the greater epistemic adequacy of this knowledge or to demonstrate that it is on the side of 'science' (and, therefore, liberation) as opposed to 'ideology'. This raises fundamental questions concerning the status of theoretical work in the social sciences, for example, whether it is possible to provide normative grounds for criticism and whether epistemological argument is the appropriate location for such discussion. To do so arguably presupposes prior knowledge of what constitutes adequate knowledge (Hindness and Hirst, 1977). In this context, attempting to provide epistemological grounds for criticism can be seen as an attempt to secure an innocent ground, a ground outside of political dispute in the context of feminist struggles.[19] The final section of this chapter will suggest that this approach is mistaken and that a more fruitful way forward for feminism, one suggested by the conjunction of feminism, sociology and postmodernism, does not involve providing epistemological arguments in an attempt to 'ground' claims to truth, but rather involves recognition of the political character of all knowledge. This suggests that the appropriate terrain of dispute is politics, sociology and anthropology and that epistemological arguments are misconceived in this context; that we cannot resolve these issues via recourse to epistemology.

Women's experiences

Turning to the second set of issues raised for methodology by feminist standpoint epistemology, the question of 'women's experiences', a further and related set of difficulties emerge. Examining the history of the second wave of the women's liberation movement from the 1960s onwards, we can see parallels between the premises of much of the theory and practice engaged here and the assumptions which underscore feminist standpoint epistemology. A brief historical excursus will therefore help to underpin my analysis of the difficulties of feminist standpoint epistemology in the attempt to base thought on 'women's experiences' and suggest that the route forward for feminist theory taken by postmodernist themes in feminist writing is neither necessarily apolitical nor a threat to feminist politics; it does dissolve the project of feminist epistemology but this is a different matter.

The second wave of the women's liberation movement based itself on the politicization of women's experiences. The most obvious and productive arena for this was consciousness-raising; women coming together and discovering that many of the problems faced are collective rather than individual. In this way Betty Friedan's 'problem with no name' (1986) became nameable as a political issue and women's consciousness of their subordination and silencing became the basis of feminism as a political movement. In the first years of the new women's movements a number of ideas developed concerning the origins of and solutions to women's oppression but the overriding idea was of a commonly experienced subordination. This commonality is perhaps best captured by the idea of 'sisterhood': the idea of feminism as a global movement based on the notion of women's shared oppression and struggle for liberation.[20]

The ideas of sisterhood and of women's liberation assume the category 'woman' and its status: the idea of woman and women's experience is formed as the ground for or basis of a political movement. This has since been challenged by the internal fracturing of women's movements on recognition that 'common sisterhood' cannot be assumed and that women are divided by differences of race/ethnicity, class, age, sexual preference, and a number of other factors; in other words, that there is no essential and shared experience of 'being a woman' unmediated by other concerns. Much of this criticism originally came from 'black' feminists who levelled the claim of imperialism against 'white' feminist analyses (see, for example, Hill-Collins, 1990; hooks, 1981; Lorde, 1984). Criticism of the universalizing and unifying tendencies of feminist thinking have also come from theoretically inspired developments within feminist work, challenging the essentialism of both feminist and non-feminist ideas in the social sciences. This latter strand of criticism has drawn its inspiration largely from developments in psychoanalytic and poststructuralist thought (see, for example, Adams and Cowie, 1990; Fuss, 1989; Riley, 1983).

In a number of ways and contexts, therefore, reliance on a politics predicated on shared identity has become problematic for feminism. In addressing political issues it is not possible to *assume* that 'sisterhood is global', that simply being a woman secures the possibility of identification with a universal project of female emancipation. This has been recognized more readily at the level of political action than at the level of theoretical reflection. (Perhaps, within feminist practice, 'sisterhood' was always recognized as partly phantasmatic? Feminism has always been a diverse, grassroots movement.) However, if we reflect upon the consequences of founding feminism on a discussion of women's experience(s) it is clear that this assumes the category of 'woman' and accepts as unproblematic the idea of 'experience' as the ground of truth. Feminist standpoint epistemology is an epistemological corollary of the politics of identity which has been so initially productive and latterly so debilitating to feminist movements.[21]

Harding and Hartsock speak of women's experience/lives as the starting point for research; we have identified some problems with this. At this point we need to ask what exactly constitutes the categories 'woman' and 'experience'? These notions have been thoroughly problematized within recent philosophy and social theory. Developing these insights, Adams and Minson (1990) criticize the assumption of an essential subject 'woman', arguing that what 'woman' is in a specific case emerges from how 'woman' is figured in a specific discourse or set of discourses; that is, there is no essential referent, no being behind becoming. Butler (1990) makes a similar point with respect to the role of identity in arguing that gender is performative. This work suggests that it is necessary to scrutinize the production of 'woman' and 'experience' within feminist accounts and else-where, in order to denaturalize assumptions about what women are.

Authenticity and the politics of identity

Returning to feminist standpoint epistemology, we can see that this mode of theorizing, grounded as it is in 'women's experiences', represents a politics of authentic identity, rather than an unsettling of the assumptions of identity. Therefore, while positing women as the subjects (and objects) of distinct knowledge has provided a challenge to the supposed universality of 'malestream knowledge', mobilized within feminist epistemology, this is problematic in that it assumes that there is a universal, whole and undistorted picture to grasp and presents the starting point and foundation for this as 'women's experiences'. The aim of a universal knowledge, a 'truer' or more complete picture remains and the foundation for this is assumed to lie in experience, a term which is not problematized.

In so far as feminist standpoint epistemology represents a politics of authentic identity based on an idea of what women really are, an awareness of the truth of women, it relies on a prefigured notion of women and therefore wrests the question of what being a woman means *from* political discussion, thus foreclosing the ground of much critical work. In other words, feminist standpoint epistemology is premised on an assumption that we can and should make a determinant judgement about what women are and on this basis, and this basis only, can we devise the outlines for emancipatory struggle. Instead I would like to suggest that there is no necessarily 'common experience' which can found feminist epistemology and politics, and that attempts to base feminist praxis on this cannot succeed in advancing the aims of women's liberation. This raises an important question: is feminism about revealing what women are and seeking change on this basis, or forcing open a space within which women might 'become' many things? If the latter, then arguably *the* central question which must remain open and under scrutiny is that of what women 'are'. A central task then lies in the constitution of political identifications with feminism as a broad range of ideas; that is, a critical role for theory must be that of aiding the constitution of communities by interrogating how women become what we are in order that we may become other than we are. From this latter point of view, an unnecessary, unwarranted and counterproductive leap is made by feminist standpoint epistemology in directly linking epistemology and politics and in reducing the latter to the former.

Before moving on to consider ways forward from this suggested by the relation of feminism with postmodernism, we can reflect upon feminist epistemology's presupposition of the subject 'woman' as an experiencing agent in terms of the models of self and of knowledge involved here. The model of self invoked by feminist epistemology is that of a foundational 'gendered' identity. It is on this basis that the particular epistemological implications of 'women's ways of knowing' is based. This then acts to fix women's identity as the ground and subject of feminist epistemology in a parallel move to that of the politics of identity. Related to this is an understanding of knowledge as liberatory; feminist epistemology operates to criticize 'masculine bias' in knowledge, demonstrating its partiality by revealing the 'authentic experiences of women' and, on this basis, forwarding 'less partial accounts'. Knowledge is seen as transformative and opposed to power/ideology: the right knowledge will set us free. Thus the conflation of epistemology and politics. At the same time, there is recognition of the inevitably situated status of the knower, that knowledge is perspectival. This produces a tension between the recognition of situatedness and a desire for objectivity. The feminist standpoint of Harding and Hartsock fills this space by assuming the subject woman and by reading from women's experiences to truth.

Postmodernism, feminism and sociology

Turning to the relationship between feminism and postmodernism, this section suggests that some of the questions and problems I have raised as emerging from the intersection of sociology–gender–feminism can be overcome from within a postmodern approach. Thus far we have seen that the empirical sociology of gender operates by *assimilating* gender into the terms of dominant sociological discourse, while feminist standpoint epistemology produces a form of epistemological *separatism* which reverses 'masculine' logic by attempting to provide a 'more objective' account based on women's lives. In the face of assimilation versus separatism, a central aim must be to transform the terms of debate. In this section, I wish to suggest that postmodern themes within feminism lend themselves to such a transformative strategy. In making this claim I take the term 'postmodernism' to refer to a set of philosophical themes indicating the impossibility of any ultimate foundation with respect to knowledge, and, accompanying this, recognizing the inevitably situated and historical character of knowledge and judgement. I will argue that this critique of foundationalism in philosophy does not entail a renunciation of central human values or feminist politics but rather opens space for such values to be given concrete instantiation. In this I follow Mouffe (1988) in suggesting that the critique of foundationalism in philosophy does not produce an apocalyptic modernism/

postmodernism but rather opens the way to a better self-understanding for modernity.[22]

Postmodern criticisms of Enlightenment philosophy often remain at the level of critique and of 'play', of theoretical specification and the deconstruction of categories. While this can be seen as having political effects, as deconstructing the division between theory and practice, I want to look to how we might develop from these discussions of the relations of sociology–gender–feminism to elaborate the reconnection of social and political theory and practice. Therefore this section will engage a series of questions arising from the foregoing discussion and aim to outline the implications of the engagement of feminism with postmodernism as characterized not by the necessary collapse of feminism, the loss of politics and acceptance of nihilism, but rather as providing space for the possibility of a new series of understandings of the politics of identity through questioning the constitution of subjectivity and suggesting the rapprochement of theoretical work in the social sciences with political practice. We will take, in turn: the question of knowledge and of foundations for theory, including the implications of the 'dissolution of the category "woman"' as the subject of feminist work; issues concerning the political implications of postmodernism; and questions flowing from this for the relation between sociology, gender and postmodernism.

Beyond feminist standpoint epistemology

We can begin by returning to feminist standpoint epistemology. This is an attempt to provide a theory of knowledge for feminism, an 'epistemological tool' for fighting domination. In this sense, it suggests an epistemological politics as a corollary of the politics of identity characteristic of much of the activity of the women's liberation movements. Reading from epistemology to politics, feminist standpoint epistemology inscribes a feminism based on a knowledge predicated on women's identity. This account of the relation of knowledge and subjectivity raises a number of ethical and political questions which this section seeks to address.

We can understand the desire underlying feminist standpoint epistemology in its attempt to read from women's experiences to provide a unique and secure ground for criticism, a foundation. From the self-understanding of feminism as a gender-based identity politics the appeal of this approach is clear. Indeed, Fuss (1989) suggests that identity politics has formed the defining problematic and *raison d'être* of much feminist thinking. However, the search for a ground outside of politics on which to base feminist argument, the search for 'innocent foundations' (Flax, 1992), is unnecessary, problematic and an example of bad faith on the part of feminism. It represents a refusal fully to think through the implications of the recognition of situatedness which is a great insight of feminism. The politics of the epistemological approach fails to recognize that feminism is implicated in the critique it offers of the knowledge produced within the social sciences and elsewhere, that there can be no innocent ground for criticism; that is, that there is and can be no ground outside of potential political contestation (Young, 1987).

We can explore the uneasy reception of postmodern ideas within feminism by focusing for a moment on the concern with the 'dissolution of the category "woman"' as a foundation for theory and politics threatened by postmodern ideas. What is this concern about? 'Postmodernism' has brought a questioning of metanarratives promising truth and the provision of conditions for the realization of universal justice, freedom and reason through 'the right knowledge'. Postmodernism therefore questions the established foundations of the political projects of the Enlightenment and in so doing is seen to threaten the ethical positions underpinned by such foundations. It undermines the foundational subject of feminism – 'woman' – and the idea of knowledge free from power which can set us free. This has brought forth a pitched battle between a postmodern fragmentation, questioning, refusal and deconstruction and attempts to hold on to Enlightenment ideas by normatively grounding political values.

The 'dissolution of the category "woman"' as a universal foundation precipitated by attention to poststructuralist and postmodern ideas is seen by many as fundamentally inimical to feminist politics (Fraser, 1989; Harding, 1987). However, it is possible to see this as the beginning of a different form of politics or engagement with the political which does not rely on essentialist categories but which focuses on questions concerning how 'woman' is figured in various social relations. Such an argument will be elaborated below. It is useful at this point to remember that the 'dissolution of the category "woman"' as an epistemological referent is not the same as arguing that gender is not a category of oppression; this is to confuse political and sociological knowledge and understanding with epistemology. It is the foundational subject of modern philosophy which is properly the target of postmodern criticism and deconstruction, not the idea of subjectivity as such;[23] that is, it is the epistemic move which is challenged, and with it the search for extra-political, 'innocent' knowledge:

> The identity of the feminist subject ought not to be the foundation of feminist politics, if the formation of the subject takes place within a field of power regularly buried through the assertion of that foundation. Perhaps, paradoxically, 'representation' will be shown to make sense for feminism only when the subject of 'women' is nowhere presumed. (Butler, 1990: 6)

The threat to metanarratives and foundational ideas of truth within postmodern philosophy has been perceived as a threat to feminism; it is, to feminism understood as based on a foundational identity. However, this is the exact point at which developing aspects of a postmodern critique provides the possibility of a critical redirection and further opening of feminist politics and feminist theory by bringing to centre stage a more thoroughgoing *questioning* of identity. For example, we could develop some of Foucault's central questions: how have we become what we are? How do we constitute ourselves in this manner? What are the costs of this? John Rajchman articulates this kind of critical thinking:

> One task for 'critical thought' is thus to expose [the costs of our self-constitution], to analyze what we did not realize we had to say and do to ourselves in order to be who we are. . . . The experience of critical thought would start in the experience of such costs. Thus before asking, or at least when asking, what we must do to behave rationally, this kind of thinking would ask: What are 'the forms of rationality' that secure our identity and delimit our possibilities? It would ask what is 'intolerable' about such forms of reason? (Rajchman, 1991: 11)[24]

This reconceptualization of the tasks of critical theory without foundations holds open space for a redirection of feminist politics; what we lose in this is the idea(l) of authenticity and truth as a ground for politics. Let me develop this for a moment. What attention to postmodernism does, in refusing closure, truth, a 'whole' story, is effectively politicize the whole terrain of struggle. For example, within the feminist movement, instead of a transcendent notion of 'global sisterhood', universal oppression and redemption from this through universal transformation (reliant on a hypostatized unity), we face a continuous ground of struggle over who and what we are and can become (and therefore the need to constitute, not presume, communities). As such, postmodernism offers the possibility of political struggle rather than a redemption from politics. It suggests that, rather than conceiving of the 'feminist movement' as a united force and facing the problem of this not being the case, instead we reconceive feminism as a permanently shifting political coalition. Identification with feminist struggles is not grounded in epistemology but in the problematization of social practices; feminism is a *political* identity to be struggled for and over. Therefore, while postmodernism offers no 'home' for a transcendental referent 'woman', this is not the same as there being no effective category; the point is to look at how 'woman' is constituted within specific domains and practices and the costs and possibilities of this (see work by Bartky, 1988; Braidotti, 1994; Butler, 1990, 1993).

The shift in the character of feminist work effected by attention to postmodern criticism can now be clarified by reflecting upon the ideas of self and knowledge at work here. Acceptance of the postmodern critique of philosophical foundations suggests a perspectival self, that identities are constituted historically and are contextually variable. The subject is therefore non-essentialist, has no a priori identity but multiple forms of identification as these are constituted through discourses, contexts of emergence, identifications, power relations, and so on. This is accompanied by recognition of no knowledge outside of history and power relations to which to appeal: knowledge is fully social and political and we are implicated in our knowledge productions, we have 'responsibility without grounds' (Flax,

1992). In this move, therefore, the focus of feminist work shifts from regarding identity as the ground of politics to the interrogation of the formation of identities and processes of exclusion, thus opening the question of identification as an active process, drawing on practical knowledges from domains such as sociology, anthropology and history.

The politics of difference

Moving beyond the assumed categories of 'woman' and 'experience' does not necessarily represent a surrender to domination, leading inexorably to the loss of feminist politics, nihilism, and so on. Rather, it offers the possibility of a new set of problematizations, politicizing the question of woman. 'The deconstruction of identity is not the deconstruction of politics; rather it establishes as political the very terms through which identity is articulated' (Butler, 1990: 148).

We can develop an account of politics from the postmodern criticisms of foundationalism by noting that postmodernism brings to the centre of discussion the questions of *political identification* and of the *constitution of communities*. This is because subjectivity and political interests are not presumed but rather are conceptualized as constituted within and through social and political life through acts of identification (see Hindess, 1986; Laclau, 1994; Laclau and Mouffe, 1985). Feminism is an achievement, but a political not an epistemic one. In the postmodern move, it is not women who are dissolved but the epistemic category as a refuge from discussion. The turn to postmodernism therefore provides the opportunity for 'gender' to become thoroughly political.

Various strategies for this politicization are suggested in the feminist literature. One suggestion is a form of 'strategic essentialism'. This is found in Harding's work in the context of her questioning whether feminists should give up the 'political benefits' which accompany claims to objective knowledge (Harding, 1987: 188). In some of her writing, Harding appears to recognize the force of postmodernist criticism and attempts to marry aspects of postmodernism with standpoint epistemology. She suggests (1993: 59) that feminism has a contradictory character: 'Feminist thought is forced to "speak as" and on behalf of the very notion it criticises and tries to dismantle – women. In the contradictory nature of this project lies both its greatest challenge and a source of its great creativity' (Harding, 1993: 59). This suggests a kind of 'strategic essentialism' – holding on to the idea of objectivity and of woman for strictly political reasons, while recognizing that this is intellectually disingenuous. Is this not, however, a case of bad faith – to recognize that these categories do not 'work' and yet to use them? Moreover, this approach fails to challenge the character of the political language in which the assumptions of rationality and universalism are countered by an unproductive charge of relativism. The dilemma here is a need to challenge conceptions of social scientific knowledge but also to engage them.[25]

In reflecting on the postmodern politicization of gender, Butler (1990) suggests a strategy of parody and subversive repetition. However, this remains individualistic: how are we to constitute political communities around feminism other than on the basis of identity? I suggest that we can move forward by recognizing the political as a site and a relation central to feminism as a form of identification. The political is both a site of contestation and a relation of difference. Difference is constitutive of the political and political identification need not be based on the philosophical foundation of a presupposed subject. The practice of politics does not presuppose unity and identity but respect and openness. This ethos is immanent to the self-understanding of feminism both as theoretical work and as a political movement. The questions which remain are how to constitute the political category of 'feminism' and how, when and why fight? But these are substantive, strategic and contextual, not theoretical questions.

The account of a new politics and engagement of feminism with sociology can be developed by focusing on the limitations of Butler's (1990) critique of modernism in social theory. This attack on modernism remains at an epistemological level and is thus incapable of fleshing out the character of a new politics. This is because Butler does not make the move from theoretical to practical reason and argument necessary to go beyond an individualism of 'subversive repetition' and 'parody', only gesturing to a coalitional politics which needs elaborating.

Feminism is a collective identification. Integral to forms of identification are forms of *practical knowledge* which reveal substantive social relations and open the ground on which it can become possible to think and act differently. The postmodern critique, restricted to theoretical reason, opens the space for practical reason and judgement (phronesis) but does not make the move itself. Integral to practical reason and judgement is the substance of sociological, anthropological and historical work. In other words, in the context of the postmodern politicization of knowledge and identity, feminism requires more not less focus on sociological knowledge. Lacking an 'epistemological fix', issues of judgement require that we engage with the substantive terrain of sociology, history, anthropology and reconnect theory and practice by rethinking our critical activity. Therefore, rather than producing useful 'tools' to fight domination, epistemological criticism sidetracks feminist argument. It blinds feminism to the constructive insights of postmodernism's criticism of Enlightenment philosophy.[26]

Feminist politics needs sociology to move from theoretical to practical reason and reflection. We need to examine how various forms of femininity and masculinity have been constituted historically and how they are constituted within contemporary power relations, in order to open a terrain on which to think differently about who we are. In this, sociology is closely linked to politics and practical reason through the need to examine and interrogate hegemonic forms of gender relations. Butler's critique opens space for such historical and sociological work, but a further delineation of the relationships between the actuality and possibility of struggles over gender relations is necessary.

Examining how hegemonic forms of gender relations are instantiated and maintained produces a form of immanent critique. This is a necessary accompaniment to Butler's suggestion of a politics of 'transgression'; in fact, such genealogies are necessary to 'perform' transgression, to know 'when to fight'. Thus, in the context of the engagement of feminist politics with postmodernism in sociology, it becomes clear that the way forward is through *practising criticism* and that this requires attention to sociology, history and politics as substantive knowledges. In this move, close study of the constitution of gender categories opens a space on which to consider the relation of the actual and potential through which subjects (as agents of knowledge) and political possibility can be articulated. The engaged, interested, that is political character of this can then be fully recognized. In the relationship between postmodernism and feminism, sociological analysis and argument finds its proper place in relation to politics.

Notes

1 The term 'postmodernism' is used here to signify recognition of the absence of ultimate foundations for knowledge.

2 These categories are internally differentiated but form distinct ways of approaching the sociological significance of 'gender'.

3 This is part of the historical trajectory of feminism as a social movement: from the 1970s women within academia began to challenge the boundaries of disciplines through refocusing them around the centrality of the overlooked character of gender and to create a politics of knowledge.

4 Examples of such work include: MacLean and Groves (1991); Scott (1984); Smart (1992); Spender (1980); Wilson (1977).

5 There are a number of strands within the sociological literature on this, from Parsonian structural-functionalism to Weberian and Marxian themes.

6 The challenge to the centrality of class analysis and attempts to rethink stratification theory according to multiple dimensions of inequality developed in the context of, and has been informed by, the emergence of feminist theoretical work. A number of authors produced work on the relation between capitalism and patriarchy, developing a 'dual systems' analysis of social stratification. Two important contributions to this development are the work of Juliet Mitchell (1975) and Heidi Hartmann (1981). In an attempt to develop an understanding of the persistence of gender oppression, Mitchell discusses the relation of patriarchy and capitalism in terms of a base-superstructure model, positing the capitalist determination of economic relations and patriarchal determination of unconscious psychic relations. Hartmann's analysis of the capitalism–patriarchy relationship is similar, proposing a 'dual system', but this account focuses on patriarchal relations operating at the level of the expropriation of women's labour by men rather than on ideology and the unconscious. She argues that housework and wage labour are central sites of women's exploitation.

7 Walby provides a useful working definition of patriarchy as 'a system of social structures, and practices in which men dominate, oppress and exploit women' (1989: 214). The term has had varied uses in social and political theory: in seventeenth century debates on the origins of political authority, it meant 'rule by the father'; Weber used it to refer to a system of government in which men rule societies through their positions as heads of households; the second wave of the women's liberation movement has used the term 'patriarchy' to refer to all

forms of male domination of women (physical, sexual, emotional, intellectual, economic and so on).

8 Recent analyses of relations between public and private life include Pateman (1988, 1989); Phillips (1991) and Showstack Sassoon (1987).

9 Walby suggests this latter form of patriarchy can then be divided according to whether it is organized around the market and the 'male model of work' or the state and citizenship. For interesting work on this, see Balbo (1987), and Hernes (1987).

10 This work, however, is not necessarily 'empiricist' in the manner suggested by Harding (1993); see later in this text and Holmwood, 1995.

11 Feminist standpoint epistemology has emerged alongside similar questions concerning the character of knowledge in both natural and social sciences generated from within the sociology and philosophy of science. See, for example, Hesse (1974); Kuhn (1970); Lakatos and Musgrave (1970) and Law (1986).

12 Or rather from the position of women; see the discussion later in this section.

13 See, for example, Haraway (1991); Harding (1986, 1987, 1991, 1993); Harding and Hintikka (1983); Hill-Collins (1990); and Smith (1987). Different authors provide quite different accounts and emphases so that, for example, the work of Donna Haraway (1991) can be situated within feminist standpoint epistemology but more accurately represents an attempt to think beyond the modernist position of Harding. See Conway (1993), for an interesting discussion of the differences between the work of Haraway and Harding.

14 Harding now recognizes distinctness of method as well as methodology and epistemology (1993, footnote 11). This appears to signal the beginning of a breakdown in her idea of feminist epistemology as distinct from feminist empiricism; see Holmwood (1995).

15 There is a shift in Harding's work from 1987 to 1993 from the use of women's experiences as a 'ground' to the metaphor of 'journey' with women's experiences as a starting point.

16 The idea of studying subjects from the point of view of their own experience is not unique to feminism but has a long history within sociology influenced by phenomenology.

17 Flax (1990) notes that this assumes that the oppressed are not in some way damaged by their experiences. Conway (1993) regards the linking of damage and truth as resting on an account of the 'ultimate victim'. Calhoun (1995) points to the way in which 'privileging lifeworld accounts' reproduces a form of the public/private distinction within feminist theory and operates as a 'metaphysics of presence'.

18 When Harding does address the issue of differences amongst women and the capacity of standpoint epistemology to think through the importance of these, she simply asserts that which needs arguing:

> the subjects/agents of knowledge for feminist standpoint theory are multiple, heterogeneous and contradictory or incoherent, not unitary, homogeneous and coherent as they are for empiricist epistemology. Feminist knowledge has started off from women's lives, but it has started off from many different women's lives; there is no typical or essential woman's life from which feminisms start their thought. Moreover, these different women's lives are in important respects opposed to each other. Feminist knowledge has arisen from European and African women, from economically privileged and poor women, from lesbians and heterosexuals, from Protestant, Jewish and Islamic women. Racism and imperialism, local and international structures of capitalist economies, institutionalized homophobia and compulsory heterosexuality, and the political conflicts between ethnic and religious cultures produce multiple, heterogeneous and contradictory feminist accounts. Nevertheless, thought that starts off from each of these different kinds of lives can generate less partial and distorted accounts of nature and social life. (Harding, 1993: 65)

19 This replicates certain moves within critical social theory in attempting to provide normative foundations for critique. See, for example, Habermas (1987), and Owen (1995).

20 For accounts and expressions of this see Coote and Campbell (1982); Friedan (1986) and Morgan (1970).

21 Harding states that feminist standpoint epistemology is not linked to the idea of identity politics because: 'marginalized lives provide the scientific problems and the research agendas – not the solutions – for standpoint theories' (1993: 62). In other words, because women's lives

are the starting point and not the end of research, Harding suggests that standpoint epistemology does not fall into the logic of identity politics. However, it is precisely as the starting point for the development of an epistemology that women's lives are foundational to feminist standpoint theory. This will either not be identitarian enough for those who want no truck with theory (remember mediation by the feminist academic) or problematic precisely because it does exhibit a similar logic to that of the politics of identity.

22 The engagement of feminism and postmodernism around issues of self and knowledge suggests a redirection of Enlightenment rather than a radical break; a redirection in which the Enlightenment story of knowledge, science, reason, progress is displaced by a focus on practical reason and judgement. This is suggested by Mouffe:

> the absence of foundation 'leaves everything as it is', as Wittgenstein would say, and obliges us to ask the same questions in a new way. Hence the error of a certain kind of apocalyptic postmodernism which would like us to believe that we are at the threshold of a radically new epoch, characterized by drift, dissemination and by the uncontrollable play of significations. Such a view remains captive to a rationalistic problematic, which it attempts to criticize. As Searle has pointed out to Derrida: 'The real mistake of the classical metaphysician was not the belief that there were metaphysical foundations, but rather the belief that somehow or other such foundations were necessary, the belief that unless there are foundations something is lost or threatened or undermined or just in question.' (1988: 38)

There are a number of themes in contemporary literature which point towards the need to develop a language and politics capable of negotiating and renegotiating difference; for example, see Tully (1995). Postmodern criticisms of Enlightenment rationalism are helpful in producing these developments, refocusing attention on history, sociology and politics and providing an alternative ethos of engagement to the attempt to constitute foundations for our arguments through epistemology.

23 In the context of its use within most feminist work, postmodernism does not imply radical contingency but lack of transcendental foundations. The point is not that there are no enduring forms of selfhood, this is necessarily so (Flax, 1990). Rather, the concern is to examine how notions of self are formed and their effects. This kind of questioning works as a form of immanent critique without need of the establishment of a prior normative framework.

24 Foucault:

> A critique is not a matter of saying that things are not right as they are. It is a matter of pointing out on what kinds of assumptions, what kinds of familiar, unchallenged, unconsidered modes of thought the practices that we accept rest. . . . Criticism is a matter of . . . show(ing) that things are not as self-evident as one believed, to see that what is accepted as self-evident will no longer be accepted as such. Practising criticism is a matter of making facile gestures difficult. (1988: 154–5)

25 Irigaray (1985) can be seen as enacting a strategic essentialism to counter the essentialism of phallocentric language; however, Irigaray does not couch this within a project of feminist science aimed at truth, her project is the refiguring of a language.

26 The critique of philosophical foundationalism is not the same as the critique of the political project of the Enlightenment; for an outline of the distinction between the epistemological project of self-foundation and the political project of self-assertion, see Mouffe (1988). Critique of philosophical foundations opens the way for a better self-understanding of modernity; to regard the loss of such foundations as the end of feminist politics is to fail to recognize that politics is centrally concerned with practical reason, not theoretical reflection.

Bibliography

Adams, P. and Cowie, E. (eds) (1990) *The Woman in Question*. London: Verso.
Adams, P. and Minson, J. (1990) 'The "Subject" of Feminism', in P. Adams and E. Cowie (eds) *The Woman in Question*. London: Verso.
Alcoff, L. and Potter, E. (eds) (1993) *Feminist Epistemologies*. London: Routledge.

Balbo, L. (1987) 'Crazy quilts: rethinking the welfare state debate from a woman's point of view', in A. Showstack-Sassoon (ed.), *Women and the State*. London: Hutchinson.

Bartky, S. (1988) 'Foucault, femininity and the modernisation of patriarchal power', in I. Diamond and L. Quinby (eds), *Feminism and Foucault: Reflections on Resistance*. Boston, MA: Northeastern University Press.

Benton, T. (1981) '"Objective" interests and the sociology of power', *Sociology*, 15(2): 161–84.

Braidotti, R. (1994) *Nomadic Subjects: Embodiment and Sexual Difference in Contemporary Feminist Theory*. New York: Columbia.

Butler, J. (1990) *Gender Trouble: Feminism and the Subversion of Identity*. London: Routledge.

Butler, J. (1993) *Bodies That Matter: On the Discursive Limits of 'Sex'*. London: Routledge.

Butler, J. and Scott, J. (eds) (1992) *Feminists Theorize the Political*. London: Routledge.

Calhoun, C. (1995) *Critical Social Theory*. Oxford: Basil Blackwell.

Conway, D. (1993) 'Das Weib an sich: the slave revolt in epistemology', in P. Patton (ed.), *Nietzsche, Feminism and Political Theory*. London: Routledge.

Coote, A. and Campbell, B. (1982) *Sweet Freedom*. Oxford: Basil Blackwell.

Crompton, R. and Mann, M. (eds) (1986) *Gender and Stratification*. Cambridge: Polity Press.

Flax, J. (1990) *Thinking Fragments: Psychoanalysis, Feminism and Postmodernisn in the Contemporary West*. Berkeley, CA: University of California Press.

Flax, J. (1992) 'The end of innocence', in J. Butler and J. Scott (eds), *Feminists Theorize the Political*. London: Routledge.

Foucault, M. (1988) *Politics, Philosophy, Culture: Interviews and Other Writings 1977–1984*. London: Routledge.

Fraser, N. (1989) *Unruly Practices*. Cambridge: Polity Press.

Friedan, B. (1986) *The Feminine Mystique*. London: Harmondsworth.

Fuss, D. (1989) *Essentially Speaking: Feminism, Nature and Difference*. London: Routledge.

Game, A. and Pringle, R. (1984) *Gender at Work*. London: Pluto.

Glendinning, C. and Millar, J. (eds) (1987) *Women and Poverty in Britain*. Brighton: Wheatsheaf.

Habermas, J. (1987) *The Philosophical Discourse of Modernity: Twelve Lectures*. Cambridge: Polity Press.

Haraway, D. (1991) *Simians, Cyborgs and Women*. London: Routledge.

Harding, S. (1986) *The Science Question in Feminism*. Ithaca, NY: Cornell University Press.

Harding, S. (1987) *Feminism and Methodology*. Milton Keynes: Open University Press.

Harding, S. (1991) *Whose Science? Whose Knowledge? Thinking From Women's Lives*. Ithaca, NY: Cornell University Press.

Harding, S. (1993) 'Rethinking standpoint epistemology: "What is strong objectivity?"', in L. Alcoff and E. Potter (eds), *Feminist Epistemologies*. London: Routledge.

Harding, S. and Hintikka, M. (eds) (1983) *Discovering Reality: Feminist Perspectives on Epistemology, Metaphysics, Methodology and the Philosophy of Science*. Dordrecht: Reidel.

Hartmann, H. (1981) 'The unhappy marriage of Marxism and feminism: towards a more progressive union', in L. Sargent (ed.), *Women and Revolution: The Unhappy Marriage of Marxism and Feminism*. London: Pluto Press.

Hartsock, N. (1983) 'The feminist standpoint: developing the ground for a specifically feminist historical materialism', in S. Harding and M. Hintikka (eds), *Discovering Reality: Feminist Perspectives on Epistemology, Metaphysics, Methodology and the Philosophy of Science*. Dordrecht: Reidel.

Hernes, H. (1987) 'Women and the welfare state: the transition from private to public dependence', in A. Showstack-Sassoon (ed.), *Women and the State*. London: Hutchinson.

Hesse, M. (1974) *The Structure of Scientific Inference*. London: Macmillan.

Hill-Collins, P. (1990) *Black Feminist Thought: Knowledge, Consciousness and the Politics of Empowerment*. Boston, MA: Unwin Hyman.

Hindess, B. (1986) '"Interests" in political analysis', in J. Law (ed.), *Power, Action and Belief: A New Sociology of Knowledge?* London: Routledge and Kegan Paul.

Hindess, B. and Hirst, P. (1977) *Mode of Production and Social Formation*. London: Macmillan.

Holmwood, J. (1995) 'Feminism and epistemology: what kind of successor science?', *Sociology*, 29(3): 411–28.

hooks, b. (1981) *Ain't I a Woman?: Black Women and Feminism*. Boston, MA: South End Press.

Irigaray, L. (1985) *Speculum of the Other Woman*. Ithaca, NY: Cornell University Press.

Kuhn, T. (1970) *The Structural Scientific Revolutions*. Chicago, IL: University of Chicago Press.

Laclau, E. (ed.) (1994) *The Making of Political Identities*. London: Verso.

Laclau, E. and Mouffe, C. (1985) *Hegemony and Socialist Strategy*. London: Verso.

Lakatos, I. and Musgrave, A. (eds) (1970) *Criticism and the Growth of Knowledge*. Cambridge: Cambridge University Press.

Law, J. (ed.) (1986) *Power, Action and Belief: A New Sociology of Knowledge?* London: Routledge and Kegan Paul.

Lockwood, D. (1986) 'Class, status and gender', in R. Crompton and M. Mann (eds), *Gender and Stratification*. Cambridge: Polity Press.

Lorde, A. (1984) *Sister/Outsider*. New York: The Crossing Press.

MacLean, M. and Groves, D. (eds) (1991) *Women's Issues in Social Policy*. London: Routledge.

Mann, M. (1986) 'A crisis in stratification theory? Persons, households/families/lineages, genders, classes and nations', in R. Crompton and M. Mann (eds), *Gender and Stratification*. Cambridge: Polity Press.

Mitchell, J. (1975) *Psychoanalysis and Feminism*. Harmondsworth: Penguin.

Morgan, R. (ed.) (1970) *Sisterhood is Powerful*. New York: Vintage.

Mouffe, C. (1988) 'Radical democracy: modern or postmodern?', in A. Ross (ed.), *Universal Abandon? The Politics of Postmodernism*. Minnesota: University of Minnesota Press.

Nicolson, L. (ed.) (1990) *Feminism/Postmodernism*. London: Routledge.

Oakley, A. (1974) *Housewife*. London: Allen Lane.

Owen, D. (1995) 'Genealogy as exemplary critique: reflections on Foucault and the imagination of the political', *Economy and Society*, 24(4): 489–506.

Pateman, C. (1988) *The Sexual Contract*. Cambridge: Polity Press.

Pateman, C. (1989) *The Disorder of Women*. Cambridge: Polity Press.

Phillips, A. (1991) *Engendering Democracy*. Cambridge: Polity Press.

Rajchman, J. (1991) *Truth and Eros: Foucault, Lacan and the Question of Ethics*. New York: Routledge.

Ramazanoglu, C. (1989) *Feminism and the Contradictions of Oppression*. London: Routledge.

Riley, D. (1983) *Am I That Name?* London: Macmillan.

Rowbotham, S. (1981) 'The trouble with "patriarchy"', in Feminist Anthology Collective (eds), *No Turning Back: Writings From The Women's Liberation Movement 1975–1980*. London: The Women's Press.

Rowbotham, S. (1992) *Women in Movement*. London: Routledge.

Sawicki, J. (1994) 'Foucault, feminism and questions of identity', in G. Gutting (ed.), *The Cambridge Companion to Foucault*. Cambridge: Cambridge University Press. pp. 286–313.

Scott, H. (1984) *Working Your Way to the Bottom: The Feminisation of Poverty*. London: Pandora.

Segal, L. (1987) *Is the Future Female? Troubled Thoughts on Contemporary Feminism*. London: Virago.

Showstack Sassoon, A. (1987) *Women and the State*. London: Hutchinson.

Smart, C. (ed.) (1992) *Regulating Womanhood: Historical Essays on Marriage, Motherhood and Sexuality*. London: Routledge.

Smith, D. (1987) *The Everyday World as Problematic: A Feminist Sociology*. Boston, MA: Northeastern University Press.

Spender, D. (1980) *Man Made Language*. London: Routledge and Kegan Paul.

Tully, J. (1995) *Strange Multiplicity: Constitutionalism in an Age of Diversity*. Cambridge: Cambridge University Press.

Walby, S. (1989) 'Theorizing patriarchy', *Sociology*, 23(2): 213–34.

Walby, S. (1990) *Theorizing Patriarchy*. Oxford: Basil Blackwell.

Weeks, J. (1987) 'Questions of identity', in P. Caplan, *The Cultural Construction of Sexuality*. London: Routledge.

Wilson, E. (1977) *Women and the Welfare State*. London: Tavistock.

Young, I.M. (1987) 'Impartiality and the civic public: some implications of feminist critiques of moral and political theory', in S. Benhabib and D. Cornell (eds), *Feminism as Critique*. Minnesota: University of Minnesota Press.

Young, I.M. (1990) *Justice and the Politics of Difference*. Princeton, NJ: Princeton University Press.

3 Racism and Postmodernism: Towards a Theory of Practice

Paul Connolly

According to Stuart Hall (1992), a discernible shift is currently taking place in black cultural politics away from the certainties associated with 'black' as a political identity towards a struggle over representation itself. The framework created by the evocation of the 'black experience', Hall maintains, has played a central political role over the past few decades as a rallying point for African/Caribbean and South Asian people struggling to highlight and challenge their marginalization within British society and their common experience of racism. However, this politics, based around the construction of an 'essential black subject' whose identity transcends ethnic, religious and cultural differences found within the 'black community', is slowly giving way to a politics centred around those very differences: a shift that Hall (1992: 253) refers to as a 'change from a struggle over the relations of representation to a politics of representation itself'.

Hall was careful, however, not to present this shift in crudely oppositional terms – the 'new' as it were simply replacing the 'old'. The social relations characterized by the marginalization and subordination of minority ethnic groups that gave rise to the essential black subject not only remain but have positively flourished with the rise of the New Right and the renewed emphasis on protecting and shoring up Britain's national identity. Struggles which problematize racism and insert it into the political sphere through reference to a collective experience of racism – the 'black experience' – therefore still play a prominent and essential political role. Rather, Hall posited that the questioning of this black experience and the emergence of what he termed 'new ethnicities' should not be seen in opposition to this earlier stage but as a fundamental part of it. As Hall (1992: 253) argued: 'as the struggle moves forward and assumes new forms, it does to some degree displace, reorganize and reposition the different cultural strategies in relation to one another'. Thus, there has emerged a struggle over two fronts: one over the continued marginalization and subordination of minority ethnic people and the other, as emerging, a struggle over their representation. The latter is, in essence, related to and has emerged out of the former.

Although Hall's comments were located within a specific debate concerning the place of 'black film' in British cinema they soon found a much wider audience. The growing dissatisfaction with the construction of the essential black subject and its inability to address the contradictions and contingencies at the heart of African/Caribbean and South Asian people's experiences in Britain came to resonate very closely with similar debates that also found expression from the late 1980s onwards (see, for instance, Cohen, 1988; Donald and Rattansi, 1992; Gilroy, 1990, 1993; Rattansi and Westwood, 1994). It is this deconstruction and de-centring of the essential black subject and its implications for theorizing racism that will provide the focus for this chapter. Some initial work at a more abstract and philosophical level has already been recently undertaken and need not be reproduced here (see particularly Rattansi, 1994). Rather, the concern of this chapter derives from my own ethnographic work (Connolly, 1997), and relates to the more concrete task of developing a theoretical frame able to cope with and increase our understanding of the complexities, contingencies and contradictions of racialized relations and identities that are uncovered once the essential black subject is set aside. I will begin this chapter with a brief and necessarily incomplete overview of some of the main theoretical issues pertinent to the present discussion that have arisen from these debates in recent years before assessing their impact on the extant literature on racism. This will provide the context within which I will offer the outlines of a theoretical frame, drawing upon and adapting the work of Pierre Bourdieu, which offers what I consider to be one of the most fruitful future directions for overcoming an essentialized and totalizing understanding of racism.

Racism, anti-racism and the 'essential black subject'

The Enlightenment project and its emphasis on the scientific search for Truth and Reason has figured prominently in discourses on 'race' over the past few centuries. The search for racial essences and the eagerness among scientists to identify, categorize and hierarchically order racial groups has been well documented in a number of important texts (see, for instance, Banton, 1987; Braham, 1992; Cohen, 1988; Husband, 1987). Moreover, this type of 'race'-thinking and the construction of various groups and peoples as the Other throughout history has meant that notions of 'Britishness' have always been racialized (see Barker, 1981; Cohen, 1988, 1992; Gordon and Klug, 1986; Miles, 1989, 1993; Rattansi, 1992). The centrality of nationhood and national identity among the British New Right that gained renewed impetus with the infamous 'Rivers of Blood' speeches of Enoch Powell in the late 1960s and can be traced through the Thatcherite era to the present hegemonic project of the struggling Major governments, are all testament to the continuing salience of 'race' to these nationalist discourses. It is against these discourses on 'race' and nationality that minority ethnic people in Britain are, at one and the same time, rendered invisible and visible. They are marginalized and excluded from official representations of what it means to be British and yet are summonsed up, in equal measure, as symbols of what being British is not; that is, as the Other. Historically the hard-working decency and reserved Christian morality of the British were therefore set against the racialized construction of the African slave as lazy, volatile and sexually promiscuous and the South Asian colonial subjects as dependent and in need of guidance. More recently, the Thatcherite hegemonic struggles which came to organize themselves around the need to revitalize Britain as a nation, came to identify Britain's decline with its loss of national identity and self-respect which were, in turn, associated with the presence of minority ethnic people in Britain and the move to multiculturalism (Parekh, 1986). Moreover, a number of moral panics were orchestrated to further emphasize certain aspects of this perceived decline that also came, inevitably, to reconstruct and reinforce these discursive constructions of the Other: from the drunken and subversive depictions of the Irish to the lawless and violent black mugger and the lazy and dependent South Asian illegal immigrant (see, for instance, Gordon and Rosenberg, 1989; Hall et al., 1978).

It was not surprising to find that, throughout this time, an anti-racist politics has emerged that aimed to challenge both the marginalization of minority ethnic people and the stereotypical construction of them as the Other. Moreover it was almost inevitable that such a politics would organize itself around the construction of a common experience of racism that would come to identify and attempt to redress the under-representation of 'black people' in Britain culturally, politically and economically. The fact that the conditions against which such a politics emerged have not significantly altered means, as Hall (1992) was at pains to point out, that the need for broader political coalitions around the 'essential black subject' remains.

These struggles were not only to be found in the political field, however, but also found expression in the sociological literature. Especially during the early 1980s in Britain, a number of writers were heavily critical of the stereotypical portrayal of minority ethnic people in research and the pathologization of their lives and cultures (see Bourne and Sivanandan, 1980; Gilroy, 1980; Lawrence, 1981, 1982; Parmar, 1981). The basic thesis that underlay these critiques was that the predominance of white, middle class researchers in academia had meant that they had little experience or understanding of racism and had therefore come to frame the research agenda from their own perspectives; one that foregrounded the uniqueness and problems of the 'black community' rather than 'white racism'. What developed out of this critique was the call for research on 'race' to locate itself within the 'black experience' and to generate appropriate research questions from this perspective (for a critical overview of some of these debates see Connolly, 1996). Partly as a result of these struggles, a significant strand of sociological research developed that came to centre itself around the emerging essentialized black subject, particularly during the early to mid-1980s, and which focused on documenting the 'black experience' of racism in Britain both quantitatively and qualitatively (see, for instance, Bhat et al., 1996; Fryer, 1984). Alongside this there emerged a number of new and innovative theoretical developments that, although being located in diverse and often essentially competing theoretical perspectives (for an overview see Rex and Mason, 1986), nevertheless tended to share a common focus which not only foregrounded the unitary 'black experience' but also located this within the context of 'white racism' in an attempt to shift the focus away from culturally deficit explanations of racial inequality. And it was out of these debates that a renewed focus on the concept of institutional racism, first proposed back in the 1960s by Carmichael and Hamilton (1967), became invaluable in problematizing the more invisible and taken-for-granted institutional processes and practices that came to disadvantage 'black people' (see, for instance, Ben-Tovim et al., 1986; Bhat et al., 1996).

Sociology, new ethnicities and the postmodern condition

The appropriation of the essential black subject within sociology has undoubtedly played a vital role in foregrounding the inherently political nature of the research enterprise and the set of taken-for-granted values that too often underpin it. Within the sociology of 'race' this has meant a progressive shift, during the 1980s, away from the construction of either marginalized or pathological accounts of minority ethnic people's lives to one that has increasingly come to foreground and problematize racism in the understanding of racial inequality and patterns of domination and subordination. However, while the essential black subject has maintained an important strategic role in the political field, its continuing presence within the field of sociology has been far more problematic. The emergence of what Lyotard (1984) has termed the 'postmodern condition' and the increasing influence of deconstructionism in sociological debates has meant that the certainties associated with the essential black subject have come under a sustained critique in recent years. Here we have witnessed a growing literature that has not only questioned the 'black experience' in terms of who was being excluded but also the certainties and generalizations that were being made about those who were included.

As regards the former, a growing body of literature has developed which has come to challenge the equation of racism with skin colour that has tended to underlie the construction of the essential black subject (Anthias and Yuval-Davis, 1992; Cohen, 1988, 1992; Miles, 1989, 1993; Omi and Winant, 1994; Rattansi, 1994). While skin colour has been and remains a central signifier in the identification and classification of people, it is neither the only nor has it always been the most prominent. Here we have seen the development of concepts such as the 'process of racialization' (Miles, 1989, 1993) and 'racial formations' (Omi and Winant, 1994) which have been increasingly appropriated and used as a way of stressing the contingent and historically specific nature of racism and its inherent contradictions as lines of inclusion and exclusion are continually being drawn and redrawn not only around skin colour but also around other signifiers including religion and nationality. Within this, some writers have gone further to argue that the equation of racism so explicitly with skin colour has led to the reification of 'race' as a social category. In this it has been argued that, within much of the sociological literature on racism, 'race' has been used in an unproblematic way which has ironically had the consequence of reflecting and reinforcing the logic of the modernist era and the associated belief that a discrete number of 'races' can be identified within the human population (Carter and Green, 1993; Miles, 1989, 1993; Small, 1993).

Moreover, there has also developed a critique around the claims made for those who have been included within the 'black experience'. Here we have seen a growing critique of the conflation of African/Caribbean and South Asian people's experiences under the essentialist catch-all heading of 'black' with the result that the important differences in terms of the nature and effects of racism as experienced by these two groups have been ignored as has, in particular, the important differences and diversity of experience *within* the South Asian population (see, for instance, Anthias and Yuval-Davis, 1992; Brah, 1991; Modood, 1988; Sahgal, 1992). Within sociology, these themes have been particularly prominent in relation to debates concerning anti-racist politics. Here, the certainties that have surrounded the construction of the 'black experience' and the corollary of 'white racism', have come under increasing criticism not only in terms of its limited theoretical base but also the adverse consequences of its impact upon anti-racist practice (see, for instance, Gilroy, 1990; Macdonald et al., 1989; Rattansi, 1992; Sivanandan, 1985).

Theorizing racism and identity

What is clear from the above discussion is that while the 'essential black subject' played a prominent role in challenging the values and assumptions of sociological research on 'race' and racism during the 1980s, its continued use is fraught with problems. While it therefore remains an important means of political mobilization, its use in sociological theories of 'race' and racism is severely limited. From the above debates we have seen the growing need to recognize the essentially open, contingent and context-specific nature of racism in contrast to the reification of the essential black subject. However, within this, I would argue that two further concerns also remain to be addressed in the extant literature. The first relates to the continued prominence of the macro/micro divide in the sociological literature. There remains a marked tendency for sociologists to approach the study of racism and its open and fluid nature *either* through a focus on more macro national-political discourses (see, for instance, Anthias and Yuval-Davis, 1992; Miles, 1989, 1993; Rattansi, 1994) *or* through a more micro, ethnographic focus (Back, 1990, 1991; Hewitt, 1986; Jones, 1988; Troyna and Hatcher, 1992). With a few exceptions (see, for instance, Back, 1993; Cohen, 1988, 1992), there has as yet been a lack of work which has engaged with the way in which discourses on 'race', manifest at various levels of the social formation, come to articulate with each other in their reproduction and the contradictions that emerge from this.

Secondly, there is still much work to be done in developing a theoretical frame that can appreciate the wider complexity of the mechanisms of power associated with racism. We need to move decisively beyond the conception of racism as simply a false ideology; a phenomenon that lives in the minds of people and manifests itself through social practices of inclusion and exclusion. Racism should not simply be understood as an irrational system of beliefs but as having its base both beyond the confines of the individual and, at one and the same time, within the body of the individual. The former is not a particularly new concern in that the need to locate people's racialized beliefs in their concrete experiences has preoccupied sociologists for a long time (see, for instance, Cashmore, 1987; Phizacklea and Miles, 1979). It is precisely because of this material basis that a growing realization has emerged within the field of anti-racist education for instance that racism cannot simply be reasoned away through rational debate (Rattansi, 1992). However, what has been far less addressed within this discussion is the way that discourses on 'race' are not only located within people's social experiences but are also expressed through time and space (Giddens, 1984; Keith and Pile, 1993; Lefebvre, 1991; Massey, 1985, 1993). In this, as Keith (1993) has so successfully demonstrated in his own ethnographic work, people's racialized beliefs and cognitive frameworks are also structured through their experience of the spatial and temporal; that is the symbolism that comes to be attached to specific places and how they come to be remembered through time. It is therefore the way that discourses on 'race' gain a material existence beyond the confines of the individual and the social and within the spatial and temporal structure of specific locales that needs to be further understood. Consequently there is a need for any future theoretical frame to be sensitive to the way that an individual's racialized beliefs and practices not only come to be expressed through the nature of particular locales but how their experience of these locales then comes to influence and shape these beliefs and practices.

Related to this topic is the need also to broaden the frame to look, at one and the same time, at how racism comes to act upon the body of individuals and their sense of identity. Racist discourses do not simply exist outside of the individual but also come to shape their sense of self. There is a need, therefore, to develop a theoretical frame that can fully appreciate the way that the power associated with racism has what Foucault (1980: 39) has called a 'capillary form of existence', that is: 'the point where power reaches into the very grain of individuals, touches their bodies and inserts itself into their actions and attitudes, their discourses, learning processes and everyday lives'.

Towards a theory of practice

It has precisely been with these issues of developing a theoretical frame that is not only able to appreciate the context-specific and contingent nature of racism but also its expression across all levels of social formation and the way that it is both inscribed through time and across space and on the bodies and very selves of individuals that I have been concerned in my own ethnographic research (Connolly, 1997). The theoretical frame that I have tentatively developed and employed and which I want briefly to outline below has therefore emerged from the grounded process of trying to develop a set of analytical tools capable of making sense of the complexities of the social worlds of, in my particular case, young children and the ways in which 'race' has come to impact upon their lives and shape their sense of identity. It is in this sense that I have found the three inter-related concepts in Pierre Bourdieu's work – that of the habitus, capital and field – most useful. For the remainder of this chapter I want to offer a brief outline of how Bourdieu has come to define and use these three concepts before setting out how I have come to refine and develop them in relation to my own work.

The **habitus** can be best seen as an analytical tool for understanding human behaviour and provides the medium through which we can conceptualize the way in which various discourses, including 'race', come to impact upon the individual and develop what was referred to earlier as its 'capillary form of existence'. In essence the habitus refers to the way we have developed and internalized ways of approaching, thinking about and acting upon our social world. Over time we come successively to learn from and incorporate the lessons of our lived experiences which help to guide our future actions and behaviour and dispose us to thinking in a certain way. This is what Bourdieu refers to as our 'habitus'. As our experience comes to be consolidated and reinforced, the habitus becomes more durable and internalized as we *habitualize* the way we think and behave. The habitus, then, is a system of

> durable, transposable dispositions, structured structures, predisposed to function as structuring structures, that is, as principles which generate and organise practices and representations that can be objectively adapted to their outcomes without presupposing a conscious aiming at ends or an express mastery of the operations necessary in order to attain them. (Bourdieu, 1990: 53)

In essence, the habitus acts unconsciously to organize our social experiences and encourages us to think and behave in certain ways – similar to Giddens' notion of practical consciousness (Giddens, 1984). The Lads in Willis' (1977) seminal study of the schooling of working class youth provide a good example of this. Their habitus has been structured by an experience of their working-class families and communities which emphasized the futility of further education and, instead, necessitated leaving school early, securing work and learning a trade. This 'reality' was at the heart of how they then came to view themselves, the utility of education and their future careers. In many ways, while they appeared to make rational choices about their future and which occupations they wanted to enter, this was guided by the unconscious aspect of their internalized experience – their habitus – that helped to limit and guide their aspirations to what was considered realistic. Staying on at school and going to university, something that is a taken-for-granted part of the middle-class habitus, was therefore something beyond the Lads' social world and lived experience.

Moreover, as Willis demonstrated in his account of the Lads' adoption of particular masculine cultural forms, their habitus in terms of one which is disposed towards the demands of manual work, was also one that they had come to 'embody'. This embodiment of the habitus is what Bourdieu refers to as the 'bodily hexis' and represents the way the habitus is 'realized, embodied, turned into permanent disposition, a durable manner of standing, speaking, and thereby of feeling and thinking' (Bourdieu, 1977: 93/4).

From this position it can be seen that the habitus provides the essential analytical tool for helping to overcome the idea that racism is simply something external to the individual or that it is little more than an irrational set of beliefs that they adhere to. Rather it is something grounded in experience and, moreover, something that comes to engrain itself within a person's very being and their own sense of self. It also, as Bourdieu intended, helps to bridge the traditional structure/agency divide that continues to preoccupy sociologists. While people come to make sense of and internalize their social position through the effects of various structures, these structures only have meaning and an existence in the way that they are reproduced through individuals acting upon their habitus. As Bourdieu argues, structures 'do not exist and do not really realize themselves except in and through the system of dispositions of agents' (quoted in Brubaker, 1985: 758).

Of course if we left it there, which is what many commentators do, then Bourdieu's work would be rightly open to charges of determinism and simplicity (see, for instance, Jenkins, 1992). How can change be understood within a theoretical framework that appears to be inherently self-fulfilling? Where has human agency gone, and how can we make sense of the contingent and inherently complex and contradictory nature of individual identities? It is here that we need to understand the relationship between the habitus and Bourdieu's other concepts of field and capital.

Capital can be understood as a range of scarce goods and resources which lie at the heart of social relations. The struggles over such resources provide the main dynamic through which social stratification and change can be understood. Bourdieu conceived of four basic types of capital: *economic* capital in the loosely Marxian sense; *cultural* capital which consists primarily of legitimate knowledge and behaviour; *social* capital which relates to resources gained via relationships and/or connections with significant others; and *symbolic* capital which basically translates as the prestige and honour that is associated with the acquisition of one or more of the other forms of capital once it has been perceived and recognized as legitimate by others (Bourdieu, 1987: 3–4). As Bourdieu outlined in his early work on education, these four types are deeply interrelated and partially transposable (see Bourdieu and Passeron, 1977). Economic capital enables people to send their children to private schools and so learn and appropriate certain valued forms of cultural capital. This cultural capital makes it possible to develop valued relationships with others (social capital) and acquire certain positions within society that are associated with particular aspects of symbolic capital and so on.

By contrast, a **field** can be best understood as a 'field of forces' (Mahar et al., 1990: 8), the social arena where struggles take place over specific resources. A field is defined primarily, therefore, in terms of the particular forms of capital present and secondarily through the relations developed around that as people struggle to acquire and/or maintain that capital. The boundaries of any particular field in terms of what is at stake and who is drawn into its domain are not fixed but inherently contested by those within the field. Thus there are as many fields as there are forms of capital. Any specific field, so identified and defined through empirical research, can be located within and/or across a number of levels of the social formation and may be quite inclusive or exclusive in terms of its size and reach.

It is this context provided by the field and capital that helps us to re-evaluate the notion of habitus in Bourdieu's work. In essence, the habitus is defined and constituted within particular fields as individuals come to learn about and internalize their position within struggles over particular forms of capital. As such, and this is a point I will develop shortly, a person has as many forms of habitus as the number of fields they inhabit. Before exploring the implications of this, however, I want to complete this pre-liminary discussion by referring to how Bourdieu understands the relation-ship between the habitus and the field. As he explains:

> The relation between habitus and field operates in two ways. On one side, it is a relation of *conditioning*: the field structures the habitus, which is the product of the embodiment of the immanent necessity of the field (or of a hierarchy of intersecting fields). On the other side, it is a relation of knowledge or cognitive construction: habitus contributes to constituting the field as a meaningful world, a world endowed with sense and with value, in which it is worth investing one's energy. (quoted in Wacquant, 1989: 44)

Competing forms of capital

It is true to say that Bourdieu's conceptions of the various forms of capital in his empirical research have been dominated by notions of class. As such, the relationship between economic capital and the acquisition of other forms of capital for working-class and middle-class people has remained a central preoccupation in his work (see, for instance, Bourdieu, 1984). This focus on class has also, I would argue, led to confusion as to whether Bourdieu understood habitus to be a universal element that people take with them to specific fields or, in the more pluralistic conception outlined above, and the one I tend to adhere to, whether each person is constituted through a number of 'habituses' (Jenkins, 1992). While he certainly argued the latter, his focus on class and its transposability between various forms of capital can lead one to interpret his work, in practice, as being more towards the former conceptualization.

I want to argue here, however, that regardless of how Bourdieu has made use of his three concepts of field, habitus and capital, they can be appropriated and re-worked to offer a more sophisticated and appropriate means by which to understand cultural formations more generally and racialized relations and identities more specifically. What I will argue here is that the concepts of field and capital can be significantly developed to take on board the complexity and contingency of social relations. This then provides the framework where the habitus can be developed to help us understand the de-centred self and therefore overcome charges of determinism and simplicity. In developing these themes for the remainder of this chapter, I will draw upon some examples gained from my own research on racism and young children.

As discussed above, when Bourdieu thought about capital he did so primarily within an analysis of class relations. As such Bourdieu defined notions of cultural and symbolic capital, for instance, in relation to those factors necessary to acquire to be successful within a capitalist society. Implicit within this is the suggestion that the working class are simply 'without' significant forms of cultural, symbolic and social capital. As a result, this creates an analytical vacuum within which the forms and dynamics of working-class culture, together with how it is produced and reproduced, are overlooked. Their social position and ways of thinking about themselves and others are simply determined by their lack of cultural and other forms of capital. I want to suggest, however, that Bourdieu's notion of capital can be developed to understand how certain subordinate groups come to develop and value their own forms of cultural, symbolic and social capital which are not only at variance with the broader forms of class-related capital but are, often, in direct conflict. How and when these forms of capital become significant depends upon the specific context – that is the particular field – in which individuals are located.

In terms of 'race', an example of this is the presence of certain black cultural forms. As I found in my own research (see Connolly, 1995a, 1995b, 1997), within the field of masculine peer group relations among working-class children, certain aspects of African/Caribbean culture came to be valued symbolically and the ability to appreciate and consume these successfully bestowed a certain amount of cultural capital on the individual

(see also Back, 1991, 1993; Hewitt, 1986; Jones, 1988). This can be understood, firstly, in terms of the way in which African/Caribbean music and
stylistics can be appropriated and used by white children and youths to
make sense of their own sense of alienation as working-class people and,
secondly, in relation to boys, how the masculinity of African/Caribbean
males has been constructed within broader racist discourses with its
emphasis on aggression, sporting competence and sexuality. However,
within the broader field of education, for example, as constituted within the
specific site of the school, such African/Caribbean cultural forms are significantly devalued and become the basis from which 'deviant' students –
i.e. those who diverge from the accepted forms of cultural capital – are
identified and disciplined (see Connolly, 1995a; Gillborn, 1990; Mac an
Ghaill, 1988; Wright, 1986).

It is in this broadening of Bourdieu's notion of capital that we can begin
to unravel the complexity and contingency of each individual's lived
experience. For working-class children, for example, it enables us to
identify a number of different and competing forms of capital that exist
both within and beyond their constitution as working class. I have already
touched upon one specific way in which 'race' can intervene within
working-class children's culture. Of course gender, and specific forms of
masculine and feminine cultural forms, also form the basis around which
certain forms of capital and their related fields are constructed. Within the
field of feminine peer group relations, the dominant and valued forms of
cultural and symbolic capital relating to femininity are transformed, within
broader male-dominated peer group relations, to signify the lack of
significant forms of masculine capital.

From this, what we are primarily interested in, in terms of 'race', is the
ways that these fields, so defined, become racialized. As I have argued
elsewhere (see Connolly, 1995a, 1995b, 1997), within the field of masculine
peer group relations among young children, 'race' enters at a number of
levels. On the one hand, as discussed above, specifically African/Caribbean
cultural forms can be valued as quintessential expressions of masculinity.
On the other hand, however, these same cultural forms can provoke a sense
of threat and insecurity among white boys who feel their own masculine
identities are being threatened and this forms the basis from which conflict
between white and African/Caribbean boys can ensue. In contrast, the
construction of South Asian boys as effeminate, or the Other in relation to
dominant forms of masculinity, within broader racist discourse often
provides the basis from which other boys come to secure their own
masculine credentials by publicly disassociating and attacking those who
have come to be symbolized as 'un-masculine'.

Moreover, these struggles over certain distinct forms of capital inevitably
become internalized over time within the individual child's habitus as they
come to develop an unconscious, practical sense of what actions and
behaviour are valued and can be capitalized on. For boys generally, this
will involve the embodiment of masculinity in the way they dress, walk,

talk and hold themselves. This embodied habitus – the bodily hexis – also becomes racialized as white, African/Caribbean and South Asian boys come to develop distinct strategies of domination, resistance and/or survival and these, in turn, become habitualized in their practical sense of themselves (see Connolly, 1995b, 1997).

Multiple identities

The de-centring of these young children's identities can be understood in the plurality of fields within which they are located and how these come in a complex manner to over-determine and influence each other. In this we can envisage a number of fields, manifest at all levels of the social formation, which act to affect and structure each other. What fields are identified and studied through particular ethnographic work and why, will depend primarily on their analytical usefulness. In my own research I drew attention to a number of fields that were pertinent in understanding the racialized identities of the young children (Connolly, 1997). These included the field of national politics and that constituted by the local housing estate, which was not only a particular site within the broader field of economics characterized by the shared relation of those on the estate to the dominant forms of economic capital (i.e. they were overwhelmingly unemployed and living in council accommodation), but the estate also became a field in its own right as the residents developed their own alternative forms of capital which they came to value and strive for through their struggle for survival. The school, situated on the estate, constituted another field organized around the dominant forms of capital associated with teaching and learning while the young children's masculine and feminine peer group relations within the school were also identified as separate fields organized around valued forms of masculine and feminine capital respectively. Once identified, the task for my own research was to unravel the complex and contradictory ways in which not only were discourses on 'race' appropriated, re-worked and reproduced in different ways within each field but also how these also came to articulate, influence and shape relations in other fields. In doing it this way the research inevitably drew out the complex and contingent nature of children's racialized identities which were continuously being drawn and re-drawn from one field of social relations to the next. Moreover, it also provided the basis from which an appreciation was gained of the ways in which discourses on 'race' came to articulate with, and be expressed through, their articulation with other discourses, whether they be on nationality predominant within the field of national politics, class and the inner city foregrounded on the local estate, age and education as found within the school, or gender as predominant within the fields of masculine and feminine peer group relations. In this sense 'race' is not simply 'added on' as just another variable to these others but is fundamentally constituted through and analysed in its articulation with them.

Moreover, as attempted in my own work, we can develop Bourdieu's account of fields to include a temporal and spatial dimension. In this we can argue that fields are not only constituted by social relations as has been the focus in Bourdieu's own work, but also can become expressed across time and through space. The school as one particular field provides an example of this. The complex set of relations that have emerged between teachers and children underlined by the pedagogical authority of the teacher can be seen to have become expressed through the spatial and temporal organization of the classroom and the school day which then acts to reinforce and reproduce that authority (see also Giddens, 1985; Shilling, 1991). This way in which social relations within any given field often come to be expressed through time and space can also be seen in relation to the estate in my own work. Here it was seen how relations on the estate and the discourses associated with it in relation to crime and the inner city have come to find expression through the built environment. Thus a number of government grants were made available during the time of my research to 'make the estate safer', principally through the erection of large steel fences and railings, the blocking off of many walkways and the fixing of security doors. The estate soon came to be experienced as a 'prison' by many of the residents and came to symbolize a crime-ridden area. These symbols, in turn, came to influence and shape the experiences of those living and working on the estate and, progressively, came to be embodied within their habitus.

Fields therefore play a crucial role in this re-working of Bourdieu's approach. Through their relationship with the habitus, they enable us to explore and unravel the essentially open and multiple identities of individuals while also providing the theoretical tools from which to understand how various discursive structures and processes come to embody themselves within the self. In relation to this it also opens up the possibility of theorizing space and time more centrally within the research.

Conclusions

This chapter, by necessity, has only been able to offer the briefest of introductions to how the important insights found in the work of Pierre Bourdieu can be adapted to offer a more sophisticated and nuanced theoretical frame for the study of racialized relations and identities. It is an approach that, I would suggest, is able to move beyond the rather closed and limited frame set by the reification of the essential black subject found in the sociological literature. The three basic concepts of habitus, capital and field not only provide the analytical tools for understanding the de-centred self but also help us to explore the ways in which discourses on 'race', at all levels of the social formation, come to articulate with each other. Moreover, they are also concepts that can aid the development of a more sophisticated understanding of power within accounts of racism.

Here, the field provides the basis from which we can come to understand how discourses on 'race' have come to be embedded across time and space while the habitus offers the analytical space for understanding how these discourses on 'race' have come to be inscribed on the bodies of individuals and within their very sense of self. However, as Bourdieu has been at pains to point out, these concepts are not offered up simply for the sake of theorizing *per se*, but are primarily intended to be applied and developed by those engaged in the practice of research. Their true value can therefore only be understood through the 'messiness' of empirical work.

References

Anthias, F. and Yuval-Davis, N. (1992) *Racialised Boundaries: Race, Nation, Gender, Colour and Class and the Anti-Racist Struggle*. London: Routledge.

Back, L. (1990) *Racist Name-Calling and Developing Anti-Racist Initiatives in Youth Work*. Research Paper No. 14. Coventry: Centre for Research in Ethnic Relations, University of Warwick.

Back, L. (1991) 'Social context and racist name-calling: an ethnographic perspective on racist talk within a South London adolescent community', *European Journal of Intercultural Studies*, 1(3): 19–38.

Back, L. (1993) 'Race, identity and nation within an adolescent community in South London', *New Community*, 19(2): 217–33.

Banton, M. (1987) *Racial Theories*. Cambridge: Cambridge University Press.

Barker, M. (1981) *The New Racism*. London: Junction Books.

Ben-Tovim, G., Gabriel, J., Law, I. and Stredder, K. (1986) *The Local Politics of Race*. London: Macmillan.

Bhat, A., Carr-Hill, R. and Ohri, S. (1996) *Britain's Black Population: A New Perspective*, 2nd edn. Aldershot: Gower.

Bourdieu, P. (1977) *Outline of a Theory of Practice*. Cambridge: Cambridge University Press.

Bourdieu, P. (1984) *Distinction: A Social Critique of the Judgement of Taste*. London: Routledge.

Bourdieu, P. (1987) 'What makes a social class? On the theoretical and practical existence of groups', *Berkeley Journal of Sociology*, 32: 1–18.

Bourdieu, P. (1990) *The Logic of Practice*. Cambridge: Polity Press.

Bourdieu, P. and Passeron, J.C. (1977) *Reproduction in Education, Society and Culture*. Beverly Hills, CA: Sage.

Bourne, J. and Sivanandan, A. (1980) 'Cheerleaders and ombudsmen: the sociology of race relations in Britain', *Race and Class*, 21(4): 331–52.

Brah, A. (1991) 'Difference, diversity, differentiation', in S. Allen, F. Anthias and N. Yuval-Davis (eds), special edition of *Revue Internationale de Sociologie*, New Series, No. 2, April.

Braham, P. (ed.) (1992) *Racism and Anti-Racism*. London: Sage.

Brubaker, R. (1985) 'Rethinking classical theory: the sociological vision of Pierre Bourdieu', *Theory and Society*, 14: 745–75.

Carmichael, S. and Hamilton, C. (1967) *Black Power: The Politics of Liberation in America*. New York: Vintage.

Carter, B. and Green, M. (1993) *Naming Difference: 'Race Thinking', Politics and Social Research*. Paper presented to the British Sociological Association Annual Conference, University of Essex.

Cashmore, E. (1987) *The Logic of Racism*. London: Allen & Unwin.

Cohen, P. (1988) 'The perversions of inheritance: studies in the making of multi-racist Britain', in P. Cohen and H. Bains (eds), *Multi-Racist Britain*. London: Macmillan.

Cohen, P. (1992) '"It's racism what dunnit": hidden narratives in theories of racism', in J. Donald and A. Rattansi (eds), *'Race', Culture and Difference*. London: Sage.

Connolly, P. (1995a) 'Racism, masculine peer group relations and the schooling of African/ Caribbean boys', *British Journal of Sociology of Education*, 16(1): 75–92.

Connolly, P. (1995b) 'Boys will be boys? Racism, sexuality and the construction of masculine identities amongst infant boys', in J. Holland and M. Blair (eds), *Debates and Issues in Feminist Research and Pedagogy*. Clevedon: Multilingual Matters in association with the Open University.

Connolly, P. (1996) 'Doing what comes naturally? Standpoint epistemology, critical social research and the politics of identity', in S. Lyon and J. Busfield (eds), *Methodological Imaginations*. London: Macmillan.

Connolly, P. (1997) *Racism, Gender Identities and Young Children*. Buckingham: Open University Press.

Donald, J. and Rattansi, A. (eds) (1992) *'Race', Culture and Difference*. London: Sage.

Foucault, M. (1980) *Power/Knowledge: Selected Interviews and Other Writings, 1972–1977*, edited by C. Gordon. London: Harvester Wheatsheaf.

Fryer, P. (1984) *Staying Power: The History of Black People in Britain*. London: Pluto Press.

Giddens, A. (1984) *The Constitution of Society: Outline of a Theory of Structuration*. Cambridge: Polity Press.

Giddens, A. (1985) 'Time, space and regionalisation', in D. Gregory and J. Urry (eds), *Social Relations and Spatial Structure*. London: Macmillan.

Gillborn, D. (1990) *'Race', Ethnicity and Education*. London: Unwin Hyman.

Gilroy, P. (1980) '"Managing the underclass": a further note on the sociology of race relations in Britain', *Race and Class*, 22(1): 47–62.

Gilroy, P. (1990) 'The end of anti-racism', in W. Ball and J. Solomos (eds), *Race and Local Politics*. London: Macmillan.

Gilroy, P. (1993) *The Black Atlantic: Modernity and Double Consciousness*. London: Verso.

Gordon, P. and Klug, F. (1986) *New Rights, New Racism*. London: Searchlight Publications.

Gordon, P. and Rosenberg, D. (1989) *Daily Racism: The Press and Black People in Britain*. London: Runnymede Trust.

Hall, S. (1992) 'New ethnicities', in J. Donald and A. Rattansi (eds), *'Race', Culture and Difference*. London: Sage.

Hall, S., Critcher, C., Jefferson, T., Clarke, J. and Roberts, B. (1978) *Policing the Crisis: Mugging, the State and Law and Order*. London: Macmillan.

Hewitt, R. (1986) *White Talk, Black Talk*. Cambridge: Cambridge University Press.

Husband, C. (ed.) (1987) *'Race' in Britain: Continuity and Change*, 2nd edn. London: Hutchinson.

Jenkins, R. (1992) *Pierre Bourdieu*. London: Routledge.

Jones, S. (1988) *White Youth, Black Culture*. Basingstoke: Macmillan.

Keith, M. (1993) *Race, Riots and Policing: Lore and Disorder in a Multi-Racist Society*. London: UCL Press.

Keith, M. and Pile, S. (eds) (1993) *Place and the Politics of Identity*. London: Routledge.

Lawrence, E. (1981) 'White sociology, black struggle', *Multiracial Education*, 9(3): 3–17.

Lawrence, E. (1982) 'Just plain common sense: the "roots" of racism', in Centre for Contemporary Cultural Studies, *The Empire Strikes Back: Race and Racism in 70s Britain*. London: Hutchinson.

Lefebvre, H. (1991) *The Production of Space* (1st edition 1974). Oxford: Basil Blackwell.

Lyotard, J.F. (1984) *The Postmodern Condition: A Report of Knowledge*. Manchester: Manchester University Press.

Mac an Ghaill, M. (1988) *Young, Gifted and Black*. Milton Keynes: Open University Press.

Macdonald, I., Bhavnani, T., Khan, L. and John G. (1989) *Murder in the Playground: The Report of the Macdonald Inquiry into Racism and Racial Violence in Manchester Schools*. London: Longsight Press.

Mahar, C., Harker, R. and Wilkes, C. (1990) 'The basic theoretical position', in R. Harker, C.

Mahar and C. Wilkes (eds), *An Introduction to the Work of Pierre Bourdieu: The Practice of Theory*. Basingstoke: Macmillan.

Massey, D. (1985) 'New directions in space' in D. Gregory and J. Urry (eds), *Social Relations and Spatial Structure*. London: Macmillan.

Massey, D. (1993) 'Politics and space/time', in M. Keith and S. Pile (eds), *Place and the Politics of Identity*. London: Routledge.

Miles, R. (1989) *Racism*. London: Routledge.

Miles, R. (1993) *Racism After 'Race Relations'*. London: Routledge.

Modood, T. (1988) '"Black" racial equality and Asian identity', *New Community*, 14(3): 397–404.

Omi, M. and Winant, H. (1994) *Racial Formation in the United States: From the 1960s to the 1990s*, 2nd edn. London: Routledge.

Parekh, B. (1986) 'The "New Right" and the politics of nationhood', in G. Cohen et al. (eds), *The New Right: Image and Reality*. London: Runnymede Trust.

Parmar, P. (1981) 'Young Asian women: a critique of the pathological approach', *Multiracial Education*, 9(3): 19–29.

Phizacklea, A. and Miles, R. (1979) 'Working-class racist beliefs in the inner-city', in R. Miles and A. Phizacklea (eds), *Racism and Political Action in Britain*. London: Routledge and Kegan Paul.

Rattansi, A. (1992) 'Changing the subject?: racism, culture and education', in J. Donald and A. Rattansi (eds), *'Race', Culture and Difference*. London: Sage.

Rattansi, A. (1994) '"Western" racisms, ethnicities and identities in a "Postmodern" Frame', in A. Rattansi and S. Westwood (eds), *Racism, Modernity and Identity on the Western Front*. Cambridge: Polity Press.

Rattansi, A. and Westwood, S. (eds) (1994) *Racism, Modernity and Identity on the Western Front*. Cambridge: Polity Press.

Rex, J. and Mason, D. (eds) (1986) *Theories of Race and Ethnic Relations*. Cambridge: Cambridge University Press.

Sahgal, G. (1992) 'Secular spaces: the experience of Asian women organising', in G. Sahgal and N. Yuval-Davis (eds), *Refusing Holy Orders: Women and Fundamentalism in Britain*. London: Virago.

Shilling, C. (1991) 'Social space, gender inequalities and educational differentiation', *British Journal of Sociology of Education*, 12(1): 23–44.

Sivanandan, A. (1985) 'RAT and the degradation of the black struggle', *Race and Class*, 26(4): 1–34.

Small, S. (1993) *Racialised Barriers*. London: Routledge.

Troyna, B. and Hatcher, R. (1992) *Racism in Children's Lives: A Study of a Mainly White Primary School*. London: Routledge.

Wacquant, L. (1989) 'Towards a reflexive sociology: a workshop with Pierre Bourdieu', *Sociological Theory*, 7: 26–63.

Willis, P. (1977) *Learning to Labour: How Working Class Kids Get Working Class Jobs*. Farnborough: Saxon House.

Wright, C. (1986) 'School processes – an ethnographic study', in S. Eggleston, D. Dunn and M. Anjali (eds), *Education for Some: The Educational and Vocational Experiences of 15–18-year-old Members of Minority Ethnic Groups*. Stoke-on-Trent: Trentham.

4 Late-Modern Criminology: 'Late' as in 'Dead' or 'Modern' as in 'New'?

Nigel South

SHOCK! HORROR! Postmodernist feminist consigns 'atavistic criminological man' to history; sociology of deviance obituary published; respected criminologists said to have published the 'longest suicide note in history'.[1]

This chapter offers some reflections on the current state and possible fate of criminology in Britain. As will be apparent from my title and opening 'headlines', there is much to examine and review. For some critics the question of whether criminology *has* a future is a matter of doubt; for others, 'crises' may occur within the field but these then have a tendency to reveal sources of further renewal. A key theme of this chapter, therefore, is the modernist preoccupation with the recurrence of 'crises' – whether within academic disciplines such as criminology, or the social world as beset for example by 'crises' of crime and control.[2] I shall first outline some differing views on the current state of late-modern (Giddens, 1990) criminology, consider several recent developments in theory, some future scenarios for crime and control, and conclude by exploring some emerging and possible items for the agenda for criminological theory at the end of the century.

Where are we now? Surveying the field

Depending on how one surveys the field and which of its famous assessors you choose to consult, criminology is either in deep crisis, close to being dead and buried, or else it has come through a period of conflict, resolution and consolidation, to reach a point of renewed vitality. For example, the late-modern pluralism of current criminology sees Carol Smart (1990), who in the 1970s was a key contributor to the development of a feminist criminology, recently declaring criminology to be an irredeemable, male-orientated, positivist project that can offer feminists little or nothing. However, at the same time, Smart continues to engage with the subject (Smart, 1995). This critique, simultaneously self-distancing yet still maintaining a dialogue,[3] is perhaps similar to Stan Cohen's continuing and continually refreshing admonitions of criminology.[4] While Cohen's assaults tend to serve as applauded stimulants to the field rather than full-scale obituaries, for the 'sociology of deviance' Colin Sumner (1994) has recently provided over 300 pages of the latter.

However, there are also major writers who, while they have contributed their own share of critique of deviancy theory and criminology in the past, are also engaged in *renewal* of the subject area. Jock Young, for example, has moved from 'new deviancy theory', through Marxism to a social democratic 'Left Realism' (Young, 1994). Young's affirmation of belief in the modernist (or late modern) project of criminology (e.g. Matthews and Young, 1992; Young, 1996) has been evident from early work with Taylor and Walton, when the book they published as *The New Criminology* (Taylor et al., 1973) signalled that the subject could be, and was to be, renewed. More recently it has been seen in his work with various colleagues on the development of the 'Realist' school of criminology (cf. Hughes, 1991) and is asserted by current work with Walton in a co-edited text *The New Criminology Revisited* (in press). In various works Ian Taylor, the other co-author of the classic 1973 text, has demonstrated the fruitfulness of opening up criminology to insights from political economy and urban sociology (Taylor, 1991, 1994a; Taylor et al., 1996), suggesting directions that I think offer a great deal for the continuing revitalization of criminology.

One other member of the 'old guard' (who, of course, were once 'young turks' but that's time, history and revisionism for you), Paul Rock, has been less sanguine about prospects for a 'new' vitality in current criminology. In several reviews of the field, Rock (e.g. 1988, 1994a: 142–7) bemoans the lack of theoretical innovation and 'iconoclasm' which he sees as characterizing the work of the 'fortunate generation' (1994a: 133–7) which did so much to challenge and change the field in Britain from the 1960s to the late 1970s. This was a period another contemporary luminary, David Downes (1988: 47–50) describes as a 'dizzying scene' and a 'paradigmatic kaleidoscope'.

Rock's observations reflect the undoubted significance of the 'new deviancy' challenge to the psychological and social pathological orientations of earlier British criminology (Garland, 1994). Perhaps it is inevitably true that the field can never again experience such a period of innovation, revelation and expansion. If so, it is now best to be *forward-looking* about what criminology may yet achieve. The current state of criminology is certainly not lacking in fertile ground for new ideas and research: theoretical conflict and competition, diversity of empirical projects and methodologies, all thrive. As we survey the many and varied contributions that make up 'end of the century' criminology, Downes' nice phrase the 'paradigmatic kaleidoscope' seems as appealing and applicable as ever.

Seeing new horizons: towards comparative criminologies?

Sheptycki, a member of a new cohort of criminologists, has also noted Rock's casting of recent entrants to the field as an epigoni of the 'fortunate generation' (1995a: 1), but importantly, Sheptycki then proceeds to outline how, for example, a *European* horizon offers many possibilities for 'new' criminological problems and prospects. European conferences, debates and cross-border studies (Ruggiero and South, 1995; Sheptycki, 1995b), suggest that possibilities for innovation exist. Sheptycki's point is a reflection of a broader awareness, in some areas of criminology at least, of the need to develop *comparative* analysis of similar and dissimilar crime and control problems. As Nelken (1994b: 223) argues, 'The introduction of a comparative aspect can help in the reformulation of central problems in criminological theory. . . . Comparative work can also breathe new life into the sociology of deviance (now rather out of fashion) because it poses the problem of how to understand the "other" without either resorting to stereotypes or denying "differences".' European, Pacific-Rim or other comparative arenas were hardly prominent in the Anglo-American discourse of the earlier 'fortunate' generation but today demand attention both theoretically and empirically. In the late 1990s, such demands (and many others, some of which I explore below), challenge and stretch criminology. All of this can represent change and opportunities for criminology rather than being interpreted as symptoms of crisis: the images within the 'paradigmatic kaleidoscope' are simply shifting again. As Ericson and Carriere (1994) observe, academic disciplines of all varieties are fragmenting, looking outward and across disciplinary boundaries, facing and responding to new intellectual currents and empirical challenges. The world has moved on and so has criminology.[5] Or perhaps not.

Strong critiques: weak impacts?

It is obviously striking that in my quick (and, I must stress, very selective) survey of recent commentators on the state of criminology, only one figure is a woman (Smart) and all males are white. To some extent this is both an accurate and misleading portrayal of the composition of contemporary British criminology. It is misleading in that key works of criticism, theory and empirical investigation have been contributed by women and non-whites, but accurate in so far as the discipline is still dominated by white males. Unsurprisingly, these characteristics of modern British criminology have been noted before (see e.g. Gelsthorpe and Morris, 1990: 7–9; Maguire et al., 1994: 11; Rice, 1990; Scraton, 1990). Yet ironically, despite the persistence of inequality of representation in the staffing of the discipline, the issues of gender and sexuality, and ethnicity, post-colonialism and 'otherness', recently attracting much discussion in mainstream sociology, hold the promise of interesting directions for theoretical and empirical work in criminology. On women/feminism and crime/criminology, this has been so from the early work of Heidensohn (1968) and Smart (1976), through to recent consideration of the significance of gendered masculinity for crime questions, (Auld et al., 1986; Groombridge, 1995; Jefferson, 1992; Messerschmidt, 1993; Newburn and Stanko, 1994). Some innovative work around criminological concerns with ethnicity and 'otherness' (Hall et al., 1978; Keith, 1993; Murji, 1994; Pryce, 1979) and with other minorities (e.g. gays: Burke, 1994; Herek and Berrill, 1992; Stychin, 1995) has been provided but this remains a seriously underdeveloped area. Perhaps after the profound (but not universal) impact of feminism on criminology (see next section), it will be in work on social 'inclusion/exclusion' and 'otherness' related to minorities and disempowered groups generally, that new ideas may arise, reflecting intellectual developments elsewhere in sociology, in cultural studies, and in the new areas of post-colonialist studies (Williams and Chrisman, 1993) and work on sexual citizenship (Plummer, 1995).

Sociological theory, feminism and criminology

From one point of view, developments in both mainstream sociological theory and feminism have opened up criminology to outside ideas and discourses in important ways in recent years. Further, while the impact of thinkers like Foucault is obvious (see e.g. Cohen, 1985; Garland, 1985; and Rock's survey of the field, 1994a: 142), to a lesser but no less important extent other sources of *social* theory such as Norbert Elias (1978, 1982), Zygmunt Bauman (1988, 1989) and others are finding expression in criminological theorizing. Of course, from another point of view, there is an accurate counter-argument that most *empirical* criminology pays little or no attention to such 'abstract' theorizing. Even the influence of feminist theory, according to Rock's survey (1994a: 147) 'has not spread very far' (cf. Hahn Rafter and Heidensohn, 1995: 4–11). Yet my own feeling is that, at the very least, the 'intellectual cultural climate' of criminology is opening up to the usefulness of a broad range of theory. Good examples are recent work by Bottoms and Wiles, generally associated with a quite conventional version of criminology but none the less forging links between the study of crime, spatial patterning and Anthony Giddens' theory of structuration (Bottoms, 1994: 639; Bottoms and Wiles, 1996)[6] and Nellis (1995), whose re-assessment of 'values for the probation service' is theoretically enlivened by use of Bauman, Giddens and others. As Heidensohn and Silvestri (1995) have observed, criminology needs to be capable of self-reflection and analysis but part of this should be remembrance of *the sources* of it's past renewals (cf. also Morrison, 1994: 136 *et passim*). Thus the

> sociology of deviance of the 1960s and 1970s had drawn on a range of theories not previously used by criminologists . . . The 'new' criminology of the 1970s (Taylor et al., 1973) claimed to be a 'fully social theory' of deviance taking neo-Marxism as well as interactionism as its revitalising life forces. Situational crime prevention, while presented as a pragmatic approach to problems, has obvious roots in rational choice theory. (Heidensohn and Silvestri, 1995: 1)

Clearly, I am an optimist about the state and future of criminology. In this spirit, in the remainder of this chapter I shall review several recent critiques and debates within criminology, interpreting them not as signs of 'crisis', but as signs of vitality.

Theory developments

Engendering criminology: deconstructing criminology?[7]

Feminism and postmodernism: a feminist critique of criminology, law and modernity   In an influential essay Carol Smart asserts that:

> the thing criminology cannot do is deconstruct crime. It cannot locate rape or child abuse in the domain of sexuality, or theft in the domain of economic activity or drug use in the domain of health. To do so would be to abandon criminology to sociology; but more importantly it would involve abandoning the idea of a unified problem which requires a unified response – at least at the theoretical level. (1990: 7)

I am not sure about all this. I have already suggested a vision of criminology as a 'broad church', quite legitimately capable of embracing a variety of positions and critical stances. Indeed, Smart's 'deconstruction' of the field of criminology none the less remains sited (and cited and celebrated) within that arena. It is therefore worth noting that, in order to criticize and 'deconstruct' 'criminology', Smart first has to 'homogenize' the subject, unifying it in an artificial manner and allowing it no space for sociological expression.

Criminology, quite evidently, merges with other knowledges and discourses in many areas and many ways (as indeed 'all subject areas overlap with others': Matthews and Young, 1992: 16). For example, to look at criminological work on illegal drug use: such work should and does look at epidemiological, health, environmental, policy and other factors (see e.g. the contributions in Dorn and South, 1987). It makes no more sense to 'deconstruct' criminological research on drugs and 'locate it' in the 'domain of health' than to deconstruct the 'domain' of the sociology of health and export the study of the newly stigmatized behaviours of smoking and heavy drinking to the sociology of deviance (if this still exists *pace* Sumner)[8]. Such substantive issues are already located in various disciplinary fields. If this misses the point, and the point is that we should deconstruct *all* sociological/criminological 'domains', then questions arise about the value of such nihilism. None the less, to engage with Smart further, I shall consider the possibilities of a 'criminology-after criminology' later in this chapter.

Undoubtedly, however, Smart must echo some of the frustration felt by criminology students when they hear of theory after theory, each of which either sounds the same as, or the opposite of, the others, and none of which ever seems to supply all the answers. For Smart then, 'The point is whether we argue that all the studies that have been carried out to date have been inadequate or whether we reappraise the very idea that we will find solutions' (1990: 76). In other words, reappraise that promise of modernity and its sciences that 'THE answers' are discoverable. For Smart, criminology can offer feminists little or nothing. Feminism would find postmodernist theory far more stimulating and useful and should simply sever links with the criminological enterprise (1990: 83–4). Criminology as it stands, even in a 'radical guise', is destined to fall into 'greater and greater complicity with mechanisms of discipline. . . . the path of radical criminology seems wedded to the modernist enterprise and is, as yet, unaffected by the epistemological sea-changes which have touched feminism and other discourses' (1990: 84). It is best to be done with it (cf. A. Young, 1992; Carrington, 1994).

Smart's critique of the 'radical guise' of some versions of criminology seems, in fact, principally to refer to a quite specific variant of recent social-democratic criminology – 'left-realism'. As I shall be returning to Smart's concerns shortly, I shall give the last word here to the 'realists'.

Left-realism argues for the value of continuing the criminological quest for understanding. This position has been elaborated by Matthews and Young (1992: 11–13, 16) in their 'reflections on realism' and their response to Smart.

> The problem with this type of critique is that of infinite regress. We might ask Smart in turn what she means by (essentialist) categories such as 'rape' and child abuse (which themselves could be endlessly deconstructed) or why rape might be better (causally?) explained in terms of sexuality rather than as a crime. . . . categories of crime are neither arbitrary nor accidental. They arise from definite social and historical relations . . . This does not mean that one should treat such categories uncritically but is to emphasize that they have a social base and cannot be defined away. (pp. 11–12)

> . . . Smart . . . claims that her critique of modernism and left-realism 'does not entail a denial of poverty, inequality, repression, racism, sexual violence and so on', but she provides little indication of how any of these problems might be practically addressed. . . . The postmodern critique of criminology melts into air. It offers deconstruction rather than reconstruction. (p. 13)

Feminism and the positivism of law For Smart, this final comment is perhaps simply a reflection of 'the problem'. Merely to attempt to 'reconstruct' criminology is to accept the patriarchal basis of criminal law, legal justice and, in turn, criminology. Even a 'feminist realism' (Mooney, 1994) would be found wanting from this point of view. To explain Smart's position just a little further it is useful to note the other arena in which she has developed her critique of positivism and patriarchy. This is the sociology of law.

In her book *Feminism and the Power of Law* (1989) Smart renders the 'quest for a feminist jurisprudence' as problematic for feminism. Here, Smart argues that although law can be used by feminists as a forum for articulating ideas, resistances, 'alternative visions and accounts' (p. 88), this implies a different use of law than the strategy of law *reform*. The search for a feminist jurisprudence relies on such reform and is hence a questionable pursuit because it 'does not *de-centre* law':

> On the contrary, it may attempt to change its values and procedures, *but it preserves law's place in the hierarchy of discourses which maintains that law has access to truth and justice*. It encourages a 'turning to law' for solutions, *it fetishizes law rather than deconstructing it*. (1989: 88–9, emphasis added)

In short, in her work on law, Smart offers further critical challenges to the project of modernist reformism. Hence Smart admires the work of those feminists who have challenged the patriarchal basis of law but is ultimately critical of their project for the way it is tied to modernity, positivism and scientific method. One of the feminist activists Smart discusses along these lines is Catherine MacKinnon.

I shall say a little more here about MacKinnon's work, partly because her campaign has stimulated other debates within feminism, criminology, cultural studies and sexual politics. At issue here are questions concerning pornography and censorship. In the early 1990s, MacKinnon was a member of a women's advocacy group in Toronto, Canada, which won a case against pornography at the level of the Supreme Court of Canada (*New York Times*, Law section, 28/2/92). The Court accepted that 'although the nation's criminal obscenity law infringed on the freedom of expression, it was legitimate to outlaw pornography that was harmful to women'. There have also been attempts to introduce anti-pornography ordinances in several US cities. However, because of their resonance with other pro-censorship positions (e.g. the politics of the moral right-wing), such campaigns do not attract *unanimous* support from feminists, either for their aims or their methods. Instead, critics observe that the fight against puritanical and discriminatory censorship, and the associated condemnation of 'other' sexual lifestyles, abortion rights, and so on, has been a long battle, often fought by those allied to feminist, gay and liberal causes (see Segal, 1994: xiv; Segal and McIntosh, 1992). For feminists to contribute to a backlash against such liberalization is shortsighted and unhelpful.

Once again, feminist debate can do much to shake-up traditional criminological assumptions, in this instance about pornography and appropriate policies. This in turn raises further issues. If the aim of some liberals and feminists has been to outlaw pornography, then the kind of questions Smart might ask would be: 'but does using male-dominated law, in the positivistic tradition, i.e. make a crime of something which is held to corrupt some and degrade others – actually alter very much?': 'will pornography go away and the degrading thoughts that men think about women suddenly change?'. At the end of the day, is nothing strengthened other than the power of traditional, positivistic law? In other words, are feminist criminological questions once again simply captured by the power of 'the masculine'?

Such questions must be left open here. However, in moving on, it is important to note that the neglect of critical thinking about gender and masculine power in criminological discourse has recently begun to receive new attention.[9]

Masculinity and crime   Criminology has recently discovered 'masculinity' (Messerschmidt, 1993; Newburn and Stanko, 1994). In one sense, of course, to say this is nonsense – criminology and the sociology of deviance have always studied deviant masculinities (e.g. as products of male socialization, aspiration and competitiveness; the social approval of male hedonism as a reward for success etc.). Indeed, part of the core of feminist critique is that past studies of the worlds of crime, deviance and youth cultures, are remarkable reflections of a particularly masculine view of the world, barely acknowledging females (see note 9). This latter deficit is now widely noted; what is new is that essentialist assumptions about masculinity are being challenged. There is not the space here to do much more than note that a sociological rethinking of 'masculinity' (Connell, 1987; Segal, 1990) may offer some promising new ways of looking at old crime questions.

One such possibility is the exploration of the significance, and implications, of male bonding and competitive masculinity for corporate/business (i.e. middle/upper class) crime. Recent work by Messerschmidt (1993) considers such inter-relationships (cf. Levi, 1994). For this author,

the fact that men control the activities of management . . . is critical to understanding corporate crime. . . . men recruit men who share similar norms, attitudes, values and standards of behaviour. . . . Foremost among these is the ability to compromise personal principles in order to move up the ladder. (pp. 133–4)

. . . when legitimate approaches fail, corporate executives are positioned to engage in specific illegitimate practices that seek to ensure not only their own, but corporate success as well. . . . Moreover, as corporate executives do corporate crime, they simultaneously do masculinity . . . . (p. 135)

Overall, however 'new' or 'old' such observations are, masculinity and its socialization are important not least because most crimes are committed by men. That is not to say '*all* crime is the fault of men or that *all* men are likely to commit crime', but the cultural socialization of males into the values of a competitive world, while arguably necessary for survival in an entrepreneurial age, also promotes cultural and experiential contradictions that can give rise to undesirable outcomes (Coote, 1993; Taylor, 1994b). This is one of the ironies of modernity – its dependence on risk, competition and enterprise, features of the modern capitalist framework which are celebrated as engines of progress yet which can also be profoundly criminogenic and anti-social in their consequences (Beck, 1992; Nelken, 1994d).

Such ironies are a source of anxiety and unease about the modern social condition. In relation to crime and control issues this is partly reflected in sociopolitical images of 'falling standards' and a 'decline in moral values' (Anderson, 1992). These concerns may be ideologically, if not realistically, addressed by familiar devices such as calls for a 'return' to the values of a more settled and less troubled past. Such 'warm beer and village green' nostalgia may also be accompanied by shrill calls to 'crack down' on those who will not conform – young offenders, single mothers etc. (Brake and Hale, 1992; Pearson, 1983; Young, 1996, 36–44). In truth, of course, such visions of neighbourhood and Arcadia are largely mythical, while tougher penal – and more iniquitous social – policies are unlikely to herald a return to a consensus society. Where then is society headed? What are the 'visions of the future'?

Crime, control and the future: some theories and speculations

What might future patterns of crime look like? Commentators of left, liberal and right persuasions might agree that the increasing growth of socially excluded, marginal groups in society, will lead to more street crime and, in response, more – and more diversified – social control and surveillance. The explanations and recommended interventions might, of course, differ (although, increasingly, they may not). Drug-related crime will continue to increase, the related profits generating significant developments in criminal organization, and expansion into legitimate commerce (Ruggiero and South, 1995). Some trends in crime suggest that business organizations are increasingly both targets for and perpetrators of criminality, related to who has access to organizational resources or is responsible for corporate success – the crimes of the middle and managerial classes. Relatedly, at various international levels the blurring of crimes committed by criminal organizations and corporate organizations will be significant (Punch, 1993; Ruggiero, 1996); while changes in global finance and trade will mean more fraud against governments, trade alliances (e.g. the European Union) and corporations. Crimes against the environment such as pollution, and resulting problems such as public health dangers, will increasingly be matters for international crime and control agendas.

In terms of future political and social control *responses* to future crime trends, there are various visions we could sample. One important criminological review of 'future trends emerging in the present' is Cohen (1985). Cohen's thesis and concerns are elaborate and expansive but one of the key metaphors he employs has been particularly influential. This is his suggestive portrayal of the growing social control system as one 'catching-up' more and more citizens in ever-larger nets of ever-finer mesh, as the spectrum of punishment extends from the prison through the community, and the variety and type of sanctions and penalties multiply.

Cohen's 'visions of social control' are bleak and pessimistic and find echoes in other dystopian predictions of the future of urban control.[10] At the same time, there are other writers who seek to map out the viability of future reformist agendas in a more hopeful spirit. To consider the former view first.

Segregation and surveillance in the late modern city   In a more recent work, Cohen (1994: 70–4) has updated his review of trends in social control. Among these, perhaps particular significance should be attached to the emergence of 'the actuarial regime' and the 'risk society' (1994: 73; cf. Feeley and Simon, 1992):

> Instead of altering individual behaviour, actuarial, surveillance and compliance regimes alter the physical and social structure in which individuals behave. This

policy . . . [it is argued] is both easier to implement than the old 'disciplinary regimes' and, ultimately, more effective.

. . . these trends . . . grafted onto new technologies and the increased surveillance capacity of modern organisations . . . – have led sociologists of social control to some grim characterisations: the age of surveillance, the classified society, the managed society, the engineered society, the suspicious society, the self-monitored society, the transparent society, the maximum-security society etc.

Writing on the future of Los Angeles, Davis (1994) outlines the application of such technological and surveillance developments in practice, and speculates on where the ongoing process of segregation in the city will lead.

In contemporary metropolitan Los Angeles a new species of special enclave is emerging in sympathetic synchronization to the militarization of the landscape. For want of a better generic appellation, we might call them 'social control districts' (SCDs). (pp. 8–9)[11]

. . . post-riot Southern California seems on the verge of creating yet more SCDs. On the one hand the arrival of the Federal 'Weed and Seed' program, linking community development funds to anti-gang repression, provides a new set of incentives for neighborhoods to adopt exclusion and/or enhancement strategies. As many activists have warned, 'Weed and Seed' is like a police-state caricature of the 1960s War on Poverty with the Justice Department transformed into the manager of urban redevelopment. The poor will be forced to cooperate with their own criminalization as a precondition for urban aid. (p. 11)

Generally, it can be argued that the interface between architecture (e.g. planning secure pathways through the dangerous city) and the directing of human action is becoming ever more significant. Again Davis' (1994) explorations of 'urban control and the ecology of fear' in post-riot Los Angeles offer a window on one future of social control. Here a strategy of segregation and surveillance has made its impact on the city. Or rather, first, it has created 'a city within a city'.

It is not only the riots of the post-Rodney King assault and trial that Davis refers to here. After rioting in 1965 and fears of greater ethnic conflict, the city's redevelopment agency began to physically segregate the new core business areas from the ghetto areas: palisades, concrete pillars, freeway walls were built, traditional pedestrian connections between the poor district and the new business district were removed, 'foot traffic in the new financial district was elevated above the street on pedways whose access was controlled by the security systems of individual skyscrapers'. All of this has, as Davis observes, 'ominous racial overtones' (p. 4).

Similarly, the extensive and comprehensive surveillance of all these areas

constitutes a virtual *scanscape* – a space of protective visibility that increasingly defines where white-collar office workers and middle-class tourists feel safe. . . . Inevitably the workplace or shopping mall video camera will become linked with home security systems, personal 'panic buttons', car alarms, cellular phones and the like, in a seamless continuity of surveillance over daily routine. Indeed, yuppies' lifestyles soon may be defined by the ability to afford *electronic guardian angels to watch over them*. (Davis, 1994: 5; original emphasis)

Deprivation, reformism and realist optimism Alternatively, from a perspective that can be seen as a form of American 'left-realism', Elliott Currie has offered a more hopeful scenario and agenda for America's inner cities and, in particular, its drug problems:

> Given the extent of the devastation inflicted on the cities and the poor by the unleashing of the strategy of inequality, there is a sense in which almost anything we do to improve the conditions of life for those most at risk could help to reduce drug abuse. But we need to make more specific choices. . . . Here then are five crucial elements of a long-term strategy . . . all of which are also both economically sustainable and congruent with a larger vision of the society we wish to achieve. (1993: 283–4)

Currie's agenda is then outlined under the following headings: 'Expanding the opportunity structure', 'Revitalizing public health care', 'Supporting families', 'Assuring shelter' and 'Rebuilding the infrastructure' (pp. 284–323), with a following evaluation of funding viability and an assertion of the realistic benefits of such programmes. Unsurprisingly, a similar spirit is present in a recent essay by Young (1996) on criminology and late-modernity:

> Crime occurs when citizenship is thwarted, its causes lie in injustice, yet its effect is, inevitably, further injustice and violation of citizenship. The solution lies not in the resurrection of past stabilities, based on nostalgia and a world that will never return, but in a new citizenship, a reflexive modernity which will tackle the problems of justice and community, of reward and individualism, which lie at the heart of liberal democracy. (1996: 33)

Britain does not (yet?) have social problems on the same scale as those evident in the inner cities of the USA. However, as debates around the 'underclass' thesis (Byrne, 1995; Morris, 1994; Morrison, 1994: 148–51) indicate, since the riots of the 1980s and early 1990s there has been a growing 'authoritarian' fear that the problems of the inner city are only just being 'contained' (Keith, 1991; Young, 1992). It is clearly arguable that sceptics and pessimists may sometimes exaggerate 'Doomsday' visions of the future; none the less, the everyday reality of the present does not seem short of indicators of the fragility of society. Whether justifiably or not, 'anxieties' about crime, control and social order are commonplace. With paramilitary policing (Jefferson, 1990) and privatization of law enforcement services (South, 1994) being among the high-profile policing and policy responses to such urban anxieties, we may yet move ever closer to the 'Robocop scenario' – the age of the 'postmodern cop' as 'urban cowboy' (Burke, 1989).

Back to theory and towards the future? A 'criminology-after criminology'?

Postmodernism, human rights and crimes against the environment

In the opening sections of this chapter, I referred to Smart's critical view that criminology is wanting in being unable to 'deconstruct itself'. As someone interested in the vitality of the subject, my initial response is obviously 'why should it?'. But Smart's critique is vitally important, for if the subject cannot engage with new intellectual currents then it is indeed lost. We should therefore, if only tentatively here, explore what the deconstructionist impetus and postmodern challenge might suggest for a 'criminology-after-criminology'. However, as well as confronting the 'epistemological sea-changes' that interest Smart, it is also important that we note several other, new, intellectual and political concerns. Broadly speaking, these include cultural, human rights and global issues. These are areas which have been largely unexplored by positivist criminology. Hence, rather than acknowledge any need to deconstruct criminology, I shall argue here that new intellectual problems within a globalized and changing late-modern world present new questions around which criminology can reconstitute itself.[12]

Postmodernism   Postmodernism was first associated with changes in architecture, art and design – away from the uniformity of modernism and toward a mixing of styles and materials, pastiche and irony; a challenge to the straightforwardness and conventions of modernism (Smart, 1990: 74–5; TCS, 1988). It celebrates fragmentation and the plurality of cultures; a greater playfulness, humour and scepticism; a world of consumerism and global communications. For some authors, the future (postmodern) image of social control is one of soft and sedating seduction by a world of consumerism and fantasy – life in Disney World (Shearing and Stenning, 1987). The future social order as envisaged by Aldous Huxley in *Brave New World* is a more accurate reflection of trends in social control than Orwell's nightmare of a totalitarian, repressive *1984*. Yet, for other commentators, one vision of postmodernity may actually be much closer to the *1984* image. Ironically, society may end up here, not because of triumphs of positivism or utilitarianism but as the result of a backlash against boundless deconstructionism. In this dystopian postmodernity, rather than the embrace of autonomy and plurality, we encounter after all, demands for the reassertion of the certainties of authority and penality. Thus Morrison has argued that

> The possibilities of postmodernism, openness, powers and freedoms, are also the possibilities of a postmodern nightmare. Lost in the midst of postmodern disjointedness, of processes so varied that no centre can be dreamt of, the process of ruling becomes authoritarian. The demands of a populace searching for meaning prioritizes basic certainties, walls, divisions, demarcations and territories to control temporal space in the void of non-meaning. (1994: 144)

Beyond speculations on the future of control, overlaps between criminology and cultural studies should also provide spaces for exploration of postmodern ideas and theories. To take just two examples, Redhead (1991) argues that past theories of *youth culture and deviance* are no longer useful. These theories claimed to look beneath or behind the surfaces of the shimmering mediascape in order to discover the 'real', *authentic* subculture, apparently always distorted by the manufactured press and television image, which in turn becomes 'real' as more and more participants act out the media stereotypes. This 'depth model' is no longer appropriate – if it ever was – for analysing the surfaces of the (post)-modern world, a culture characterised by shallowness, flatness and 'hyper-reality'. (1991: 94)

Perhaps then, what is needed is a 'Cultural Criminology' (Ferrell and Sanders, 1996), sensitive to postmodern style and practices yet remaining 'a criminology', even if transgressively so:

Bending or breaking the boundaries of criminology to construct a cultural criminology in this sense does not undermine contemporary criminology as much as it expands and enlivens it. Cultural criminology widens criminology's domain to include worlds conventionally considered exterior to it: gallery art, popular music, media operations and texts, style. In the same way, it introduces criminology into contemporary debates over these worlds, and defines criminological perspectives as essential to them. (1996: 17)

Representation, media and discourse would naturally be central to such a criminology:

For good or bad, postmodern society exists well beyond . . . discrete, linear patterns of action and reaction. Rather, . . . criminal events, identities, and styles take life within a media-saturated environment, and thus exist from the start as moments in a mediated spiral of presentation and representation. (1996: 14)

But – can *postmodernism* say anything *constructive* about *responding* to social conflict, crime and social problems?

Postmodernism can be seen as conservative: rejecting modernist agendas for reform and progress. Yet intellectually, postmodernism is also characterized as liberating, precisely *because* it challenges assumptions about historical inevitabilities, the march of progress and 'Grand Narrative' views of history. Postmodernism allows that different perspectives involve different interests and different criteria of significance.[13]

The US cultural commentator Todd Gitlin (1989) has developed an optimistic and useful perspective on postmodernity and social issues, which suggests that we do not have to retreat from aspiration but that there *can* be an agenda for social and political action in the postmodern world. He asks 'how then can we develop a workable political point of view for the post modern era?' With regard to a form of social intervention that is a control of 'excesses', Gitlin suggests we need a 'politics of limits' rooted in three 'protections'.

1 The Ecological – the earth must be protected against exploitation and damage caused by humanities' activities.
2 The Pluralist – the social group must be protected against domination by other social groups whether by cultural exclusion, economic power or social marginalization; pluralism is encouraged.
3 The Libertarian – the individual must be protected against domination by larger groups.

A politics of limits respects multiplicity over hierarchy and difference over deference. Or, as Morrison (1994: 144) similarly argues, 'the attainment of solidarity in the context of diversity and difference demands a new metaphysics, an awareness in which a generality is struggled for which embraces plurality.[14]

So – what might a postmodern concern with post-traditional-criminology issues look like?

Morrison (1994: 143) argues that, 'the problematic of postmodern criminology will be how to create and sustain a social solidarity which takes pragmatism as its epistemology and plurality and contingency as its foundational ontology'. To apply Gitlin's version of postmodernism, *limits* and *protections* must be respected even within a postmodern world of diversity. Only if these *are* respected can individuals be free to express self-identity/ies, enjoy freedom of movement, rights of participation and citizenship. It follows that, in some way, these limits must be consensually and pragmatically enforced. This could therefore represent a new shift in the history of regulation and punishment: from the 'spectacle of punishment' in the age of the sovereign power, to the individualized penal servitude of the bureaucratic criminal justice system of modernity – to a postmodern mix of lifestyle, cultural and penal censures and sanctions.[15] For example: electronic tagging (your home is your prison); financial regulation (the extra-legal policing of consumerism); the medieval past resurrected in the present, e.g. 'Parish Constables' and Citizen Watch patrols, and the return of the chain-gang in Alabama alongside the building of a new generation of 'ultimate security' prisons. A postmodern image of social control might also have a *global character*: consider the ways in which the role of the United Nations has changed in recent years and disappointment over its inability to be a successful international peacekeeping, 'police force' (Fisas, 1995), as in the conflicts in former-Yugoslavia and Rwanda. Global environment problems and global crimes such as money laundering washed through the 24-hour a day banking system (South, 1992) also need global coordination of laws and other responses.

Domestically, continuing trends in 'decentralization' and 'privatization' reflect Conservative government policy to distance the state further from the administration of punishment and control (e.g. privately run prisons, private security policing; Johnston, 1992; Ryan and Ward, 1992; South, 1988, 1994). In such a context, traditional appeals to state law via the national courts may no longer be adequate and appeals for justice may increasingly need to invoke international principles of human rights and see appellants turning to *supra-national* human rights courts (Turner, 1993). Conservative, bourgeoise notions of justice are outmoded, and in a post-Marxist world we cannot appeal to socialist ideals, so the ideologies and institutions of modernity have had their chance and failed (Morrison, 1994; 150–1). Regard for international human rights (1) would reflect diversity, (2) is not tied to the sovereignty of individual nations, (3) is a global standard breaking away from national histories of exploitation, colonialism and nationalism.[16]

There is a small but growing literature on postmodernism and criminology (substantial critical responses are Hunt, 1991 and Lea, (in press)). My own speculations are merely suggestive of issues for debate between those who would strengthen and argue a future for late-modern criminology and those who would postmodernize in order to deconstruct the subject.

Just to take the theme of human rights issues a little further here (or, more accurately, a great deal further but in limited space), I wish to draw attention to two further areas for the consideration of late-modern criminology.

Human rights and the future of the planet

One area is that to which Stan Cohen (1993) has recently drawn attention, the neglect of the criminological study of the suffering and atrocities committed in cases of human rights violations. The other area concerns the relationship between the human rights of current and future generations, and the imperatives of maintaining a liveable and sustainable planet.

Human rights and crimes of the state As Stan Cohen (1993: 491) observes: 'whatever the concept of human rights means, it has become a dominant narrative. Arguably, with the so-called death of the old meta-narratives of Marxism, liberalism and the Cold War, human rights will become *the* normative political language of the future.' Entailed here are 'numerous policy issues of policing, enforcement and international law'. Given the complexity and sheer scale of the issues, violence and offences to be confronted here, Cohen (1993: 495) acknowledges that it is quite 'understandable why mainstream criminology is reluctant to become too immersed in these debates. Their absence in "left-realist" criminology is stranger to explain. After all, the ontological base here is a realist philosophy which starts with harm, victimization, seriousness, suffering and supposed indifference to all this by the adolescent left idealism of the 1960s.'

The proposition here is that a revitalized, late-modern criminology for 'the end of the century' must take seriously those crimes which are truly 'the crimes of the twentieth century': the 'gross violations of human rights', that include genocide, mass political killings and rape by agents of the state (p. 492).

Cohen goes on to consider several reasons for the strength or weakness of popular support for human rights causes. One question which he raises is 'how far concerns for international standards of human rights are related to concerns about global environmental protection?'. My own view is that there should be an intimate relationship between these two concerns. It is to this second area that I briefly turn.

Global environmental protection and future human rights The argument here is that alongside human rights, environmental concerns will also enter into the 'normative political language of the future'. Issues here include the human rights and victim status of those who live with the impact of environmental degradation today, and the rights of future generations and the sustainability of the planet they will inherit. As Ferris eloquently puts the case:

> Post-enlightenment liberalism and socialism which shaped the parameters of contemporary thinking about social policy [and much criminology] were both premised on the conquest of nature. It is becoming very difficult to evade awareness of the costs of this 'victory'. Rather than liberation from the historic bonds of scarcity we have to recognise at least the possibility of the destruction of the planet. . . . Ecological movements worldwide have drawn attention to the problems and placed the idea of limits on the policy agenda [NB discussion of Gitlin earlier]. It is no longer a question of saving 'socialism' or 'capitalism' but humanity itself on a threatened planet. (1991: 26)

In the process of the industrialization of the twentieth century world, numerous crimes, violations, deviations and irregularities have been perpetrated against the environment. As Snyder (1991: 226 *et passim*) observes,

> The paucity of action taken thus far on environmental issues portrays vividly the power of the corporate sector. This is an area . . . which challenges the lifestyle and philosophy which is the basis of all capitalist systems – the idea that humans have a right to make use of all the resources of the planet, that other life forms such as animals and birds are there to serve our needs, and that we have no long-term obligations to future generations or to the natural world.

Criminology has barely begun to consider the questions and challenges raised here.

Conclusion

It may be that disciplinary boundaries *per se* are increasingly becoming meaningless for criminology, as for other fields of study. Such fragmentation cannot be resisted (Ericson and Carriere, 1994) but can perhaps be understood within a reflexive framework (Nelken, 1994c). However, as Ferrell and Sanders (1996) observe in laying out their proposals for a new 'cultural criminology', such breaking of boundaries can be positively constructive for a field of study, strengthening rather than destructively deconstructing.

This chapter has moved from what are, in the scheme of things, relatively mundane to rather grander questions about the 'state of criminology'. To conclude, I shall return to my opening theme – 'where are we now?'

Crises and confidence in criminology The now repetitious announcement of crises in criminology (Heidensohn and Silvestri, 1995) ironically brings to mind Cohen's (1972) critique of society's episodic embrace of moral panics: every now and then, it seems, criminology feels the need to declare a state of crisis. As in the case of societal anxiety attacks, the accompanying diagnostic apparatus is quickly produced – articles, books, seminars, debates with snappy titles ('Whither, whether, wither criminology?'), conference plenary sessions and so on. And then – as panics do – concerns wane, debates melt away.

One development which will be interesting for the further revitalizing of British criminology is the impact of its very own 'demographic time-bomb'. The influence of the 'fortunate generation' who took up their new posts in the 1960s and 1970s has certainly and evidently been considerable. Yet few of that talented generation have referred to the fact that many of them will start to retire from their posts in the next decade.[17] The spaces that will be opened up will be of intellectual significance, as well as importance in terms of offering employment possibilities that may help change the gender and ethnic composition of the discipline.

My final observation must be that late-modern criminology seems to be in a rather vigorous state of good health: producing new directions, reflexive debate and exploring its own history with confident sophistication (Beirne, 1993; Rock, 1994b). Though clearly many others disagree, I think students should engage with the field in a spirit of optimism. Late-modern criminology is certainly not 'late' as in 'dead', but flourishing, alive and well.

Notes

1 See Smart, 1990; Sumner, 1994; Jefferson, 1995. On the other hand, the book Jefferson is reviewing, *The Oxford Handbook of Criminology* (Maguire et al., 1994; second edition forthcoming) can be seen as a testimony to the healthy diversity and productivity of current criminology.

2 This chapter is principally concerned with developments in theory, with some reference to observations and speculations on the future of crime and control. Examination of the broad literatures, diversities and 'crises' of contemporary crime and control issues cannot be included here. For a very useful and up-to-date review see Muncie and McLaughlin (1996).

3 See the Introductory chapter to Smart's (1995) collected essays for an intellectual autobiography, charting the changing nature of her critical dialogue with criminology and the sociology of law.

4 Cohen's relationship with criminology is nicely hinted at by the ambiguous title of a collection of his essays – *Against Criminology* (1988).

5 For some similar points, see Cohen (1994) writing in the same volume. On *some* other recent developments see: on postmodernism, Henry and Milovanovic, (1991, 1994); on trends in theory, Nelken (1994a); on international variations in feminist criminology, Hahn Rafter and Heidensohn (1995).

6 Bottoms and others writing on crime prevention do, however, retain a narrow view of what the term 'environmental criminology' might suggest, although not without acknowledging that this may have 'its problems, especially in an era of "green" issues' (Bottoms, 1994: 586, fn. 3). I shall suggest later that crimes *against* the *natural environment* (as opposed to crimes committed within the *built* environment), represent a significant new dimension for criminology to embrace at the end of the twentieth century.

7 Heidensohn and Silvestri (1995: 14) have usefully offered definitions of these terms: 'By engendering the agenda we mean that gender issues and especially the gendered nature of a considerable amount of crime has been acknowledged – domestic violence, for instance. "Deconstruction" is the process of rethinking the meaning and categorisation of terms and topics so that none can be assumed to have substance. Thus the very terms "women" and "crime" have been challenged and presented as problematic.'

8 For a nice example of the sociologies of deviance and health 'meeting', see Conrad and Schneider, 1980.

9 For some earlier critiques of masculinity/masculinism in youth culture studies and criminology, see Dorn and South, 1983; McRobbie, 1980.

10 For readers who like a good detective story but need some academic justification for such enjoyment, Kerr (1992) is a powerful fictional speculation on various enforcement and other social trends into the next century, also managing to embrace feminism, the Frankfurt School, a nice joke on the resurrection of Lombrosian positivism and much else.

11 Davis nicely 'remodels' the Chicago School's 'zonal model of the city' as it might apply to late-modern Los Angeles.

12 See e.g. Cohen, 1994, on the challenges to Anglo-American and European discourses of criminology when faced with the problems of 'the politics of reconstruction' in, for example, Eastern Europe and South Africa.

13 Thanks to David Owen for this point.

14 Note, amidst all this celebration of the 'newness' of postmodernism, remarkable echoes of symbolic interactionism (pluralism, anti-essentialism etc.: cf. Plummer, 1990) and Young's (1975: *passim* and p. 91) manifesto for a 'working class criminology': 'Forms of deviancy occur as attempts to create unhampered and livable space. . . . a tenderloin of the city where a sense of "the possible" breaks through the facticity of what is.'

15 Thanks here to Nicholas Dorn for shared discussions and speculations on postmodernism and policing some years ago; and see also Sumner, 1994.

16 Ideas suggested in an unpublished talk on 'postmodernism' by Bryan Turner, *Essex Postgraduate Conference*, Clacton 1990.

17 I have seen only Downes (1988: 45) and Heidensohn (and Silvestri, 1995: 21) remark on this.

References

Anderson, D. (ed.) (1992) *The Loss of Virtue: Moral Confusion and Social Disorder in Britain and America*. London: Social Affairs Unit/National Review Books.

Auld, J., Dorn, N. and South, N. (1986), 'Irregular work, irregular pleasures: heroin in the 1980s', in R. Matthews and J. Young (eds), *Confronting Crime*. London: Sage.

Bauman, Z. (1988) 'Is there a postmodern sociology?', *Theory, Culture and Society*, 5(2/3): 217–38.

Bauman, Z. (1989) *Modernity and the Holocaust*. Cambridge: Polity Press.

Beck, U. (1992) *The Risk Society: Towards a New Modernity*. London: Sage.

Beirne, P. (1993) *Inventing Criminology: Essays on the Rise of 'Homo Criminalis'*. Albany, NY: SUNY Press.

Bottoms, A. (1994) 'Environmental criminology', in M. Maguire, R. Morgan and R. Reiner (eds), *The Oxford Handbook of Criminology*. Oxford: Oxford University Press.

Bottoms, A. and Wiles, P. (1996) 'Crime and policing in a changing social context', in W. Saulsbury, J. Mott and T. Newburn (eds), *Themes in Contemporary Policing*. London: Policy Studies Institute.

Brake, M. and Hale, C. (1992) *Public Order and Private Lives: The Politics of Law and Order*. London: Routledge.

Burke, F. (1989) 'Panic killing (cops)', in A. Kroker, M. Kroker and D. Cook (eds), *Panic Encyclopedia*. London: Macmillan.

Burke, M. (1994) *Coming Out of the Blue*. London: Cassell.

Byrne, D. (1995) 'Deindustrialisation and dispossession: an examination of social division in the industrial city', *Sociology*, 29(1), 95–115.

Carrington, K. (1994) 'Postmodernism and feminist criminologies: disconnecting discourses?', *International Journal of the Sociology of Law*, 22: 261–77.

Cohen, S. (1972) *Folk Devils and Moral Panics*. London: Paladin.

Cohen, S. (1985) *Visions of Social Control*. Cambridge: Polity Press.

Cohen, S. (1988) *Against Criminology*. New Brunswick, NJ: Transaction Books.

Cohen, S. (1993) 'Human rights and crimes of the state: the culture of denial', reprinted in J. Muncie, E. McLaughlin and M. Langan (eds) (1996), *Criminological Perspectives*. London: Sage.

Cohen, S. (1994) 'Social control and the politics of reconstruction', in D. Nelken (ed.) (1994), *The Futures of Criminology*. London: Sage.

Connell, R. (1987) *Gender and Power*. Cambridge: Polity Press.

Conrad, P. and Schneider, J. (1980) *Deviance and Medicalization: From Badness to Sickness*. St Louis: C.V. Mosby.

Coote, A. (1993) 'The problem with crime is a problem with men', *Independent*, 16 February.

Currie, E. (1993) *Reckoning: Drugs, the Cities and the American Future*. New York: Hill and Wang.

Davis, M. (1994) *Beyond Blade Runner: Urban Control – the Ecology of Fear*. Open Magazine Pamphlet series. New York: The New Press.

Dorn, N. and South, N. (1983) *Of Males and Markets: A Critical Review of Youth Culture Theory*. London: Middlesex Polytechnic.

Dorn, N. and South, N. (eds) (1987) *A Land Fit for Heroin? Drug Policies, Prevention and Practice*. London: Macmillan.

Downes, D. (1988). 'The sociology of crime and social control in Britain, 1960–87', in P. Rock (ed.), *A History of British Criminology*. Oxford: Oxford University Press.

Elias, N. (1978) *The History of Manners*. New York: Pantheon.

Elias, N. (1982) *State Formation and Civilization*. Oxford: Basil Blackwell.

Ericson, R. and Carriere, K. (1994) 'The fragmentation of criminology', in D. Nelken (ed.), *The Futures of Criminology*. London: Sage. pp. 89–109.

Feeley, M. and Simon, J. (1992) 'The new penology: notes on the emerging strategy of corrections and its implications', *Criminology*, 30(4): 452–74.

Ferrell, J. and Sanders, C. (1996) *Cultural Criminology*. London: Northeastern University Press.

Ferris, J. (1991) 'Green politics and the future of welfare', in N. Manning (ed.), *Social Policy Review*. London: Longman.

Fisas, V. (1995) *Blue Geopolitics: The United Nations Reform and the Future of the Blue Helmets*. London: Pluto.

Garland, D. (1985) *Punishment and Welfare*. Aldershot: Gower.

Garland, D. (1994) 'Of crimes and criminals: the development of criminology in Britain', in M. Maguire, R. Morgan and R. Reiner (eds), *The Oxford Handbook of Criminology*. Oxford: Oxford University Press.

Gelsthorpe, L. and Morris, A. (1990) 'Rethinking criminology and the feminist critique', in L. Gelsthorpe and A. Morris (eds), *Feminist Perspectives in Criminology*. Buckingham: Open University Press. pp. 7–9.

Giddens, A. (1990) *The Consequences of Modernity*. Cambridge: Polity Press.

Gitlin, T. (1989) 'Postmodernism defined, at last!', *Utne Reader*, Summer, 34: 52–61.

Groombridge, Nic (1995) 'Tough talk: masculinities and crimes, some reflections on men researching men'. Paper to the British Criminology Conference, University of Loughborough.

Hahn Rafter, N. and Heidensohn, F. (eds) (1995) *International Feminist Perspectives in Criminology*. Buckingham: Open University Press.

Hall, S., Jefferson, T., Clarke, J., Critcher, C. and Roberts, R. (1978) *Policing the Crisis*. London: Macmillan.

Heidensohn, F. (1968) 'The deviance of women: a critique and an enquiry', *British Journal of Sociology*, xix: 2.

Heidensohn, F. and Silvestri, M. (1995) 'The conformity of criminology'. Paper to the British Criminology Conference, University of Loughborough.

Henry, S. and Milovanovic, D. (1991) 'Constitutive criminology: the maturation of critical theory', *Criminology*, 29(2): 293–316.

Henry, S. and Milovanovic, D. (1994) 'The constitution of constitutive criminology: a postmodern approach to criminological theory', in D. Nelken (ed.), *The Futures of Criminology*. London: Sage. pp. 110–33.

Herek, G. and Berrill, K. (eds) (1992) *Hate Crimes: Confronting Violence against Lesbians and Gay Men*. London: Sage.

Hughes, G. (1991) 'Taking crime seriously?', *Sociology Review*, November, 18–22.

Hunt, A. (1991) 'Postmodernism and critical criminology', in B. Maclean and D. Milovanovic (eds), *New Directions in Critical Criminology*. Vancouver: Collective Press.

Jefferson, T. (1990) *The Case against Paramilitary Policing*. Milton Keynes: Open University Press.

Jefferson, T. (1992) 'Wheelin' and stealin", *Achilles Heel*, Summer.

Jefferson, T. (1995) 'Review of M. Maguire, R. Morgan and R. Reiner (eds) 1994, *The Oxford Handbook of Criminology*', *Sociology*, 29(2): 372–4.

Johnston, L. (1992) *The Rebirth of Private Policing*. London: Routledge.

Keith, M. (1991) '"Policing a perplexed society"?: No-go areas and the mystification of police–black conflict', in E. Cashmore and E. McLaughlin (eds), *Out of Order? Policing Black People*. London: Routledge.

Keith, M. (1993) *Race, Riots and Policing*. London: UCL Press.

Kerr, P. (1992) *A Philosophical Investigation*. London: Chatto and Windus.

Lea, J. (1996) 'Criminology and postmodernism', in P. Walton and J. Young (eds), *The New Criminology Revisited*, in press. London: Macmillan.

Levi, M. (1994) 'Masculinities and white collar crime', in T. Newburn and E. Stanko (eds), *Just Boys Doing Business? Men, Masculinities and Crime*. London: Routledge.

Maguire, M., Morgan, R. and Reiner, R. (eds) (1994) *The Oxford Handbook of Criminology*. Oxford: Oxford University Press.

Matthews, R. and Young, J. (1992) 'Reflections on realism', in J. Young and R. Matthews (eds), *Rethinking Criminology: The Realist Debate*. London: Sage.

McRobbie, A. (1980) 'Settling accounts with subcultures: A feminist critique', *Screen Education*, 39.

Messerschmidt, J. (1993) *Masculinities and Crime: Critique and Reconceptualisation of Theory*. Lanham: Rowman and Littlefield.

Mooney, J. (1994) 'The Prevalence and Social Distribution of Domestic Violence: an Analysis of Theory and Method'. PhD Thesis, University of Middlesex.

Morris, L. (1994) *Dangerous Classes*. London: Routledge.

Morrison, W. (1994) 'Criminology, modernity and the "truth" of the human condition: reflections on the melancholy of postmodernism', in D. Nelken (ed.), *The Futures of Criminology*. London: Sage. pp. 134–53.

Muncie, J. and McLaughlin, E. (1996) *The Problem of Crime*. London: Sage.

Murji, K. (1994) 'Drugs: "scare in the community"', *Community Care*, 1–7 June, pp. 2–8.

Nelken, D. (ed.) (1994a) *The Futures of Criminology*. London: Sage.

Nelken, D. (1994b) 'Whom can you trust? The future of comparative criminology', in D. Nelken (ed.), *The Futures of Criminology*. London: Sage. pp. 220–43.

Nelken, D. (1994c) 'Reflexive criminology?', in D. Nelken (ed.), *The Futures of Criminology*. London: Sage. pp. 7–42.

Nelken, D. (1994d) 'White collar crime', in M. Maguire, R. Morgan and R. Reiner (eds), *The Oxford Handbook of Criminology*. Oxford: Oxford University Press. pp. 356–92.

Nellis, M. (1995) 'Probation values for the 1990s', *Howard Journal of Criminal Justice*, 34(1): 19–44.

Newburn, T. and Stanko, E. (eds) (1994) *Just Boys Doing Business? Men, Masculinities and Crime*. London: Routledge.

Pearson, G. (1983) *Hooligan: A History of Respectable Fears*. London: Macmillan.

Plummer, K. (1990) 'Staying in the empirical world: symbolic interactionism and postmodernism', *Symbolic Interaction*, 13(2): 155–60.

Plummer, K. (1995) *Telling Sexual Stories*. London: Routledge.

Pryce, K. (1979) *Endless Pressure: A Study of West Indian Lifestyles in Britain*. Harmondsworth: Penguin.

Punch, M. (1993) 'Bandit banks: financial services and organized crime', *Journal of Contemporary Justice*, 9(3): 175–96.

Redhead, S. (1991) 'Rave off: youth, subcultures and the law', *Social Studies Review*, 6(3): 92–4.

Rice, M. (1990) 'Challenging orthodoxies in feminist theory: a black feminist critique', in L. Gelsthorpe and A. Morris (eds), *Feminist Perspectives in Criminology*. Buckingham: Open University Press.

Rock, P. (1988) 'The present state of criminology in Britain', in P. Rock (ed.), *A History of British Criminology*. Oxford: Oxford University Press.

Rock, P. (1994a) 'The social organization of British criminology', in M. Maguire, R. Morgan and R. Reiner (eds), *The Oxford Handbook of Criminology*. Oxford: Oxford University Press.

Rock, P. (ed.) (1994b) *History of Criminology*. Dartmouth: Aldershot.

Ruggiero, V. (1996) *Organized and Corporate Crime in Europe: Offers that Can't be Refused*. Aldershot: Dartmouth.

Ruggiero, V. and South, N. (1995) *Eurodrugs: Drug Use, Markets and Trafficking in Europe*. London: UCL Press.

Ryan, M. and Ward, T. (1992) 'From positivism to postmodernism: some theoretical and strategic reflections on the evolution of the penal lobby in Britain', *International Journal of the Sociology of Law*, 20: 321–35.

Scraton, P. (1990) 'Scientific knowledge or masculine discourses? Challenging patriarchy in criminology', in L. Gelsthorpe and A. Morris (eds), *Feminist Perspectives in Criminology*. Buckingham: Open University Press.

Segal, L. (1990) *Slow Motion: Changing Masculinities, Changing Men*. London: Virago.

Segal, L. (1994) *Is the Future Female?*. London: Virago.

Segal, L. and McIntosh, M. (eds) (1992) *Sex Exposed: Sexuality and the Pornography Debate*. London: Virago.

Shearing, C. and Stenning, P. (1987) 'Say Cheese!: From the Panopticon to Disney World', in C. Shearing and P. Stenning (eds), *Private Policing*. Beverly Hills, CA: Sage.

Sheptycki, J. (1995a) 'Folk devils and Eurocops: criminological problems and prospects for understanding transnational crime and policing in Europe'. Paper to the British Criminology Conference, University of Loughborough.

Sheptycki, J. (1995b) 'Transnational policing and the makings of a postmodern state', *British Journal of Criminology*, 35: 4.

Smart, C. (1976) *Women, Crime and Criminology*. London: Routledge.

Smart, C. (1989) *Feminism and the Power of Law*. London: Routledge.

Smart, C. (1990) 'Feminist approaches to criminology or postmodern woman meets atavistic man', in L. Gelsthorpe and A. Morris (eds), *Feminist Perspectives in Criminology*. Buckingham: Open University Press. pp. 70–84.

Smart, C. (1995) *Law, Crime and Sexuality*. London: Sage.

Snyder, L. (1991) 'The regulatory dance: understanding reform processes in corporate crime', *International Journal of the Sociology of Law*, 19: 209–36.

South, N. (1988) *Policing for Profit: The Private Security Sector*. London: Sage.

South, N. (1992) 'Moving murkey money: drug trafficking, law enforcement and the pursuit of criminal profits', in D. Farrington and S. Walklate (eds), *Offenders and Victims: Theory and Policy*. London: British Society of Criminology/Institute for the Study and Treatment of Delinquency.

South, N. (1994) Privatizing policing in the European market: some issues for theory, policy and research', *European Sociological Review*, 10(3): 219–33.

Stychin, C. (1995) *Law's Desire: Sexuality and the Limits of Justice*. London: Routledge.

Sumner, C. (1994) *The Sociology of Deviance: An Obituary*. Buckingham: Open University Press.

Taylor, I. (ed.) (1991) *The Social Effects of Free Market Policies*. Hemel Hempstead: Harvester Wheatsheaf.

Taylor, I. (1994a) 'The political economy of crime', in M. Maguire, R. Morgan and R. Reiner (eds), *The Oxford Handbook of Criminology*. Oxford: Oxford University Press.

Taylor, I. (1994b) 'The Gun Club: men, firearms and the new economic order', *Sociology Review*, 3(4): 10–14.

Taylor, I., Evans, K. and Fraser, P. (1996) *A Tale of Two Cities*. London: Routledge.

Taylor, I., Walton, P. and Young, J. (1973) *The New Criminology: For a Social Theory of Deviance*. London: Routledge.

TCS (1988) *Postmodernism*. Double issue of *Theory, Culture and Society*, 5(2/3): June.

Turner, B. (1993) 'Outline of a theory of human rights', *Sociology*, 27(3): 489–512.

Walton, P. and Young, J. (eds) (in press) *The New Criminology Revisited*. London: Macmillan.

Williams, P. and Chrisman, L. (eds) (1993) *Colonial Discourse and Post-Colonial Theory*. London: Prentice-Hall.

Young, A. (1992) 'Feminism and the body of criminology', in D. Farrington and S. Walklate (eds), *Offenders and Victims: Theory and Policy*. London: BSC/ISTD. pp. 62–79.

Young, J. (1975) 'Working class criminology', in I. Taylor, P. Walton and J. Young (eds), *Critical Criminology*. London: Routledge.

Young, J. (1992) 'Riotous rage of the have-nots'. *Independent on Sunday*, 19 July.

Young, J. (1994) 'Incessant chatter: recent paradigms in criminology', in M. Maguire, R. Morgan and R. Reiner (eds), *The Oxford Handbook of Crimonology*. Oxford: Oxford University Press.

Young, J. (1996) 'Writing on the cusp of change: a new criminology for an age of late modernity', in P. Walton and J. Young (eds), in press.

5 Law, Politics and the Social Sciences

Alan Hunt

Law and the social sciences: an uneasy relation

The intellectual discourses about law of the twentieth century have always exhibited an ambivalence about the relationship between law and the social sciences. Parallel discourses have traversed academic legal debates, one seeking to integrate law with the rising hegemonic influence of the social sciences and the other concerned to preserve the normative value of the asserted autonomy of law.[1] Generally 'autonomy' has been the predominant view, largely because of its 'fit' with the institutional and professional isolation of law. From this stance 'law as social science' positions have been seen as mildly subversive because they risk the subsumption of law into more diffuse categories such as 'social control' or 'regulation', in which law loses its distinctiveness and its claim to professional preeminence. The other 'danger' of viewing law as part of the social sciences has been that it threatens the sharp distinction between law and politics. The separation of law from politics is conceived of both as a social fact and as a paramount value. Conventional legal theory focuses attention upon legal techniques conceived of as non-political, neutral and rational decision procedures that are applied to social conflicts, typically conceived of in the form of interparty litigation. In liberal theory law is viewed as sustaining and policing an imagined boundary between law and politics. This view is associated with an assumption that a major role of law is to provide the least system-disturbing mechanism of conflict resolution. This conception is frequently associated with a view of law as a steering mechanism operating through the provision of rules which allow for conflict avoidance by positive channelling of social behaviour.

Yet conventional legal thought was never simply a view of legal autonomy conceived in terms of the separation of law and politics. This descriptive claim has long been invested with normative significance. Thus the discourses of the rule of law and separation of powers have always been more than mere description; they have also functioned as vehicles for the political legitimation of liberal conceptions of the social and political order.

The central feature of the legal culture of liberalism involves a conception of law as a purposive enterprise in which state law is conceived as first selecting its targets and then aspiring to organize, rule or otherwise govern major fields of liberal-democratic society. Having selected its field of operation, law must construct it in such a way as to render it amenable to legal governance. For example, law aspires to governance over politics, but the dispersion and heterogeneity of politics makes it significantly ungovernable; to overcome this difficulty, 'politics' itself is constructed in a truncated fashion, as the decisions of a range of legally identified roles within specifiable institutional settings, in order to render it a suitable subject of legal governance. Thus administrative law seeks to exercise governance over a legally identified conception of governmental decisions while constitutional law sets up in judgment over the boundaries of legislative and administrative competence. In general, social relations must first be legally constructed as a prior condition for legal intervention. This point is significant in drawing attention to the fact that law is not simply a mechanism that seeks to bring under its governance pre-existing social relations, but that law both constitutes and is constituted by social relations.

Law proclaims itself sovereign. The sovereignty of law is not a matter of external political fact, as held by the legal positivist tradition stretching from Austin to H.L.A. Hart and beyond; rather sovereignty is an aspiration to which law lays claims and which it must vigilantly guard against all challenges. Ronald Dworkin provides the most explicit contemporary articulation of legal sovereignty, what he calls 'law's ambition for itself'. His project is proclaimed through the celebration of 'Law's Empire' of which judges, jurists and lawyers 'are the subjects of law's empire, liegemen to its methods and ideals' (Dworkin, 1986: vii). This imagery is best understood as a defence of what I have elsewhere termed 'legal imperialism' (Hunt, 1992). In its most innocent form 'legal imperialism' denotes the role assigned by Dworkin and, more generally, by liberal legal theory, to law as the impersonal sovereign that replaces the monarchical sovereignty of absolutism. In its more developed form the imagery of legal imperialism seeks to capture the substance of the 'problematic of legitimacy' which takes the central problem about the relationship between law and politics to be whether or not the exercise of power is legitimate or illegitimate. Dworkin assigns to law the task of acting as the guardian of the boundary between state and civil society. Law, through the agency of rights bestowed on legal subjects, makes possible a form of politics in which the capacity of the state exists within prescribed and controllable boundaries.

There has always been a tension at the heart of the long-running debate between autonomy and the law as social science discourses. On the one hand the liberal commitment to the rule of law induces a commitment to the idea of legal autonomy. In this guise law is the neutral umpire who enforces rules of the game of constitutional politics, that is a politics that imposes constraint upon both political actors and the state as a special political actor. In this conception the law is given an elevated and central space within the institutional arrangements of society. In this vision of sovereignty law can and must do everything. Dworkin, for example, exhibits a remarkable confidence in the capacity of law to realize political and ethical goals. His confidence is founded on what can only be regarded as a naive faith in the capacity of law to check and control political power. Law holds out the great dream of social peace.

> We have an institution [law] that calls some issues from the battleground of power politics to the forum of principle. It holds out the promise that the deepest, most fundamental conflicts will once, some-place, finally, become questions of justice. (Dworkin, 1986: 71)

More generally the call of 'law as integrity' expresses the desire for an escape from both personal preferences and political conviction. This fear of politics and the corresponding dream of discovering a mechanism for resolving political problems by some means other than politics is deeply embedded in the problematic of legitimacy and is endemic within the liberal tradition.

On the other hand, another dimension of modernity enjoins a commitment to the idea of law as a purposive technique of modern governance, as a mechanism of instrumental rationality, the prime means for the realization and legitimation of the immense reach of projects of governance touching almost every arena of social life. The expansion of legislation as a primary vehicle of governance embraces not only the traditional arenas of governmental action, but has become increasingly a presence in the field of private governance, and institutions of all types employ legislative techniques in which policies and programmes take legislative form. This key role of legislation should not be thought of as simply a technique of government; its significance is wider, in that legislation has increasingly become a key site of political contestation. Many – but still by no means all – contemporary conflicts occur around the legislative processes in so far as social movements advance their interests in the form of legislative demands.[2] Social and political debates take the form of alternative legislative programmes – classically illustrated in the myriad forms of the contest between pro- and anti-abortion forces.

This expanded conception of the law as a fundamental technique of modern government has enjoined numerous responses, varying in their degree of anxiety as to the implications. Concern over these tendencies has come from both the left and the right. Early on Dicey commented that the expansion of purposive ('collectivist') legislation posed an incipient, but not inevitable, threat to the common law (Dicey, 1905). More recently, Hayek has identified the expansion of instrumental legislation as the main vehicle of the precipitous forward march of the 'constructivist fallacy', namely that planned social engineering is either possible or desirable (Hayek, 1973–79). From a very different perspective Habermas has expressed concern that as the range, scope and detail of legal intervention expands it produces a general movement towards an expanding 'juridification' of social life.[3] This idea refers to the process by which the state intervenes in areas of social life in ways which limit the autonomy of individuals or groups to determine their own affairs and threatens the further colonization of civil society ('the lifeworld') (Habermas, 1987: 356–73). More generally we can identify 'legalization' as a general feature of high modernity (the period of the

Keynesian welfare state). Legalization is also a distinctive feature of what
Stephen White aptly describes as 'postmodern modernity' (White, 1989).
The neo-liberal political 'revolution' has – thus far – failed to deliver on
one of its key promises to 'roll back the state' and reduce the scope and
scale of 'regulation'.

While legalization is only one enduring tendency within the development
of modern governance it can serve as a signifier for all the trends in the
development of legal mechanisms and institutions which have formed
the backdrop against which the sociology of law formed, developed and
currently engages. To the emergence of this academic enterprise I now turn.

The institutionalization of the sociology of law

These theoretical reflections on the rise of juridification need to be viewed
for the light they throw on the development of the academic enterprise that
responds to the labels 'sociology of law', 'law and society movement' and
'socio-legal studies'. This development is not the usual story of the
emergence of a sub-discipline, followed by academic institutionalization
and barrier-building to defend territory and ward off other sub-disciplines.
The sociology of law did not start life as a specialized sub-discipline in the
way that the sociology of the family or the sociology of religion did. Rather
its existence has always had a primary link to the Law Schools. Sociology
of law was born in the Law School rather than in the Sociology Department. Only after its institutionalization has the field found a recognized
niche as a sub-discipline of sociology.

Growing up as it did, as a reaction against the dominant tradition within
the Law Schools, the sociology of law had, from the outset, a radical self-
conception in so far as it sought to challenge the narrow positivism and
complacency of the Law Schools which served to provide not only
professional training, but to sustain the intellectual legitimacy of the legal
order. The most important manifestation of this critical edge is to be seen
in the persistence of the 'gap problem' as the focus of attention. The official
texts of law offered the promise of 'justice'; yet the 'law in action' always
fell short of the promise of the 'law in books'[4]. Thus the central problematic for the sociology of law was whether or not this 'gap' between promise
and reality could be overcome (Abel, 1980; Nelken, 1981). Throughout the
1960s and 1970s the debate was between those who held that by careful
policy analysis and skilled drafting the 'gap' could be closed and those
more radical spirits who insisted that the 'gap' was itself a constitutive
characteristic of law. In the course of this controversy a mass of valuable
descriptive work was produced which charted the operative practices of
legal institutions and personnel. Epitomizing this style of work is the classic
finding that small-claims courts function as debt collecting agents for credit
companies and not for the consumers whom they were supposed to aid, or
that legal representation serves not so much to advance the interests of

clients as to 'cool them out', accommodating them to the interests of the court (Blumberg, 1967; Caplovitz, 1974).

The weakness inherent in 'gap' studies is that they were too closely tied to an acceptance of the view that legislation was a vehicle for social change. Gap studies tend towards instrumentalism and, at the same time, express what Sarat aptly describes as a 'thinly veiled moral outrage' that law's results should differ from its declared purposes (Sarat, 1985). In the 1970s a more radical shift manifested itself. A full-frontal critique of law ensued in which law was conceived as an agency of capitalist rule. Some of these accounts verged on simplistic conspiracy theories (Lefcourt, 1971) while others were more sophisticated (Balbus, 1973).

From this period emerged a more significant debate which focused on the attempt to grasp the complex role of law viewed from the standpoint of class and political relations. The most dramatic intervention, and one that remains a reference point down to the present, was Edward Thompson's *Whigs and Hunters* (1975), in which he defends the 'bourgeois' concept of the rule of law as operating to modulate the exercise of state power even in the era of the maximum intensity of repressive law, epitomized by the infamous 'Black Act'. With this came the discovery and re-discovery of Gramsci; hegemony became an important organizing concept and the thesis that the legal order played a significant part in the constitution of the hegemonic projects of modern liberal-democratic states. More generally this Gramscian renaissance was associated with a shift of focus from the coercive character of class and political relations to one which perceived 'ideology' as an ever-present and decisive component of the social order. This embracing of ideology as a key concept directed attention to a wider canvas through which law was to be approached. It moved the focus of interest away from the mechanisms of legal institutions to a broader canvas in which law was implicated in the formation of popular consciousness. Since the concept of ideology was central to the burgeoning of Western Marxism from the late 1960s, associated in particular with the names Althusser and Poulantzas, there was a period in which debates about law moved outside a narrow sub-disciplinary realm and became part of wider theoretical and political debates. Despite this opening up of enquiries about law the looming presence of Gramsci's concept of hegemony always tended towards the positing of a unitary focus of attention, presented variously as 'the state' or 'the ruling class'.

While these debates occupied the left, the process of the academic institutionalization of the sociology of law proceeded steadily. The main feature was a shift of the institutional location of the sociology of law from Law Schools to sociology and anthropology departments (and to a lesser extent political science departments); the 'sociology of law' and 'anthropology of law' became recognized sub-disciplines. At the same time there occurred the consolidation of both national and international academic associations. Linking these developments was the securing of regular research funding.

With the partial 'liberation' of the sociology of law from the Law Schools went the emergence of a general intellectual concern to break with the role of acting as the handmaiden of orthodox legal studies. Typically this involved a rift with 'internalism', the insider's view of law and commitment to the problems and concerns of the legal community defined in terms of professional and judicial interests. This shift was primarily affected by efforts to avoid 'law' as the unproblematic object of enquiry. In place of internalism there emerged various strategies of treating 'law' as a particular case of some wider social phenomenon. The most pervasive form of this response was to treat law as a particular instance of, for example, 'disputing', thereby pointing towards a problematic which compared law as a dispute mechanism with other such mechanisms (Ellickson, 1991; Felstiner et al., 1981; Galanter, 1983). The dispute focus led rapidly to an enthusiasm for informal approaches to dispute resolution which persists to the present with the expansion of the mediation industry. The dialectic of formalism versus informalism has been a refractory theme within the sociology of law (Abel, 1982; Harrington, 1984; Trubek, 1984).

Another conceptualization locating law as a social phenomenon of even older provenance is the 'social control' model which reappears in many forms, the most recently influential being Foucault's (1977) focus on 'discipline'. It should be noted that the related models of 'regulation' and 'governance', to be discussed below, involve essentially similar strategies of approaching law as an instance of a more general social process.

The institutionalization of the sociology of law brought with it an increasingly pronounced orientation to social policy considerations. Embedded in the constructivist projects of law in the modernist 'age of statutes', in which legislation is unambiguously viewed as an agency of social change, the sociology of law becomes increasingly concerned with the design of law reform measures. Variant forms of this style of work have been 'effectiveness studies' concerned with assessing the goal-effectiveness of legal change in meeting social policy objectives (Abel-Smith and Stevens, 1968; Ross et al., 1970; Sarat, 1985). Closely related are 'process studies' focusing not so much on substantive rules, but rather on the administration of legal regulation which results in significant failure to realize declared policy objectives (Cicourel, 1968; Feeley, 1980). Paralleling concerns with effectiveness and process with a more historical inflection, 'emergence studies' have explored the making of many major pieces of legislation; they span Marx's classic analysis of the mid-nineteenth century English factory legislation to studies of the US civil rights legislation of the 1960s (Bumiller, 1988; Marx, 1961; Sunstein, 1990). These studies all tend to varying degrees of scepticism about constructivist legal projects.

More recently the traditions of effectiveness and process studies resonate in an important debate about the contribution that projects of legislative reform can make to contemporary social movements. With varying intensity the civil rights movement, feminism and environmental movements have debated what part demands for legislation should have in their programmes. Each movement has produced positions both favouring and decrying use of legislative strategies. These controversies have been reflected in their most general form in the 'rights debate' which found its first expression in early writings from the critical legal studies movement and which continues to excite controversy down to the present (Bartholomew and Hunt, 1990).

While the sociology of law had by the 1980s achieved a considerable measure of security through its institutionalization, it has not escaped the self-doubts and uncertainties that afflict postmodern modernity. Epistemological doubts about the viability of truth-claims and the consequent tendency to adopt relativist stances are as evident in this field as in all the social sciences. However, the arrival of postmodern anxiety in the sociology of law has had a distinctive lineage. The 'critical legal studies' (CLS) movements which emerged in the late 1970s moved quickly from a Marxist-influenced leftism to a deconstructivism with radical politics.[5] For nearly a decade the focus on debate shifted back to the Law School context in which CLS has been born where the enemy remained the 'black-letter lawyer' wedded to literalist forms of interpretation. During this period the law and society movement consolidated itself. Its leading journals tended to eschew theoretical debates and concentrated on solid empirical studies.[6] The impact of postmodernist thought was limited to the espousal of legal pluralism which had few of the destabilizing thrusts characteristic of the wider postmodernist interventions (Galanter, 1981; Santos, 1987).

The most distinctive and constructive developments in contemporary sociology of law are ones that take relativism seriously by attending to law as a cultural phenomenon as a means of grounding the theoretical insights of legal pluralism. This trend has manifested itself in some rich studies of 'law in everyday life' or 'law and community' studies (Greenhouse, 1986; Greenhouse et al., 1994; Macaulay, 1987; Merry, 1990; Sarat and Kearns, 1993). This work sustains significant links to the older realist tradition, but is focused not so much on 'law in action' within legal institutions, but rather on 'law in the community', deploying concepts of legal culture and legal consciousness. This strand has close affinity with theoretical strands that variously make use of ideas of relational or constitutive theory which seeks to grasp the way in which law both constitutes social relations and is, in turn, constituted through social practices and discourses (Hunt, 1992; Merry, 1992). Thus, despite some of the narrowing effects that have been associated with the institutionalization of the law and society movement, it has sustained a commitment to a fully social theory of law.

Beyond the juridification thesis

I will develop the argument that sociology of law can today secure its commitment to a sociological project by means of a focus on law and governmentality which involves a return in a new and richer form to the enduring problematic of the relation between law and politics. This requires a focus on the interaction of legal and non-legal forms of governance.

The starting place for this interrogation is provided by the work of Michel Foucault (1977); it is not so much a matter of applying Foucault, but rather of transforming some of his key insights into the relation between law and power. He started out from the contention that traditional forms of political power were, in some important and distinctive sense, legal whereas the modern forms of disciplinary power are in some significant sense non-legal in character.[7] I have elsewhere offered an extended critique of this account on the grounds that it proposes a generalized expulsion of law from modernity (Hunt, 1992). This version of the connection between law and political power and between discipline and non-legal power is, although flawed, significant in its own right as a substantive account of some features of modernity. This characterization of the modalities of power provides a powerful rejoinder to the widely accepted theories of advancing juridification; it requires us at least to hesitate before too readily embracing the common sense view, one shared by everyone from Hayek to Luhmann and Habermas, that modernity is characterized by a generalized quantitative expansion of legal regulation.

Foucault constructs his subsequent account of modern governmental rationality by contrasting it to the form of rationality that characterized the European experience from the sixteenth through to the eighteenth century. This form of rationality which precedes modernity is difficult to name. Foucault designates it as 'reason of state', where the accumulation of the power of the state becomes an end in itself.[8] There is here a distinction, implied though not developed, namely, the idea of a shift from pre-modern to modern modes of regulation which take the form of a governmental style that emphasizes a commitment to the necessity of the positive regulation of an expanded conception of the polity and economy through projects of policing that know little of the modern dichotomy between the public and the private and which assertively involve, to use his own phrase, 'the government of the self'.

Foucault constructed a picture of the emergence of governmental reason.[9] We can understand Foucault as coming to grips with what Gordon calls 'real liberalism' (Gordon, 1991). Real liberalism is contrasted with the more abstract and ideological construct of *'laissez-faire'* which overemphasizes state abstentionism. To focus on 'real liberalism' allows us to direct attention to the actual mechanisms of regulation and governmental conduct rather than on this presumed abstentionism. Gordon suggests that Foucault's sketch of modern governmental rationality is to be found in the combination of 'security' and 'liberty'.

The emergence and rise to a predominant focus of concern with 'security' forms, according to Foucault, a dominant component of modern governmental rationality. It is embedded in the shift from a view of individuals as 'subjects' to one in which they are conceived as the bearers of 'interests', that is, they are economic subjects. Subjects or citizens (subjects of the state) are considered only in so far as the state requires to regulate their conduct or to demand performance from them; military conscription and imposition of taxes are two significant instances. 'Real liberalism' is characterized by Foucault as a 'totalizing unity of the juridical sovereign' (quoted in Gordon, 1991: 22).

The individual considered as a bearer of interests requires the state to take cognizance of those interests, in their multiplicity and complexity. It is manifest in the notion of a deontological liberalism in which the state abstains from judging the merit or worth of individual interests and seeks to remain neutral as between the different life-plans that people pursue. 'Security' functions not by negative prescription or refusal, but rather through the specification of a range of tolerable variation. Thus liberalism constructs a complex governance, within which political, economic and juridical instances of subjectivity are dispersed.

The association of 'security' with 'liberty' marks not merely the rise to prominence of rights discourses, but involves the idea that the systematic realization of political and juridical rights is an essential condition of good government itself as a precondition for the persistence, stability and prosperity of both economic and political governance. Gordon succinctly captures this governmental role of rights. '[D]isrespect of liberty is not simply an illegitimate violation of rights, but an ignorance of how to govern' (1991: 20). This concern with rights and the conditions of prosperity can be seen as reaching a high point in Keynesian economic strategy in which the attempt to master cyclical economic crisis and to secure its emblematic goal of full employment are conceived as preconditions of both economic prosperity and of political stability – as the manifestation of good government.

My purpose is not to debate the merits of the idea of 'security-liberty'; for present purposes I will assume the utility of this characterization of the distinctive form of modern governmental rationality. I will make use of the 'security-liberty' thesis to pose the question: *what part does law play in modern governmental rationality?*

As a start we can begin by discarding some earlier answers to this question. Foucault is explicit in rejecting any special emphasis upon 'constructualism' as the distinctive legal form of modernity.[10] Similarly excluded is the preoccupation, that Foucault attributes to Marx, with the role of law as legitimizing state coercion. While I think both the characterization and the consequent exclusion of these positions is too sweeping and I suggest that any full examination would need to give them more detailed consideration, I will stick with Foucault in order to explore where this train of thought leads even though in doing so some potentially significant differences with Foucault's views will emerge.

Foucault's account of the place of law in the transition to modern governmental rationality exhibits a distinct and significant shift in his position.[11] He starts by equating law with sovereignty and the juridical monarchy. His focus on the rise of the 'new disciplines' is marked by a shift away from state power towards arenas that are characteristically 'less legal'. He points to two distinct tendencies. The first is a version of the widely held view that counterposes law and regulation, seeing the rise of purposive law and of administrative regulation as signalling a decline or demise of law. The second tendency conceives of law functioning increasingly as a norm, that is, as a general standard, and offers a rather commonplace and one-sided account of the role of law in contemporary society that focuses attention on the rise of open-ended standards which, when linked to administrative regulation, create an expanded space for official discretion. In another version this description recalls Weber's anxiety about the rise of substantive rationality over formal legal rationality (Weber, 1966).

Despite the important traces of modernity that Foucault reveals, there is something either unsatisfactory or incomplete about his account of the part played by legal practices. A more adequate account would need to stress a persisting plurality of the forms of law. Only one facet of this process is characterized by the rise of substantive justice and discretion, epitomized in welfare legislation. This trend is matched by a persistent increase in the range, scope and detail of legal intervention which produces a general movement towards an expanding legalization and juridification of social life. Also significant is an increase in the particularistic character or positivization of law laying down detailed rules for a host of specialized areas of activity, for example, in detailed provisions concerning welfare, construction standards, product safety, credit transactions, and so on. Alongside these developments, exhibiting features of both the above trends, is the complex phenomenon of the advancing constitutionalization expressed in many and varied extensions of both the forms and types of entrenched rights that go far beyond the classical political and property rights of the constitutionalism of the eighteenth and nineteenth centuries.

There are hints by Foucault of a different conceptualization, one we can locate as the retreat from a transition from 'law to disciplines' to a new focus on 'law and regulation' (1978: 144). This shift emerges most clearly in his short paper on 'Governmentality' (1979). In this phase of his work the earlier expulsion of law from modernity is significantly modified. Now his conception of law focuses on the purposive rationality of the legislative output of representative legislatures. He emphasizes the increasing particularism of regulatory instruments. The previous conception of law as a totalizing and transcendent unity is superseded by historically specific production of regulatory devices that mediate between state and civil society and between state and individual.

My goal is to explore this general field of governance in a way that will develop an expanded conception of the role of law in these processes. What is required is a conception of law that is compatible with a perspective that conceives law as a complex of varied forms that provide major mechanisms through which governance is practised. In the first instance the model of law as regulation can be seen as a shift towards an emphasis on public law which focuses on the varied means whereby extensive fields of social life are made subject to regulatory intervention. This view requires immediate modification to our conventional conception of 'public law'. Rather than being bounded by the activities of territorial states – whether national, provincial or local – the conception of the public which we need includes the regulatory activity of territorial states, the immense regulatory productivity of quasi-state institutions, professional and institutional agencies and the regulatory activity of economic agencies. In taking note of the range and diversity of these activities two main effects should be noted: first, that the pertinence of the distinction between the public and the private can only be maintained by problematizing its complexity. One response to the limitations of the public/private dichotomy has been a revival of interest in the distinction between state and civil society with the advocacy of an apportionment of powers to a multiplicity of public spheres between state and civil society (Habermas, 1989; Keane, 1984).

Much of the debate around these perceptions of major shifts in the conceptualization of modern society has been preoccupied with the implications of the proliferation of the regulatory complex for the fate of the rule of law. This debate has taken a variety of forms, but perhaps its most general form is one in which the passing of 'autonomous law' is viewed as being supplanted by increasingly bureaucratic regulation. Others have adopted a less pessimistic response and have seen positive potential in the diversification of the forms of legal regulation (Luhmann, 1985; Teubner, 1986). I will suspend any normative judgement on these different visions of the trajectory of modern law; instead I will focus attention on their implications for a more modest role for legal theory conceived as providing the conceptual tools for understanding a complex process in which our received concepts and theories have become impediments to understanding. My project is to articulate a conception of law that starts out from an interrogation of the law as a mode of governance.

At the heart of this endeavour is a concern to give full recognition to the lessons of legal pluralism, namely, that we should recognize the diversity of legal phenomena and avoid falling into the presumption of a unitary or totalizing 'Law', while at the same time avoiding assuming a general dispersal of law as a mere medium of regulatory intervention. The processes of diversification and of centralization exist in complex tension. Provisionally we can express the role of the central state-law apparatuses as being continually engaged in a project of regulatory unification. This project is pursued with varying intensity and commitment and is never more than partially successful. The unificatory project is always present and must inform our theorization of law just as must our recognition of the reality of legal pluralism.

The rediscovery of legal pluralism has been important in drawing attention to the diversity of legal orders, but there has been a tendency towards a certain over-reaction. In challenging a unitary conception of state-law, attention has tended to shift away from the distinctive importance of state-law. The importance of state-law and state power on which I want to insist is their capacities, never fully realized but as ever-present projects, for unification, concentration, globalization and consolidation. This chapter explores whether it is possible to retain the insights of legal pluralism and to focus on 'governance' in order to identify the new forms of dispersed and localized power and, at the same time, to retain a continuing appreciation of the significance of state-law.

Law and the condensation of power

I will explore the connection between law and power, and the question of the part played by state-law in the unification or condensation of the dispersed arena of social power, by defending the general thesis that the key link between law and modern power is that law plays the organizational and ideological role of providing the always unstable and incomplete unification of dispersed social power.

There is one important respect in which I want to depart significantly from Foucault. His concern to focus on localized or capillary power exposes him to the objection that he ignores the significance of the state and other forms of centralized and institutionalized power. My sense is that there is a broad post-Foucauldian consensus that any adequate social or political theory has to take account of both 'big power' and 'local power'. The really difficult question is to find an adequate way of grasping their mutual articulation and interaction. The weakness of Foucault's project is that in putting 'local power' on to the agenda he appears to ignore or to understate the importance of the processes that aggregate or condense power in centralized sites.[12] This is not just a matter about trying to 'bring the state back in' (Evans et al., 1985) and, I would add, with it state law; it is perhaps more significant that it is economic power which is dramatically and revealingly absent from Foucault's work. Yet there is no dispute that Foucault recognized the existence of major or global dominations.

In the important essay 'The Subject and Power' he seems to recognize that he has perhaps gone too far in stressing the diffusion of power:

> [W]hat makes the domination of a group, a caste, or a class . . . a central phenomenon in the history of societies is that they manifest in *a massive and universalizing form, at the level of the whole social body*, the locking together of power relations with relations of strategy and the results proceeding from their interaction. (1982: 226; emphasis added)

Foucault's most significant attempt to grapple with the condensation of power emerges in his development of a very distinctive conception of 'strategy'. In a very characteristic formulation he argues that

> domination is organized into a more-or-less coherent and unitary strategic form; that dispersed, heteromorphous, localized procedures of power are adapted, re-enforced and transformed by these *global strategies* . . . [H]ence one should not assume a massive and primal condition of domination, a binary structure with

'dominators' on one side and 'dominated' on the other, but rather a multiform production of relations of domination which are partially susceptible of integration into *overall strategies*. (1980: 142, emphases added)

This approach has yielded valuable insights into the way in which two or more technologies of power interact to produce a structural coupling in which the resulting forms of power cannot be deduced from the individual techniques, for example, when the combination of law and medicine results in a distinctive regulation of the body. But this emphasis on the combination of techniques of power does not necessarily offer an account of how the diffuse techniques of power relate to and are aggregated in the massive institutional presence of state, military and economic apparatuses. It is important to attend to the persistent aggregation of dispersed powers, and that they are focused particularly around institutional practices, of which the state is one, among others, of these sites of condensation. I want to go further, to argue that it is both possible and desirable that attention be directed to exploring the distinctive forms of this condensation. These forms of power condensations, of course, have historical dimensions, which allow us to focus attention on the changing forms of their combination.

Law, politics and power

One immediate implication of my discussion has been to resist the temptation to counterpose 'law' and 'politics'. Rather, law and politics are both techniques of power – but this does not imply the elision of law and politics. Rather it proposes a mode of analysis that focuses attention on the specificity of the techniques of power and it proposes a political analysis that engages with the appropriateness of the distinct modes of regulation for the governance of different fields of social relations. Such an approach makes it possible to engage in constructive debate about the reasons for welcoming or resisting specific ways of regulating whatever may be the political object of our enquiry.

Let me be more concrete and use the currently topical issue of sexual harassment to illustrate my point. One way of posing the question of sexual harassment is to consider its limits. One tendency is concerned to construct both the analysis of harassment on some operationalizable notion of harm or 'social injury' which is distinctively 'sexual' in character. This approach is to be distinguished from an alternative which seeks to broaden the notion of sexual harassment to include a range of behaviours 'offensive' to their 'victims' (for example, sexist speech).[13] What is involved in this debate is not just a matter of an attempt to construct or to reconstruct a legal regime; rather it involves a political question about 'legal strategy', about the distinctively political advantages and disadvantages of this and other potential strategies.

My preference for the former (or narrower) approach to sexual harassment is that it provides sustainable grounds for the criminalization of specific practices where an injury condition can be established in a manner consistent with 'normal' canons of legal proof. Let me hasten to add that my reason for favouring this strategy is not that I want a 'weak' sexual harassment law. I suggest that the attempt to construct a broader conception which embraces all forms of gender-related offensive conduct is misguided because it confuses the politics of gendered relations, which I suggest should be viewed primarily as a field of ideological or symbolic politics, rather than as a target for legal regulation. The broader strategy of seeking to criminalize offensive behaviour has the major disadvantage of conceding the intellectual and moral high-ground to its opponents by presenting itself as a reinvention of an anti-sexual 'social purity' movement that was characteristic of one major strand of nineteenth century feminism.[14] This brief discussion of sexual harassment is intended not as a substantive contribution to that topic, but rather to indicate the wider political pertinence of a more elaborated model of the concept 'mode of governance'.

Modes of governance: a theorization of law and politics

I now return to explore the connection between state, law and power and do so by conceiving the processes of governance. The immediate attraction of a focus upon governance is that it avoids, or more accurately refuses, the coercion/consent opposition. The governance approach does not need to take sides in this old debate; it encompasses modalities that transcend the coercion and consent dichotomy.

The focus on governance remains close to the concern with the linkage between power and knowledge in its emphasis on the role of information, expertise, policies and strategies. It involves the deployment of specific knowledges encapsulated in legal or administrative forms of interventions in specific social practices whose resultants have consequences for the distribution of benefits and detriments for the participants in the social practices subject to regulation. A further feature of governance should be stressed in order to avoid falling into a purely technicist or instrumental conception. Every instance must be understood as encompassing some dimension of moral regulation or, to use Foucault's related concept, 'normalization'. Moral regulation is not simply a variety of regulation but it is a more or less significant dimension of all regulation.[15] By extension it follows that all governance involves the suppression, marginalization or repudiation of alternative ways of being, whilst encouraging or promoting other realities. This view of governance is diametrically opposed to any technicist view of regulation.

In my usage governance is not a sub-species of law, but rather it is a distinctive type of social process with respect to which legal aspects may or may not be present. It refers to a specific style of purposive, instrumental practices. It is now time to look more closely at governance. I will sketch the elements of a general concept of a mode of governance.[16] Governance is always intentional (even though its results may be unintended and its project may end in failure); thus the first step is the constitution of an object of governance. There are no natural or ready-made social objects and hence no ready-made objects of governance; their existence is always the outcome of some active process which creates that which is to be regulated. It follows that if objects of governance can be created, then they can similarly be dismantled and abandoned. The selection and de-selection of objects of governance are often primary sites of political contestation.

A second general feature of governance is that it involves the designation, identification or creation of agents who are charged with a range of functions ranging from the collection and recording of information, inspection, surveillance, reporting, initiation of enforcement action and a host of other activities.

The third general feature of the process revolves around the production of regulatory knowledge. Only after some social phenomenon or social practice has been constructed in such a way that it can be studied, quantified and measured does it become possible for it to be treated as a suitable candidate for regulation. Whilst these processes are worthy of more detailed attention and probably justify distinctions being made between different 'modes of production of knowledge', my present purpose is served if I stress the increasingly significant role played by law in the process of the production of knowledge. In general, law enters into the processes of the production of knowledge more and more routinely, and this applies to state, public and private agencies which are increasingly organized around the collection of systematic regulatory knowledge. Legislation both stipulates and ordains the knowledge to be collected, as well as stipulating limits to its deployment (e.g. data protection and freedom of information), and prescribes the parameters of the knowledge to be collected. And again it is important to note that these parameters and boundaries are frequently the subject of political and administrative contestation.

The production of regulatory knowledge serves to link the creation and constitution of 'objects of governance' with a third aspect of governance, namely, the formation of strategies of governance. Not only is knowledge 'produced' but it must also be transformed into a form that is capable of being expressed as a regulatory policy or strategy, which in turn is capable of being incorporated into legislative form.[17] Thus the production of a regulatory mechanism involves some definite limitations upon the strategies that may ultimately find legislative expression.

An important dimension of the merit claimed for the governance approach to theorizing law is that it locates law within a wider context. Governance takes distinctive forms (the forms of governance) that have at least five significant features: identification of an object, conferment of powers upon agents, specification of decision-procedures, identification of policy objectives and the stipulation of rewards or sanctions.

The governance approach thus focuses attention on social ordering as the outcome of the interaction between multiple modes of governance. Its major contribution to the theorization of law is to pose the question of the form and manner of the legal component of any field of governance in such a way that foregoes any assumption that the role played by law can satisfactorily be understood by reference to its own rules or procedures as satisfactorily specifying its relation with other modes of governance. One important consequence is that a governance approach systematically denies the possibility of grounding a theory of law in the assumption of legal autonomy; in this respect the approach is at variance with most traditional jurisprudential models. It also departs in significant respects from the currently influential theories of autopoiesis or of self-referentiality (Luhmann, 1985; Teubner, 1988) that fail to allow sufficient space for the unruly clash and competition between different mechanisms of governance.

The concept of 'modes of governance' thus provides a potentially fruitful way of thinking about the complex mechanisms of social ordering and their interaction. Further, it allows us to explore the particular contribution made by specifically legal mechanisms. But the most important benefit is that it facilitates an account that remains sensitive to the variation in modes of governance and of local power, whilst at the same time allowing attention to be retained upon the role of state-law in the concentration and condensation of power relations.

Distinct modes of governance may be identified that are relatively autonomous in the sense that the type of governance that exists is not directly determined by the type of social relation that is its object of governance. One important exemplification of the argument in favour of the relative autonomy of modes of governance is that it allows us to take account of changing historical forms. The example that has been most extensively studied is the regulation of labour. What is clear from the history of labour relations is that the form of governance has varied significantly over time and that the major determinant of that variation from coercive command power of capital through to collective bargaining and grievance procedures is the relative power of labour and capital (Henry, 1987; Woodiwiss, 1990).

Regulatory systems interact and should not be considered in isolation. This introduces a new dimension of considerable importance, namely, the role played by law in drawing and sustaining boundaries, and a role which will return us to the theme of the connection between law and politics. There is a literal sense in which law, and most explicitly property law, demarcates and enforces boundaries; but this notion of boundary maintenance has a wider significance. Workplace boundaries have a special import precisely because of the critical significance of the division between work and politics within capitalist economies; it is here that the historically important distinction is established between the incorporation of the working class within the polity whilst excluding workers from full participation in the work place.

Considerable ideological significance flows from the sustenance of the apparently natural exclusion of workers from the same participatory rights within the enterprise that the struggle for the franchise secured in the political realm; indeed the struggle for democratic participation rights in the enterprise has become an important element of modern radical politics. The same considerations apply to struggles over property forms such as those between traditional property forms and the much debated 'new property' (Reich, 1964). It is not that law creates these boundaries but rather that once in place they are protected and reinforced by both legal ideology and legal practices. This suggests the broader thesis that one characteristic feature of the connection between law and governance is that law serves to demarcate and secure the boundaries between distinct fields of governance such that the specificity of different fields is reinforced.

This analysis of law in terms of the project of securing contested 'boundary markers', to use E.P. Thompson's phrase (Thompson, 1975), is not without its problems. Jennifer Nedelsky argues that the persistence of the 'boundary' metaphor reinforces separation and impedes highlighting of relationships and connectedness (Nedelsky, 1990). Her problematization of boundaries connects with the important and persistent theme raised by the tradition of 'legal form' analyses, of which other important examples are Pashukanis' commodity form theory (Pashukanis, 1980) and the CLS' 'critique of rights' (Tushnet, 1984). This line of enquiry extends Nedelsky's argument and, maybe, deepens her objections since it suggests that the boundary metaphor is not simply characteristic of liberal legalism, but also plays an influential role in radical theory. In the latter case it is used not as an endorsement of the existing legal relations, but as a call for those boundaries to be differently located, for example by challenging the exclusionary zone of private property rights in favour of securing a protected arena of social rights. I leave open for future reflection whether the analysis of law as a mode of governance needs to develop a conceptual framework that does not rely on the metaphor of 'boundaries'. For the time being I will continue to make use of boundary conceptions in returning to propose a reconceptualization of the linkages between law and politics.

The general thrust of a theory constructed around the concept mode of governance is that it avoids two dichotomies, that of law versus regulation, and of law versus politics. In the place of these conventional dichotomies it proposes the exploration of a general field traversed by competing, sometimes complementary, but often conflicting, practices.[18] For my present concerns I will focus attention on just two of these sets of practices, legal and political, which are themselves not conceived as unitary. The claim made for this style of analysis is that it facilitates descriptive analysis, by exploring the forms of combinations of practices in the governance of specific fields of governance, and it also enables prescriptive analysis, by making possible both policy and strategic prescriptions to propose changes in the governance of any selected object of enquiry. Thus, for example, in addressing current controversies over the regulation of abortion it suggests an analysis of the concrete articulation of medical, legal and moral discourses and practices that point towards a prescriptive politics which proposes, for example, a de-medicalization of abortion practices. This style of enquiry is especially suited to the development of political strategies that avoid either according a general priority to legal regulation (as does liberal legalism) or, conversely, a projected exclusion of legal regulation (as does radical legal theory). It is important to avoid the polarization of a debate pitched at a very general level of abstraction which, in crude terms, sets up a 'for' or 'against' law debate that is incapable of any constructive resolution and is doomed for ever to play out a long-distance slugging match. A more constructive approach can be indicated by applying the theoretical approach outlined here to one of the most pressing instances of the dynamic of law-and-politics.

Notes

1 I discuss this classical lineage of legal thought during the first half of the century under the rubric of 'the sociological movement in law' in Hunt, 1978.

2 A recent Canadian instance illustrates the pervasiveness of legislative politics. A family whose daughter was raped and murdered launched a campaign for legislative intervention and the case resulted in a judgment in which the Supreme Court ruled that the police had no power to compel a suspect to provide specimens suitable for DNA analysis. Protracted campaigning resulted in all-party support for legislation expanding police powers in the collection of human tissue.

3 The concept of juridification was first employed by the social-democratic jurist Hugo Sinzheimer and subsequently taken up by Otto Kirchheimer. I am grateful to Gunther Tuebner for introducing me to the work of Sinzheimer; for a useful introduction see Kahn-Freund, 1981. Kirchheimer used the term to indicate the way in which law comes to be used as a means of neutralizing political conflicts by subjecting them to formal legal regulation (Kirchheimer, 1969).

4 This preoccupation with the gap problem provides the most important intellectual linkage of sociology of law to the pre-Second World War work of the 'American realists' (Fisher et al., 1993).

5 I have elsewhere argued that the key shift in the orientation of CLS can be traced to an exchange between Duncan Kennedy and Peter Gabel published in 1984 (Gabel and Kennedy, 1984; Hunt, 1986).

6 See in particular for the USA the *Law and Society Review* and for the UK the *Journal of Law and Society*.

7 It should be stressed that Foucault does not suggest any simple displacement of law by discipline; indeed he is at pains to show how the problematic of law and sovereignty persists. This idea he captures with his insight that modernity has 'not yet cut off the King's head' (1980: 121).

8 A slightly different periodization can be found in 'Governmentality': here he identifies the stages of state formation as (i) state of justice or 'society of law', (ii) administrative state or 'society of regulation', and (iii) the 'governmental state' (1979: 21).

9 Foucault's reflections on this question were fragmentary and largely unpublished; for this reason I rely upon Colin Gordon's reconstruction (Gordon, 1991).

10 There are a variety of versions of the contractualism thesis; they include such diverse views as Sir Henry Maine's well-known 'status to contract' thesis (Maine, 1905), Pashukanis' 'commodity form' account (Pashukanis, 1980), and Weber's association between rational law and economic predictability (Weber, 1966).

11 For fuller elaboration of Foucault's treatment of law, see Hunt and Wickham, 1994.

12 For a fuller critique of the problem of the condensation of power and its link to Foucault's account of 'strategy', see Hunt, 1992; Hunt and Wickham, 1994.

13 To be offended is not to be injured. Some strands of radical feminism have sought to establish a link between offence and injury by arguing that pornography may be construed as silencing women and thus 'injuring' their right to freedom of speech (MacKinnon 1984); for a criticism of this argument see Dworkin, 1991.

14 For an important recent study of social purity see Valverde, 1991.

15 The idea of moral regulation is most fully developed by Corrigan and Sayer who demonstrate that each stage in the process of state formation is associated with a distinctive form of moral regulation. They emphasize the dual character of moral order as being both externally regulative and internally constitutive and as such has impact not only on social practices, but also on the formation of identities and subjectivities (Corrigan and Sayer, 1985: 194).

16 For fuller elaboration of the conception of a mode of governance, see Hunt, 1993: ch. 13.

17 I use the term 'legislative' broadly to refer to any process which 'transforms' regulatory knowledge into the form of procedures, ordinances, regulations, rules and statutes whether in public or private institutions.

18 The further elaboration of this approach would require attention to the classification of 'modes of governance'; this chapter does not make any attempt to undertake this task and indeed it suffers from the limitation of working with such ready-made categories as legal and political modes of governance. Further, elaboration would require the disruption of such taken-for-granted categories.

References

Abel, R. (1980) 'Redirecting social studies of law', *Law and Society Review*, 9: 805–9.

Abel, R. (1982) 'The contradictions of informal justice' in Richard Abel (ed.), *The Politics of Informal Justice*, vol. I: *The American Experience*. New York: Academic Press.

Abel-Smith, B. and Stevens, R. (1968) *In Search of Justice*. London: Allen Lane.

Balbus, I. (1973) *The Dialectics of Legal Repression: Black Rebels Before the American Criminal Courts*. New York: Russell Sage Foundation.

Bartholomew, A. and Hunt, A. (1990) 'What's wrong with rights?', *Journal of Law and Inequality*, 9: 501–58.

Blumberg, A. (1967) 'The practice of law as a confidence game', *Law and Society Review*, 1: 15.

Bumiller, K. (1988) *The Civil Rights Society: The Social Construction of Victims*. Baltimore, MD: Johns Hopkins University Press.

Caplovitz, D. (1974) *Consumers in Trouble: A Study of Debtors in Default*. New York: Free Press.

Cicourel, A. (1968) *The Social Organization of Juvenile Justice*. New York: John Wiley.

Corrigan, P. and Sayer, D. (1985) *The Great Arch: English State Formation as Cultural Revolution*. Oxford: Basil Blackwell.

Dicey, A.V. (1905) *Law and Public Opinion*. London: Macmillan.

Dworkin, R. (1986) *Law's Empire*. Cambridge, MA: Harvard University Press.

Dworkin, R. (1991) 'Two concepts of liberty', in E. and A. Margalit (eds), *Isaiah Berlin: A Celebration*. London: Hogarth Press.

Ellickson, R.C. (1991) *Order Without Law: How Neighbors Settle Disputes*. Cambridge, MA: Harvard University Press.

Evans, P., Rueschemeyer, D. and Skocpol, T. (1985) *Bringing the State Back In*. Cambridge: Cambridge University Press.

Feeley, M. (1980) *The Process is the Punishment*. New York: Basic Books.

Felstiner, W., Abel, R. and Sarat, A. (1981) 'The emergence and transformation of disputes: naming, blaming, claiming . . . ', *Law and Society Review*, 15: 631.

Fisher, W.W., Horwitz, M. and Reed, T. (1993) *American Legal Realism*. New York: Oxford University Press.

Foucault, M. (1977) *Discipline and Punish: The Birth of the Prison* [1975]. New York: Pantheon Books.

Foucault, M. (1978) *The History of Sexuality*, vol. I. *An Introduction*. New York: Pantheon Books.

Foucault, M. (1979) 'Governmentality' [1978], *Ideology and Consciousness*, 6: 5–21.

Foucault, M. (1980) *Power/Knowledge: Selected Interviews and Other Writings 1972–1977* (ed. Colin Gordon). Brighton: Harvester Press.

Foucault, M. (1982) 'The subject and power', in H. Dreyfus and P. Rabinow (eds), *Michel Foucault: Beyond Structuralism and Hermeneutics*. Chicago: University of Chicago Press. pp. 208–26.

Gabel, P. and Kennedy, D. (1984) 'Roll over Beethoven', *Stanford Law Review*, 36: 1–55.

Galanter, M. (1981) 'Justice in many rooms: courts, private ordering and indigenous law', *Journal of Legal Pluralism*, 19: 1–47.

Galanter, M. (1983) 'Reading the landscape of disputes: what we know and don't know (and think we know) about our allegedly contentious and litigious society', *UCLA Law Review*, 31: 4–71.

Gordon, C. (1991) 'Governmental rationality', in G. Burchell, C. Gordon and P. Miller (eds), *The Foucault Effect: Studies in Governmentality*. Hemel Hempstead: Harvester Wheatsheaf.

Greenhouse, C. (1986) *Praying for Justice: Faith Order and Community in an American Town*. Ithaca, NY: Cornell University Press.

Greenhouse, C., Yngvesson, B. and Engel, D.M. (1994) *Law and Community in Three American Towns*. Ithaca, NY: Cornell University Press.

Habermas, J. (1987) *The Theory of Communicative Action*, vol. II. *Lifeworld and System*. Boston, MA: Beacon Press.

Habermas, J. (1989) *The Structural Transformation of the Public Sphere: An Inquiry into a Category of Bourgeois Society*. Cambridge, MA: MIT Press.

Harrington, C. (1984) *Shadow Justice: The Ideology and Institutionalization of Alternatives to Courts*. Westport, CT: Greenwood Press.

Hayek, F.A. von (1973–79) *Law, Legislation and Liberty* (3 vols). London: Routledge and Kegan Paul.

Henry, S. (1987) 'Disciplinary pluralism: four models of private justice in the workplace', *Sociological Review*, 35: 279–319.

Hunt, A. (1978) *The Sociological Movement in Law*. London: Macmillan.

Hunt, A. (1986) 'The theory of critical legal studies', *Oxford Journal of Legal Studies*, 6: 1–45.

Hunt, A. (1992) 'Law's empire or legal imperialism', in A. Hunt (ed.), *Reading Dworkin Critically*. New York: Berg.

Hunt, A. (1993) *Explorations in Law and Society: Toward a Constitutive Theory of Law*. New York: Routledge.

Hunt, A. and Wickham, G. (1994) *Foucault and Law: Towards a New Sociology of Law as Governance*. London: Pluto Press.

Kahn-Freund, O. (1981) *Labour Law and Politics in the Weimar Republic* (eds Roy Lewis and Jon Clark). Oxford: Basil Blackwell.

Keane, J. (1984) *Public Life in Late Capitalism: Toward a Socialist Theory of Democracy*. Cambridge: Cambridge University Press.

Kirchheimer, O. (1969) *Politics, Law and Social Change: Selected Essays of Otto Kirchheimer* (eds F.S. Burin and K.L Shell). New York: Columbia University Press.

Lefcourt, R. (ed.) (1971) *Law Against the People: Essays to Demystify Law, Order and the Courts*. New York: Random House.

Luhmann, N. (1985) *A Sociological Theory of Law*. London: Routledge and Kegan Paul.

Macaulay, S. (1987) 'Images of law in everyday life: the lessons of school, entertainment, and spectator sport', *Law and Society Review*, 21: 185–218.

MacKinnon, C. (1984) 'Not a moral issue', *Yale Law and Social Policy Review*, 2: 321.

Maine, Sir Henry (1905) *Ancient Law: Its Connection with the Early History of Society and its Relation to Modern Ideas.* London: Routledge.

Marx, Karl (1961) *Capital: Vol 1.* Moscow: Foreign Languages Publishing House.

Merry, S.E. (1990) *Getting Justice and Getting Even: Legal Consciousness Among Working-Class Americans.* Chicago: University of Chicago Press.

Merry, S.E. (1992) 'Culture, power, and the discourse of law', *New York Law School Law Review*, 37: 209–25.

Nedelsky, J. (1990) 'Law, boundaries, and the bounded self', *Representations*, 30: 162–89.

Nelken, D. (1981) 'The "Gap Problem" in the sociology of law: a theoretical review', *Windsor Yearbook of Access to Justice*, 1: 35–61.

Pashukanis, E. (1980) *Pashukanis: Selected Writings on Marxism and Law* (eds. P. Beirne and R. Sharlet). London: Academic Press.

Reich, C. (1964) 'The new property', *Yale Law Journal*, 73: 733.

Ross, L.H., Campbell, D. and Glass, G.V. (1970) 'Determining the social effects of a legal reform: the British "Breathalyser" crackdown of 1967', *American Behavioral Scientist*, 13: 493–509.

Santos, Boaventura de Sousa (1987) 'Law: a map of misreading. Toward a postmodern conception of law', *Journal of Law and Society*, 14: 279–302.

Sarat, A. (1985) 'Legal effectiveness and social studies of law: on the unfortunate persistence of a research tradition', *Legal Studies Forum*, 9: 23–31.

Sarat, A. and Kearns, T. (eds) (1993) *The Law in Everyday Life.* Ann Arbor: University of Michigan Press.

Sunstein, C. (1990) *After the Rights Revolution: Reconceiving the Regulatory State.* Cambridge, MA: Harvard University Press.

Teubner, G. (ed.) (1986) *Dilemmas of Law in the Welfare State.* New York: Walter de Gruyter.

Teubner, G. (ed.) (1988) *Autopoietic Law: A New Approach to Law and Society.* Berlin: Walter de Gruyter.

Thompson, E.P. (1975) *Whigs and Hunters: The Origin of the Black Act.* London: Allen Lane.

Trubek, D.M. (1984) 'Turning away from law', *Michigan Law Review*, 82: 824–35.

Tushnet, M. (1984) 'An essay on rights', *Texas Law Review*, 62: 1363–403.

Valverde, M. (1991) *The Age of Light, Soap and Water: Social Purity and Philanthropy in Canada, 1885–1925.* Toronto: McClelland and Stewart.

Weber, M. (1966) *Law in Economy and Society* (ed. Max Rheinstein). Cambridge, MA: Harvard University Press.

White, S. (ed.) (1989) *Life-World and Politics: Between Modernity and Postmodernity.* Southbend, IN: University of Notre Dame Press.

Woodiwiss, A. (1990) *Rights v. Conspiracy: A Sociological Essay on the Development of Labour Law in the United States.* Oxford: Berg.

SCIENCE AND TECHNOLOGY

6 The Sociology of Science and Technology after Relativism

Ralph Schroeder

Within sociology, the study of science and technology is still a relatively small specialism. Nevertheless, it is an important area since this is where the status of scientific knowledge is arbitrated – whether we mean by this knowledge about the natural or about the social world. This is also one of the reasons why the sociology of science and technology is worth considering in a collection that aims to present some current directions in the discipline. This chapter will be concerned with the affinities between relativism in the sociology of science and in postmodernism; but first, it will present an alternative to these forms of relativism.

It used to be the case that discussions of the workings of natural science and of technology were confined to the sociology of science. Recently, however, postmodernism has also come to dwell on the possibilities created by scientific and technological change. Notions such as 'cybersociety' (Jones, 1995) and 'cyberculture' (Escobar, 1994) have proliferated. With this postmodern turn to science and technology, postmodernism has also adopted ideas from the sociology of science about the social or cultural determination of knowledge. So, for example, we find the argument that all knowledge is always already culturally shaped or constructed made in similar ways by postmodern theorists and by sociologists of science and technology.[1] The implication, that more space ought to be given to marginalized or hitherto underrepresented forms of knowledge, appears to follow in both cases (Law, 1991: 2–3).

With hindsight, this stance can now be seen as part of a longer-term heritage which has sought to defend the position that sociology is a culture-centred pursuit which deals with meaning – against the coldness and impersonality of a positivistic or scientistic sociology which allegedly cannot cope with meaning. This heritage will no doubt endure. It is worth noticing, however, that within the study of science and technology, the stance that has been adopted *vis-à-vis* knowledge has completely flip-flopped in recent decades: whereas it used to be argued that social and cultural forces determine knowledge and technology, nowadays it seems that science and technology *as* culture determine social life.[2] The broader culture-centred heritage has undergone a parallel shift; from Marxist and structuralist arguments about the social determination of culture and knowledge, to the notion of culture (or knowledge) as a shaper of identities, subjectivities and the like. One feature that postmodern theories and recent theoretical standpoints in the sociology of science and technology therefore share is relativism, or the notion that there are no independent criteria for the validity of knowledge.[3]

Whatever the contribution of these culture-centred theories[4] to sociology may be (and large areas of sociology remain oblivious to postmodernism), they have now gained a prominent place in sociological theory. Put differently, postmodern relativism is now a major theoretical tradition within sociology – perhaps one with many subsidiary schools and rival factions and leaders – but a well-established tradition nevertheless. Outside of this, there is currently little in the way of an intellectual centre or counter tradition in sociological theory. The 'positivist dispute in sociology' (Adorno et al., 1976) may once have ranged a faction of scientistically inclined social scientists on one side against neo-Marxists (who regarded science as ideology) and heremeneutics on the other. Recently, however, no non-culture-centred rival theoretical tradition has been able to come into the foreground. This is partly because no epistemological premises could possibly embrace or unite the many theoretical positions in contemporary sociology, which range from individualistic rational choice theories to holistic neofunctionalism; nor is there much common ground among these hardy perennials who regard themselves as a-theoreticist. In this sense then, postmodernism has succeeded; it has moved from the margin of sociological theory to the centre.

The aim of this chapter is not to grope towards a rival 'post-post' tradition; nor is it to spell out why it is impossible to devise knowledge claims in sociology which somehow override the knowledge claims of scientific knowledge (though we shall come back to both topics). Instead, I want to outline a position in the sociology of science and technology which goes beyond relativism, and secondly, to link both the relativist and non-relativist conceptions of knowledge to their respective social roles. If there has come to be a wide gulf between culture-centred understandings of science and technology as against those which regard science and technology as separable from culture and society, then, as we shall see later, this gulf is also reflected in the different consequences of the advance of knowledge in natural and in social science.

Science, technology and the 'Great Divide'

Studies in the sociology of science and technology tend to be case studies of particular scientific problems, laboratories, or artefacts. These studies tend not to address the question of the relation between science, technology and social change at the macro level. But it is impossible to divorce these two levels; without a conception of the role of science and technology in modern society as a whole, it is impossible to recognize the contribution of specific instances of scientific and technological advance at the level of everyday life. Hence we shall first have to examine macro-social change.

The two central questions on the macro level, which are completely intertwined, are to do with whether science and technology play a unique role in modern or industrial society on the one hand, and whether they have an autonomous impact on the other. It is only the second which is typically dealt with in the sociology of science and technology. The first has been tackled within a number of disciplines, foremost among them history (Smith and Marx, 1994), economic history (Inkster, 1991; Mokyr, 1990) and economics (Nelson, 1994). The combination of both questions has also raised important issues in philosophy (Trigg, 1993: 149–71) and anthropology (Horton, 1970). The debates in these disciplines do not, however, overlap with those that have recently been taking place in the sociology of science and technology.[5]

Within these fields (although it is the opposite in the sociology of science and technology) there is an emerging consensus that the role of science and technology in modern or industrial society has had unique social consequences or concomitants. Regardless of whether the emphasis is on how science and technology foster industrial development (Inkster, 1991), or how they produce economic growth more narrowly conceived (Mokyr, 1990), economic historians recognize that the industrial revolution of the nineteenth century is a watershed in the role of science and technology in society. The importance of this is that we can say that science and technology are not everywhere and at all times determined by the societies around them, but that instead, because of the consequences of scientific and technological advance during this period, their relation with society changed too.

It is not possible to go directly from this argument to the autonomy of scientific and technological change. The further step is to say that another feature of modern or industrial society is sustained economic growth. This feature sets it apart from traditional or pre-industrial societies. If we *now* combine these two – the uniqueness of this type of economic growth and the unique growth of scientific knowledge and of technological development in industrial society – to say that there is a causal relationship between them, then there will nevertheless be an element of circularity in this argument.[6] There may, however, be good reasons for this circularity: if it were not for the fact that scientific knowledge (and with it, technology of a certain type) can be separated from non-scientific belief systems in this way, it is difficult to see how any distinction between science and other kinds of belief systems could be made. Similarly, if the material basis of societies which have undergone the transformation of industrialization could not be separated from those which had not, there would be little point in setting modern or industrial societies apart at all. Be that as it may, the implication of this argument is that a separation can be made between the social world and the world of scientific knowledge and physical artefacts, a separation which, as we shall see, bears importantly on how the relation between science and technology and social change is conceptualized on the micro or everyday level.

The autonomy of science and technology follows at this point, since their consequences, at least on this occasion, are different from those elsewhere. Yet now we need to ask, what is the significance of this autonomy? Marx thought that the main importance of science and technology lay in their capacity to transform the mode of production, but as MacKenzie has pointed out, this is too narrow since it leaves out, among other things, domestic and military technology (1984: 499, n. 84). There is, moreover, an ongoing debate over the sense in which Marx allowed for the autonomous impact of science and technology – if at all (Bimber, 1994; MacKenzie, 1984). In any case, if the autonomy of science and technology has been established by reference to its association with economic growth, this does not preclude that there are consequences of this autonomy apart from merely economic ones.

Weber's ideas can take us further here. Weber regarded science and technology as central to the process of 'disenchantment', or the increasing extension of instrumental rationality throughout the social world (Brubaker, 1984: 29–35; Schroeder, 1995). This means that there are always two sides to the advance of science and technology: on the one hand, the advance of instrumental rationality, or of seeking the most efficient means to achieve a given end, entails an increasing mastery over the natural and social worlds; on the other, this process also brings about the increasing impersonality of the external conditions of life. Thus the consequences of scientific and technological advance are not just economic ones; they apply to all areas of social life.

Realism and anti-realism

Weber's notion of disenchantment pertains to modern or industrial society generally and it specifies a pattern that accompanies all scientific and technological change within this type of society. But what if we want to identify the consequences of a specific advance in scientific knowledge or the implications of a particular new technological artefact? Here it becomes useful to draw on Hacking's discussion of science. Hacking contends that modern science 'has been the adventure of the interlocking of representing and intervening' (1983: 146). 'We shall count as real', he writes, 'what we can use to intervene in the world to affect something else, or what the world can use to affect us' (1983: 146). This can be extended to technology, except that in this case, we are dealing with physical artefacts rather than with knowledge since, as Agassi has pointed out, 'at the very least . . . the implementation of any technique whatsoever involves both physical and social activities' (1985: 25; cf. Bimber, 1994: 88). In other words, techno-logical artefacts are where the social and the natural or physical worlds meet, but technology always involves (physical) hardware. Paraphrasing Hacking's conception of science, we can now say that modern technology has been the adventure of the interlocking of refining and manipulating since technological advance consists of the process whereby artefacts are continually being modified in order to enhance our mastery of the world.[7]

This conception of science and technology enables us to identify the contribution that specific advances in scientific knowledge and technological artefacts make to the process of disenchantment because it allows us to say what gains have been made in each case by instrumental rationality. This view of scientific and technological advance is therefore 'realist' inasmuch as it rests on the notion that scientific knowledge is separable from the world and that artefacts are physical objects. Yet it also takes into account the effect of this advance on the social world by means of Weber's concept of disenchantment. The sociology of science and technology translates the one into the other; that is, it translates the ways in which knowledge intervenes in the world and artefacts manipulate it into the ways in which the external conditions of social life become increasingly governed by how knowledge and technology are deployed.[8]

This realist approach to science and technology cannot be divorced from the macro level. The reason for this is that it is only once a distinction has been made between culture and science, or between a sphere of cognition whose validity is independent of social life ('realism' tells us only that knowledge is separate from the world, not what the significance of this separation is), that we can operationalize realism by identifying the separate realm of knowledge and of physical artefacts that is to be investigated. It can be noted in passing that this argument does not apply the other way round: realism at the concrete level of the study of the impact of specific areas of scientific knowledge or of technology is not essential at the macro level since realism here adds nothing to the argument that modern or industrial society is characterized by a unique mode of cognition.

To this we must add that the relation between science and technology has been variable. Until recent times, the two were not closely linked (Collins, 1986: 113). In the course of the twentieth century, however, they have become increasingly intertwined. Another feature of science and technology in this century has been that science has on a number of occasions become 'big science' (Galison and Hevly, 1992; Price, 1963), such as particle physics or the human genome project, while technological artefacts have become part of 'large technological systems' (Hughes, 1987), as, for example, with electrification and telecommunications. In these cases, it is necessary to tackle simultaneously the large-scale social implications of science and technology on the one hand, and how these focus the attention of a large part of the research and development community and require an immense mobilization of social resources on the other. This means, too, that in these cases the examination of the disenchanting consequences of scientific and technological advance must encompass a wide range of simultaneous developments.

Yet these features only pertain to certain types of scientific and technological advance. Others, like smaller-scale laboratory research or stand-alone domestic technologies, will require different points of departure. The study of science and technology has so far consisted of various approaches stemming from a number of disciplines and different strengths have emerged within them. There are, for example, historical studies which delineate the emergence of individual new technologies (MacKenzie, 1990). Or in economics, general models have been developed to gauge how utilitarian calculations may shape the diffusion of new technologies (Arthur, 1989). What is still missing are the sociological frameworks which steer a middle course between historical case studies and general theories. In other words, there is no systematic sociological framework which – without falling into the determinism of social and cultural shaping, or the determinism of science and technology as culture, both of which remain wedded to relativism – specifies the appropriate level for examining the interplay between scientific and technological advance and the social structures which they shape and which they are shaped by.[9]

One of the reasons for this shortcoming is that the sociology of science and technology has been perennially driven by the question of determinism, of scientific and technological versus social determinism. But if the relationship between science and technology and social life is always a question of levels, then it is important to go beyond this duality: for different kinds of scientific and technological advances it will be necessary to address different aspects of the interrelationship between the two sides. In the case of 'big science' or 'large technological systems', for example, it may be necessary to focus on the institutional momentum that has built up behind the research and development efforts. For consumer electronics, on the other hand, it may be necessary to examine the feedback loops between research on new devices and the domestic contexts in which they are used (Silverstone and Hirsch, 1992). No doubt there are many different ways in which scientific and technological advances translate into everyday settings and it is impossible to determine, a priori, whether science and technology or social forces do the shaping. What *is* clear from the outset, however, is that there will always be two sides to this interplay; the side of an ongoing 'adventure' of representing and intervening, or of refining and manipulating, and the side of disenchantment, or of an advance in instrumental efficacy and of the depersonalization of the external conditions of life.

The sociology of science and technology has been stuck on the question of determinism because it has sought foundations in epistemological questions; that is, it has tried to address the relation between science and technology and society from a particular epistemological vantage point. The problem with this is that epistemology cannot yield such foundations. As Gellner has pointed out, if we explain the workings of science in modern society in the manner that has been proposed here, then realism adds nothing to the legitimation of the scientific worldview (1988: 202–3). Hacking's realism, too, is without such foundations: what part of the world science represents or intervenes in, or what part of a technological artefact is refined and what it manipulates – these matters are left open. The only assumption that is made is that the world is separable from knowledge (but this is an assumption which social science also has to make) and, in the case of technology, that this world is the physical one (which is true in so far as the investigation is concerned with artefacts).

Put differently, this kind of realism is not foundational because it is a precondition of any form of enquiry which seeks to impose order upon the world. The objects of this kind of enquiry, on the other hand, are constantly being redefined and reshaped by the advance of science and technology and this, again, is true of both natural and social science. We can therefore also foresee an end to the necessity of adopting this kind of realism; namely in a society in which it is also no longer necessary to impose order on the natural and social worlds, or one in which the central sociological significance of disenchantment has come to an end.

In attempting to assert their epistemological priority over science and technology, the sociology of science and technology and the postmodern approach to knowledge have been overstepping their limits. They have tried to produce a theoretical account which tries to fix or encompass the role of knowledge in the world. This standpoint necessarily presupposes anti-realism, or the idea that knowledge is not possible outside of the confines of a particular society or culture. Such anti-realist presuppositions are inescapable for the view that science and technology are always already shaped by culture or by social forces – and vice versa. As has been shown, however, the social reality of science and technology demands realism in order to be able to gauge the social consequences of scientific and technological advance.

The persistence of the two cultures

A realist standpoint does not make it impossible to reflect on the social preconditions for the growth of scientific knowledge; in other words, it does not rule out a sociology of scientific knowledge. There are a number of competing explanations for the rise of modern science and of the scientific revolution, but the outlines of this process and its main causes are well known (Collins, 1994a: 161–5; Sanderson, 1995: 317–32). In terms of the content of scientific knowledge, on the other hand, the sociology of science may be unique, but this, according to Collins, is because 'scientists are likely to be ideologists for the idealized view [of science] which best supports their own prestige. Only in the sociology of science does this ideological interest happen to coincide with our [the sociologist's] analytical interest in what really goes on' (Collins, 1992a: 271). But again, this shared interest does not prevent sociology from putting scientific knowledge into its social contexts.

The social preconditions for the advance of sociological knowledge, on the other hand, are less well known. As Collins has argued, the social science disciplines gained increasing independence with the rise of an autonomous institutional base in the universities, particularly during the nineteenth century.[10] In recent decades, moreover, the university system has undergone a massive expansion, leading to extreme specialization and to an increasing insularity of the academic world. Thus most of the output of the social sciences is now addressed to other members of the academic community, and the self-contained nature of academic discourse and the growth in output have become mutually reinforcing.

The post-war period has also seen an enormous growth in the culture and entertainment industries, providing a steady stream of new material that demands comment. This factor has given a boost to culture-centred theories in the social sciences. There may also be an intrinsic appeal in the content of culture-centred theories: explicating the significance of science and technology as tools for cultural domination or for cultural renewal could be regarded as more exciting than explaining the contribution of scientific and technological advance to economic growth, for example, or its relation to military power, areas which may be more difficult and which may also, by comparison, seem more mundane. Finally, Collins has noted that there is a Durkheimian 'truth' to postmodernism inasmuch as the self-referentiality and self-doubt about the efficacy of knowledge in postmodernist theory correspond to the reality of an increasingly inward-looking and at the same time un-overseeable supply of intellectual output (1992b: 94).

Apart from the conditions for the advance of sociological knowledge, what of its consequences? Although a large body of knowledge has been accumulated in sociology, it belabours the obvious to say that this has not had the same kind of effect as knowledge in the natural sciences. There may be some truth in Giddens' view that sociological knowledge often goes unrecognized since it has come to be taken for granted in our everyday self-understandings (1987). It may also be, as Collins has pointed out, that the main role of sociology has been to lend support to conflicting positions in disputes over social policy (1994a: 170). Nevertheless, unlike advances in natural science and technology, there is no direct translation of advances in sociological knowledge into the external environment, nor does social science enjoy the same kind of status among the public as its opposite number.

We can now return to the issues raised at the outset of this chapter. As I noted earlier, relativism has come to occupy a central place in sociological theory by focusing on epistemological issues. This is due to the high premium that is placed in relativist social thought on the sphere of culture. At the same time, this exclusive focus on the subject matter of culture – how culture shapes and is shaped by social life – has given this theoretical tradition a restricted niche within sociology. There is now a large body of sociological and postmodernist writing dealing with the cultural significance of science and technology, but there is little discernible sense in which these build on one another, partly because, if science and technology are seen as cultural products, there may indeed be a wide variety of meanings attached to them, and partly because, as I mentioned earlier, there has been vacillation in the underlying epistemological claims. Other areas of sociology have in the meantime moved on regardless of these culture-centred theories and they have registered cumulative advances both in theory-building and in substantive research. Historical sociology is a good example (Collins, 1994a: 168–9; Lloyd, 1993: esp. 201–20): in this area, scholarship has been cumulative in the sense that studies build on one another in terms of the refinement of concepts and causal models as well as in the assessment, scope and accumulation of the evidence to support them.

Culture-centred theorists have argued that a cultural understanding of science and technology radically blurs or redraws the line between nature and culture, between technology and society, between humans and non-humans, and other such boundaries.[11] This, in turn, it is claimed, will reshape these boundaries in society-at-large. Yet it is difficult to see how such shifts could take place unless they would resonate with wider changes in public attitudes towards science and technology. And even if it were possible to detect such shifts on the horizon, it would be difficult to foretell where they might lead: if we think, for example, of changing attitudes to nature in historical perspective, then, as Thomas (1983) has shown, such changes, whereby, in early modern England, the underlying conception of the natural world practically reversed itself, took several centuries. The idea that redrawing boundaries within the world of academic social science will radically change public perceptions of nature and of science is therefore somewhat optimistic – quite apart from the limitations on the diffusion of sociological knowledge.

It might be objected at this stage that there is nevertheless considerable scepticism and disquiet about science and technology in contemporary society. If this is so, could this not be an indication of a more far-reaching shift in our conception of science and technology? To put this into context, we need to return to the two levels discussed earlier, the macro level of industrial society and the level on which the sociological investigation of particular scientific or technological endeavours takes place. This distinction also applies to public attitudes towards science and technology: the macro level link between scientific and technological advance and economic growth, even though it is much discussed in academic social science, is not very prominent in our everyday life. On the level of our everyday dealings with science and technology, on the other hand, there has indeed been a growing wariness which has manifested itself, for example, in the increasing prominence of environmental issues and in concerns about advances in medical technology. Thus there is a disjunction between the everyday world and the features which characterize industrial society at the macro level (although this may be true of many concepts pertaining to industrial society, viz. the 'division of labour').[12]

The reason for this disjunction can be traced to the fact that we have inherited our beliefs about science and technology from a different age, from the Enlightenment and the Industrial Revolution, in which scientific and technological advance were associated with progress. Progress in knowledge, in turn, was associated with advancement towards a better society. To put this inheritance into perspective, we can recall the more ambivalent attitude towards science and technology contained in Weber's notion of disenchantment: science and technology enhance instrumental rationality, but they also lead, as he put it on one occasion, to an 'external uniformity of life style' ([1921] 1980: 64). Once the double-edged nature of this advance is restored at the macro level, it may also be easier to understand our more immediate misgivings about science and technology. Nevertheless, these misgivings should not obscure the implicit taken-for-grantedness of scientific and technological advance, however much this may have become the wallpaper of modern society rather than the new furniture. It has often been pointed out that taking this advance for granted is as characteristic of postmodernism and relativist practitioners of the sociology of science and technology as it is of everyone else.

Thus we find the two cultures still as separate as they were in 1959 when Snow put forward this formulation ([1959] 1964). It is possible that the more empirically oriented social sciences have moved closer to the natural sciences and in this way they may have played a role in extending instrumental rationality. Whether they will also be more influential within the academic community in the long run than the culture-centred theories that have been discussed here is difficult to say; perhaps 'theory' represents the commanding heights of the intellectual economy in sociology and exercises an influence that is out of proportion to its size. Be that as it may, the tension between the two cultures is bound to keep generating cultural hopes and fears about scientific and technological advance since these are ways of making sense of a process which might otherwise seem to lead, to speak with Weber, to 'an ever more devastating senselessness' (1948: 357).

The implication of the conception of science and technology outlined in the previous sections is that sociology, too, should meet (or at least approximate) the criteria for the validity of knowledge which govern the natural sciences. There will no doubt continue to be debates over what exactly this entails, although there is widespread agreement about key requirements, for example, 'the presence of well-articulated hypotheses and their systematic testing', or the use of 'careful observation by publicly checkable methods' (Gellner, 1985: 125–6).[13] The fact that adherence to these requirements does not generate the same kind of rapidly moving research front as the natural sciences cannot be counted as arguments against the adoption of scientific methods; the results of adopting these methods are evidently different.

Finally, the argument that social scientific knowledge cannot posit claims about the validity of knowledge which override the claims of the natural sciences does not entail that sociology should be uncritical towards science and technology. Even if the effects of both types of knowledge are different in practice, a realist standpoint does not predispose the sociologist of science and technology to the view that their effects are beneficial or harmful, or to a particular political position (such as the view that science and technology can be good or bad depending on how we use it, which is commonly regarded as the 'liberal' position). If a realist standpoint suggests that specific scientific and technological advances have specific disenchanting effects, then here, as in other areas of social science, it will be possible to assess these effects and take appropriate measures.

To recapitulate: there has recently been a convergence between a sociology of science and technology and postmodernist theory whereby both focus on the cultural significance of science and technology. By seeing science and technology as part of culture, scientific and technological change can be enlisted as vehicles for cultural criticism or to set an agenda for cultural renewal. These culture-centred theories are part of a long-standing anti-scientistic tradition in sociological theory and the social bases of this tradition ensure its continued survival. The social reality of scientific and technological advance, however, is not cultural but mainly economic and its impact lies in the extension of instrumental rationality throughout social life. This Weberian and realist perspective on science and technology can also be applied to sociology in the sense that the advance of sociological knowledge, though it has contributed to the growth of scientific knowledge, does not have the same instrumental effects. Even so, there is considerable momentum behind the advance of sociological knowledge, and while the strength of cultural theories will wax and wane, the growth of knowledge is a cumulative process. Whether it matters that sociological knowledge has done more to help us make sense of the social world, and thereby provided a basis for thinking about and confronting the options that lie ahead – rather than to explain and transform it – is another question.

Notes

1 For this convergence, see, for example, Law (1991). He writes that the 'epistemologies of all these programmes', including studies of science and technology and postmodernism, have in common a 'denial of absolutism' (1991: 7).

2 Woolgar (1988) presents an overview of ideas about the social and cultural shaping of science. For similar ideas about technology, see MacKenzie and Wajcman (1985). The view that science and technology *as* culture shape social life has been put forward, for example, by Latour (1993) and Haraway (1991).

3 Within the sociology of science, relativism mainly pertained to scientific knowledge. More recently, however, it has also become a feature of studies of technology. Woolgar (1991), for example, wants to treat technologies as 'texts'.

4 'Culture-centred theories' is awkward, but it would be misleading to say 'cultural theories' since the ideas under discussion have been housed as much in sociology (and more recently in anthropology) as in cultural studies.

5 An exception here are anthropological studies of technology, which have moved very close to recent (postmodern) developments in the sociology of science and technology (Pfaffenberger, 1992). But in these anthropological studies, too, the larger questions that are addressed here have been avoided.

6 This argument about the relation between science and economic growth has been made by Gellner (for example, 1985: 115–16, 1988: 17–18). Gellner himself has noticed the pulling-oneself-up-by-one's-own-bootstraps nature of the argument (1985: 89–93). For the merits and limitations of this argument, see Schroeder (1996a).

7 Hacking (1983) illustrates the 'interlocking of representing and intervening' with various examples from the laboratory sciences. In the case of technological artefacts, examples of the interlocking of refining and manipulating can be found in Hughes' accounts of how artefacts are made more robust before they leave the laboratory so that they can withstand the tougher conditions in the world outside, and how these conditions, in turn, are imported into the laboratory (1987: 62–3; cf. Collins 1993: 316–17).

8 An application of these ideas to the case of virtual reality technology can be found in Schroeder (1996b).

9 An important exception is Fuchs' (1992) study, which focuses on the meso level of organizations and offers a (non-relativistic) sociological account of the bases of scientific knowledge.

10 This paragraph and the next are based on Collins (1994b: 3–46 and 1992b: 92–4).

11 Again, Latour (1993) and Haraway (1991) stand out as examples.

12 The same may be true for sociological knowledge; it is easy to lose sight of large-scale social scientific advances from the vantage point of being in the midst of what seem to be shifting and non-cumulative changes in academic fashion. In this regard, natural scientists may have a different perspective inasmuch as their 'slow boring of hard boards', to borrow a phrase from Weber (1948: 128), yields a stronger sense of steady advance.

13 It is unclear how much light the philosophy of science can shed on the validity of scientific method in the sense discussed here. Whether, for example, Popper and Kuhn tell us much about how the validity of science is illustrated in the practice of scientists or the consequences of their work will no doubt continue to be a matter of debate among philosophers.

References

Adorno, T., Albert, H., Dahrendorf, R., Pilot, H. and Popper, K.R. (1976) *The Positivist Dispute in German Sociology*. London: Heinemann Educational Books.

Agassi, J. (1985) *Technology, Philosophical and Social Aspects*. Dordrecht: D. Reidel.

Arthur, B. (1989) 'Competing technologies, increasing returns, and lock-in by historical events', *The Economic Journal*, 99: 116–31.

Bimber, B. (1994) 'Three faces of technological determinism', in M.R. Smith and L. Marx (eds), *Does Technology Drive History? The Dilemma of Technological Determinism*. Cambridge, MA: MIT Press. pp. 79–100.

Brubaker, R. (1984) *The Limits of Rationality: An Essay on the Social and Moral Thought of Max Weber*. London: George Allen & Unwin.

Collins, R. (1986) *Weberian Sociological Theory*. Cambridge: Cambridge University Press.

Collins, R. (1992a) 'Symposium on the "Hard Program" in the sociology of scientific knowledge. Replies and objections', *Social Epistemology* 6(3): 267–72.

Collins, R. (1992b) 'On the sociology of intellectual stagnation: the late twentieth century in perspective', *Theory, Culture and Society*, 9: 73–96.

Collins, R. (1993) 'Ethical controversies of science and society: a relation between two spheres of social conflict', in T. Brante, S. Fuller and W. Lynch (eds), *Controversial Science: From Content to Contention*. Albany, NY: SUNY Press. pp. 301–17.

Collins, R. (1994a) 'Why the social sciences won't become high-consensus, rapid-discovery science', *Sociological Forum*, 9(2): 155–77.

Collins, R. (1994b) *Four Sociological Traditions*. New York: Oxford University Press.

Escobar, A. (1994) 'Welcome to Cyberia – notes on the anthropology of cyberculture', *Current Anthropology*, 35(3): 211–31.

Fuchs, S. (1992) *The Professional Quest for Truth*. Albany, NY: SUNY Press.

Galison, P. and Hevly, B. (eds) (1992) *Big Science*. Stanford, CA: Stanford University Press.

Gellner, E. (1985) *Relativism and the Social Sciences.* Cambridge: Cambridge University Press.

Gellner, E. (1988) *Plough, Sword and Book.* London: Collins Harvill.

Giddens, A. (1987) 'What do sociologists do?', *Social Theory and Modern Sociology.* Cambridge: Polity Press. pp. 2–21.

Hacking, I. (1983) *Representing and Intervening.* Cambridge: Cambridge University Press.

Haraway, D. (1991) 'A cyborg manifesto: science, technology and socialist feminism in the late twentieth century', in *Simians, Cyborgs and Women.* London: Free Association Books. pp. 149–81.

Horton, R. (1970) 'African traditional thought and western science', in B. Wilson (ed.), *Rationality.* Oxford: Basil Blackwell. pp. 131–71.

Hughes, T. (1987) 'The evolution of large technological systems', in W. Bijker, T. Hughes and T. Pinch (eds), *The Social Construction of Technological Systems.* Cambridge, MA: MIT Press. pp. 51–82.

Inkster, I. (1991) *Science and Technology in History – an Approach to Historical Development.* Basingstoke: Macmillan.

Jones, S. (ed.) (1995) *Cybersociety: Computermediated Communication and Community.* London: Sage.

Latour, B. (1993) *We Have Never Been Modern.* Hemel Hempstead: Harvester Wheatsheaf.

Law, J. (1991) 'Introduction: monsters, machines and sociotechnical relations', in J. Law (ed.), *A Sociology of Monsters.* London: Routledge. pp. 1–23.

Lloyd, C. (1993) *The Structures of History.* Oxford: Basil Blackwell.

MacKenzie, D. (1984) 'Marx and the machine', *Technology and Culture*, 25: 473–502.

MacKenzie, D. (1990) *Inventing Accuracy: A Historical Accuracy of Nuclear Missile Guidance.* Cambridge, MA: MIT Press.

MacKenzie, D. and Wajcman, J. (eds) (1985) *The Social Shaping of Technology.* Milton Keynes: Open University Press.

Mokyr, J. (1990) *The Lever of Riches – Technological Creativity and Economic Progress.* Oxford: Oxford University Press.

Nelson, R. (1994) 'Evolutionary theorizing about economic change', in N. Smelser and R. Swedberg (eds), *The Handbook of Economic Sociology.* Princeton, NJ: Princeton University Press. pp. 108–36.

Pfaffenberger, B. (1992) 'Social anthropology of technology', *Annual Review of Anthropology*, 21: 491–516.

Price, Derek de Solla (1963) *Little Science, Big Science.* New York: Columbia University Press.

Sanderson, S. (1995) *Social Transformations: A General Theory of Historical Development.* Oxford: Basil Blackwell.

Schroeder, R. (1995) 'Disenchantment and its discontents: Weberian perspectives on science and technology', *Sociological Review*, 43(3): 227–50.

Schroeder, R. (1996a) 'From the Big Divide to the Rubber Cage: Gellner's conception of science and technology', in J. Hall and I. Jarvie (eds), *The Social Philosophy of Ernest Gellner.* Amsterdam: Editions Rodopi. pp. 427–43.

Schroeder, R. (1996b) *Possible Worlds: The Social Dynamic of Virtual Reality Technology.* Boulder, CO: Westview Press.

Silverstone, R. and Hirsch, E. (eds) (1992) *Consuming Technologies: Media and Information in Domestic Spaces.* London: Routledge.

Smith, M.R. and Marx, L. (eds) (1994) *Does Technology Drive History? The Dilemma of Technological Determinism.* Cambridge, MA: MIT Press.

Snow, C.P. ([1959] 1964) *The Two Cultures: And A Second Look*, 2nd edn. Cambridge: Cambridge University Press.

Thomas, K. (1983) *Man and the Natural World – Changing Attitudes in England 1500–1800.* London: Allen Lane.

Trigg, R. (1993) *Rationality and Science: Can Science Explain Everything?* Oxford: Basil Blackwell.

Weber, M. (1948) *From Max Weber: Essays in Sociology*. London: Routledge and Kegan Paul.

Weber, M. ([1921] 1980) *Gesammelte Politische Schriften*, 4th edn. Tübingen: J.C.B. Mohr.

Woolgar, S. (1988) *Science: The Very Idea*. Chichester: Ellis Horwood.

Woolgar, S. (1991) 'The turn to technology in the social studies of science', *Science, Technology and Human Values*, 16(1): 20–50.

CULTURE AND MEDIA

7 Social Theory and Cultural Studies

Douglas Kellner

By the nineteenth century what Herbert Marcuse had described as 'affirmative culture' was the dominant concept of culture in Western societies. In this concept, the realm of the beautiful and aesthetic enjoyment were separated from everyday life and celebrated as higher realms of ideal values. For Marcuse (1968: 88ff.), this elevated form of 'affirmative culture' referred to 'the culture of the bourgeois epoch which led in the course of its own development to the segregation from civilization of the mental and spiritual world as an independent realm of value that is also considered superior to civilization'. The concept of an autonomous 'high' culture was given a highly influential articulation in the writings of Matthew Arnold (1963), who described the goal of culture to cultivate 'perfection' in human beings as the result of its 'sweetness and light' which would be brought to the public through cultural education and protect it from 'anarchy' and 'barbarism'.

Culture for Arnold was 'the best that has been thought or known in the world everywhere' and would save humanity from the ravages of industrial civilization. This manifestly idealist concept thus distinguished 'culture' from 'civilization' which was used to describe all the material conditions and practices of everyday life ranging from cuisine to economics. Culture, by contrast, referred to a higher realm of purely ideal values. This elevated concept of culture was punctured by anthropological studies that expanded the concept of culture to include much of what had been contained in the concept of civilization. By the 1930s, even cultural conservatives like T.S. Eliot were providing broader conceptions of culture in harmony with the anthropological perspective of culture as bound up with the totality of a people's way of life. After polemically engaging Arnold's idealist concept of culture, for instance, Eliot writes:

> the reader must remind himself, as the author has constantly to do, of how much is here embraced by the term *culture*. It includes all the characteristic activities and interests of a people: Derby Day, Henley Regatta, Cowes, the Twelfth of August, a cup final, the dog races, the pin table, the dart board, Wensleydale cheese, boiled cabbage cut into sections, beetroot in vinegar, nineteenth century Gothic churches and the music of Elgar. (1949: 104)

Eliot goes on to say that this concept of culture is obviously not unified, thus anticipating the later rupturing of culture into class and subcultural categories carried out by British cultural studies and later post-structuralist theory. The quote from Eliot therefore suggests that by the post-war era, the distinction between culture and civilization, between the realm of the ideal/spiritual and the material, was collapsed into a broader and more inclusive concept of culture. Precisely, this expansive concept has been taken up by a number of contemporary theoretical perspectives with consequences for the study of culture that I will explore in this chapter.[1] In particular, I want to argue for a sociology of culture and cultural studies that interrogates a wide range of cultural phenomena from opera and high modernism, to media culture and the practices of ordinary people. I will propose taking culture as a continuum and reject divisions into high or low, popular and elite, categories. In addition, I will propose methods for a cultural studies concerned with such a broad range of phenomena. I will argue for the need to incorporate social theory into cultural analysis, as well as for the importance of culture for contemporary social theory. First, however, I want to reflect on the problematic approach to culture in some versions of sociological theory.

Social theory and culture

Classical social theory attempted to chart the relationships between the economy, polity, society and culture of the rapidly developing modern societies that emerged with the second industrial revolution in the nineteenth century (see Antonio and Kellner, 1992). Several of the founding fathers of classical theory – such as Marx, Weber and Durkheim – did pay attention to cultural phenomena and took culture seriously; this is certainly true of Marx's theory of ideology, Weber's studies of religion and other cultural forms and Durkheim's studies of cultural norms and forms like religion. Classical theory attempted to analyse the interrelationships between culture and society and the important social functions of culture. Moreover, Marx, Durkheim, Weber and other classical theorists had a multiperspectival model that analysed the interaction of society, culture, economics and politics.

Classical theory tended to analyse systems of social differentiation and complexity, which allegedly marked the specificity of modern societies. On this model, modern Western societies were characterized by social differentiation, by the development of separate spheres of existence developing their own logic and structures – such as the economy, polity, society, culture. Following this model, post-Second World War sociological theory conceptualized culture as an increasingly differentiated realm, parallel to social differentiation within the social sphere, which in turn was delineated into increasingly complex social functions, social norms and the individualization and autonomy of persons, accompanied by increasingly differentiated forms of community, of culture, of communication and political association.

This widely held paradigm of social differentiation as the defining feature of modern societies saw the task of social theory as to explore the domain of the social. In particular, post-Second World War sociological theory wanted to develop sociology as a science within the academic division of labour and abstracted the domain of the social as the central focus of its endeavours. Accordingly, with some exceptions, sociological theory tended to neglect culture as an important domain and to attribute it secondary importance in the constitution and the nature of modern societies. Moreover, those theorists such as Parsons who did pay attention to culture abstracted the domain of the cultural and social from the economic and the political, thus severing the forms of economic and political determination characteristic of the classical theories of Marx and Weber.

Since the 1960s' contestation of existing institutions, discourses and forms of knowledge, however, some social theorists have begun taking culture seriously and reconceptualizing the nature and functions of culture. Consequently, a variety of new approaches to the study of culture have emerged both inside and outside the field of sociology. Insurgent sociologists, deriving from the new social movements of the 1960s and 1970s, saw the importance of culture in manufacturing consent to racism, sexism and contemporary capitalism – including its imperialist wars – and began to study culture more intently than the previous generation of sociologists. Indeed, a variety of individuals from many disciplines began focusing on the culture–society nexus and began producing a variety of cultural theories and politics – as I will argue in this chapter.

Some of the new cultural theories contested the existing academic division of labour in which sociology of culture, for instance, was a sub-discipline of the field of sociology rather than as a contested terrain where economic, political, social, cultural and other forces intersected. Other approaches to the sociology of culture, however, merely used existing paradigms to interpret cultural phenomena – Marxian, Weberian, Parsonian, or whatever. Yet the emergence of a new transdisciplinary space to study culture is evident in such diverse arenas as British cultural studies, German critical theory, French post-structuralism, feminism and women's studies, multiculturalism and race studies, gay and lesbian studies, and many varieties of postmodern theory. Overcoming the standard academic division of labour alluded to above, these approaches articulate the relations between culture and society in a variety of promising perspectives, some of which I discuss in this study – whereas other contributors will discuss some of the other new approaches to culture that I listed above.

Against the concept of the separation of the social as the object of sociological theory, I will argue for a model of social theory that analyses the concrete and complex interactions between the social, cultural, economic and political dimensions. This is the model of Marx and Weber, as well as, more recently, of the critical theory of the Frankfurt School, British cultural studies and postmodern theory. I will draw on all these traditions in the following discussion, stressing the similarities in their breaking of disciplinary boundaries and thus taking culture seriously as they map out the interrelationships between the social, culture, economics and politics in the constitution of contemporary societies.

My argument will be that those traditions that transcend disciplinary boundaries and provide transdisciplinary and multiperspectival approaches are productive for sociological study of culture. The Frankfurt School, I will argue, developed the first important analyses of media culture and a multiperspectival approach to study all cultural phenomena, but their approach is vitiated by a too rigid distinction between high and low culture and questionable assumptions about the nature of both mass culture and of media audiences. British cultural studies in turn overcomes the Frankfurt high/low culture distinction and develops more promising perspectives on media culture and its audiences. But British cultural studies, I will argue, falls prey to a form of cultural populism and fetishism of the popular, and then takes a problematic postmodern turn. Yet postmodern theory, I suggest, is also useful in calling attention to new configurations and functions of culture, although it tends in some versions to erase economic, political and social dimensions of cultural production and reception, and thus to engage in a new form of cultural and technological determinism. I will therefore ultimately suggest the need for a multiperspectival approach that draws on various contemporary positions, but that overcomes the specific limitations of each.

The Frankfurt School and the culture industries

Currently, the study of culture within the field of sociology is bifurcated between a textualist approach and more empirical approaches. The culturalist approach is largely textual, centred on the analysis and criticism of texts as cultural artefacts, using methods primarily derived from the humanities. A social science-based sociology of culture, by contrast, employs empirical methodologies, ranging from straight quantitative research, empirical studies of specific issues or domains, or more broadly historical research. These conflicting approaches point to a bifurcation of the study of culture into warring paradigms with competing models and methods. Yet there are, I will argue, some contemporary approaches to culture that do not bifurcate the field in the first place, but present models of ways to study its interconnection within the broader fields of the economy, society, politics and history.

To a large extent, the Frankfurt School inaugurated critical studies of mass communication and culture and developed an early model of cultural studies (see Kellner, 1982, 1989a, 1995a). During the 1930s, the Frankfurt School developed a critical and transdisciplinary approach to communications studies, combining analysis of political economy of the media, cultural analysis of texts, and audience reception studies of the social and ideological effects of mass culture and communications.[2] They coined the term 'culture industries' to signify the process of the industrialization of mass-produced culture and the commercial imperatives which drove the system. The critical theorists analysed all mass-mediated cultural artefacts within the context of industrial production, in which the commodities of the culture industries exhibited the same features as other products of mass production: commodification, standardization and massification. The products of the culture industries had the specific function, however, of providing ideological legitimation of the existing capitalist societies and of integrating individuals into the framework of mass culture and society.

Adorno's analyses of popular music, Lowenthal's studies of popular literature and magazines, Herzog's studies of radio soap operas, and the perspectives and critiques of mass culture developed in Horkheimer and Adorno's famous study of the culture industries provided many examples of the usefulness of the Frankfurt School approach. Moreover, in their theories of the culture industries and critiques of mass culture, they were the first to systematically analyse and criticize mass-mediated culture and communications within critical social theory. They were the first social theorists to see the importance of what they called the 'culture industries' in the reproduction of contemporary societies, in which so-called mass culture and communications stand in the centre of leisure activity, are important agents of socialization, mediators of political reality and should thus be seen as major institutions of contemporary societies with a variety of economic, political, cultural and social effects.[3]

Furthermore, they investigated the cultural industries in a political context as a form of the integration of the working class into capitalist societies. The Frankfurt School were one of the first neo-Marxian groups to examine the effects of mass culture and the rise of the consumer society on the industrial working classes which were to be the instrument of revolution in the classical Marxian scenario. They also analysed the ways in which the culture industries and consumer society were stabilizing the contemporary capitalism and accordingly sought new strategies for political change, agencies of political transformation and models for political emancipation that could serve as norms of social critique and goals for political struggle. This project required rethinking the Marxian project and produced many important contributions – as well as some problematical positions.

The Frankfurt School theorists contributed also to developing a sociology of high culture and interrogated cultural artefacts ranging from popular music to Schoenberg and Stravinsky. One of their early projects in the 1930s was to develop a critical sociology of literature (see Lowenthal in Bronner and Kellner, 1989: 40ff.) and Adorno's four volumes of literary essays provide important exercises in socially contextualizing literature and appraising its effects (collected in two English-language volumes in Adorno, 1991 and 1992). His study of Wagner (1981) also provides important contributions to the sociology of culture, as do his many works in music sociology. In addition, both Adorno and Walter Benjamin wrote extensively on avant-garde movements and attempted to develop theories which appraised the critical and emancipatory potential of art.

The Frankfurt School analysis of culture thus spanned a wide range of products, but tended to divide culture into high and low categories, a problematical dichotomy that should be superseded for a more unified model which takes culture as a spectrum and applies similar critical methods to all cultural artefacts ranging from opera to popular music, from modernist literature to soap operas. In particular, the Frankfurt School model of a monolithic mass culture contrasted with an ideal of 'authentic art', which limits critical, subversive and emancipatory moments to certain privileged artefacts of high culture, is highly problematic. The Frankfurt School position that all mass culture is ideological and homogenizing, having the effects of duping a passive mass of consumers, is also objectionable. Instead, one should see critical and ideological moments in the full range of culture, and not limit critical moments to high culture and identify all of low culture as ideological. One should also allow for the possibility that critical and subversive moments could be found in the artefacts of the cultural industries as well as the canonized classics of high modernist culture that the Frankfurt School seemed to privilege as the site of artistic opposition and emancipation.[4] One should also distinguish between the encoding and decoding of media artefacts, and recognize that an active audience often produces its own meanings and use for products of the cultural industries.

Thus, there are serious flaws in the original programme of critical theory which requires a radical reconstruction of the classical model of the culture industries (Kellner, 1989a, 1995). This would include: more concrete and empirical analysis of the political economy of the media and the processes of the production of culture; more empirical and historical research into the construction of media industries and their interaction with other social institutions; more empirical studies of audience reception and media effects; and the incorporation of new cultural theories and methods into a reconstructed critical theory of culture and the media. Of course, individuals are doing many of these things outside of the Frankfurt School tradition, but often without sociologically contextualizing their studies and relating their findings to the project of critical social theory and social transformation.

A sociology of culture thus requires critical social theory to interpret, contextualize and provide grounds for critique for the findings of empirical and historical research. On the other hand, critical social theory needs to engage in historical and empirical research into the fields of culture and communication and modify and develop their social theory in line with the results of the findings. Such an enterprise would involve the merging of theoretical construction with empirical research and would require the reconstruction of the classical theories of the Frankfurt School. Cumulatively, such rethinking would update the critical theory of society and its activity of cultural criticism by incorporating contemporary developments in social and cultural theory into its enterprise.

Yet precisely the critical focus on media culture from the perspectives of commodification, reification, ideology and domination provides a perspective useful as a corrective to more populist and uncritical approaches to 'popular culture' which surrender critical perspectives. Although the Frankfurt School approach is partial and one-sided, it does provide tools to criticize the ideological and vulgar forms of media culture and the ways that it provides ideologies which legitimate forms of oppression and domination. Ideology critique is a fundamental constituent of cultural studies and the Frankfurt School is valuable for inaugurating systematic and sustained critiques of ideology within the cultural industries.

Moreover, on the level of metatheory, the Frankfurt School work preceded the bifurcation of the field of media studies and thus provides a model to overcome contemporary divisions in the study of media, culture and communications.[5] Their studies dissected the interconnection of culture and communication in artefacts that reproduced the existing society, positively presenting social norms and practices and legitimating the dominant organization of society. The Frankfurt School carried out their analysis within the framework of critical social theory, thus integrating communication and cultural studies within the context of study of capitalist society and the ways that communications and culture were produced within this order and the roles and functions that they assumed.[6]

The contribution of British cultural studies

After the Second World War, Raymond Williams popularized the expanded conception of culture and the need to think together 'culture and society' in a series of publications that helped produce British cultural studies. He polemicized against the concept of the masses which he claimed was both condescending and elitist – as well as overly homogenizing, covering over real and important differences between individuals and groups – a theme that came to run through the cultural populism which helped shape and distinguish British cultural studies.

In work inaugurated by the University of Birmingham Centre for Contemporary Cultural Studies – founded in 1962 by Richard Hoggart and Stuart Hall – British cultural studies developed a variety of critical approaches for the analysis, interpretation and criticism of cultural artefacts which overcame some of the limitations of the Frankfurt School that I noted.[7] British cultural studies systematically rejected high/low culture distinctions and took seriously the artefacts of media culture, thus overcoming the elitism of the Frankfurt School. Likewise, they overcame the limitations of the Frankfurt School notion of a passive audience in their conceptions of an active audience that creates meanings and the popular. Yet it should be pointed out that Walter Benjamin – loosely affiliated with the Frankfurt School, but not part of their inner circle – also took seriously media culture, saw its emancipatory potential, and posited the possibility of an active audience. For Benjamin (1969), the decline of the aura – the sense of originality, uniqueness and authenticity – under the pressures of mechanical reproduction helped produce a public able more actively and critically to engage a wide range of cultural phenomena. He argued that, for instance, the spectators of sports events were discriminating judges of athletic activity, able to criticize and analyse plays, players, strategies, and so on. Likewise, Benjamin postulated that the film audience as well can become experts of criticism and critically dissect the construction, meanings and ideologies of film.

Yet one could argue that we need to think together the concepts of the active and manipulated audience to grasp the full range of media effects, thus avoiding both cultural elitism and populism. While audiences do create their own meanings they often do so under determinant conditions and are conditioned to find pleasure in certain artefacts and codes (i.e. the happy endings of Hollywood films and much television, the transformation of everyday life into song and colour in musicals, the thrills of horror films, special effects, and so on). Moreover, audiences are conditioned to produce meanings in certain ways and the concept of the active audience underplays the obvious seduction and fascination of media culture. Thus, I would propose articulating the extreme populist conception of the active audience with earlier notions of the manipulated audience to understand more fully the complex interactions between texts and audiences in media culture (Kellner, 1995a).

Despite their differences, like the Frankfurt School, the work of the Birmingham School of cultural studies is also transdisciplinary and subverts academic boundaries by combining social theory, cultural analysis and critique, and politics in a project aimed at a comprehensive criticism of the present configuration of culture and society oriented towards fundamental social transformation. Like the Frankfurt School, British cultural studies situates culture within a theory of social production and reproduction, specifying the ways that cultural forms served either to further social domination or to enable people to resist and struggle against domination. It analysed society as a hierarchical and antagonistic set of social relations characterized by the oppression of subordinate class, gender, race, ethnic and national strata. Employing Gramsci's model of hegemony and counterhegemony, it sought to analyse 'hegemonic', or ruling, social and cultural forces of domination and to seek 'counterhegemonic' forces of resistance and struggle.

For Gramsci, societies maintained their stability through a combination of force and hegemony, with some institutions and groups violently exerting power to maintain social boundaries (namely the police, military, vigilante groups, etc.), while other institutions (like religion, schooling, or the media) serve to induce consent to the dominant order through establishing the hegemony, or ideological dominance, of a specific type of social order (such as liberal capitalism, fascism, white supremacy, democratic socialism, communism, or whatever). Hegemony theory thus involved both analysis of current forces of domination and the ways that specific political forces achieved hegemonic power (like Thatcherism or Reaganism) *and* the delineation of counterhegemonic forces, groups and ideas that could contest and overturn the existing hegemony.

Birmingham cultural studies aimed at a political project of social transformation in which location of forces of domination and resistance would aid the process of political struggle. Richard Johnson, in discussions at a 1990 University of Texas conference on cultural studies, stressed that a distinction should be made between the postmodern concept of difference and the Birmingham notion of antagonism, in which the first concept often refers to a liberal conception of recognizing and tolerating differences, while the notion of antagonism refers to structural forces of domination, in which asymmetrical relations of power exist in sites of conflict. Within relations of antagonism, oppressed individuals struggle to overcome structures of domination in a variety of arenas. Johnson stressed that the Birmingham approach always defined itself as materialist, analysing sociohistorical conditions and structures of domination and resistance. In this way, it could be distinguished from idealist, textualist and extreme discourse theories which only recognized linguistic forms as constitutive of culture and subjectivity.

Thus, British cultural studies presents an approach that allows us to avoid cutting up the field of culture into high and low, popular versus elite, and to see all forms of culture as worthy of scrutiny and criticism. It enables approaches to culture that force us to appraise the politics of culture and to make political discriminations between different types of culture that have different political effects. It brings the study of race, gender and class into the centre of the study of culture and communications and adopts a critical approach that, like the Frankfurt School, but without some of its flaws, interprets culture within society and situates the study of culture within the field of contemporary social theory and oppositional politics.

From the beginning, the work of the Birmingham group was oriented towards the crucial political problem of their age and milieu. Their early focus on class and ideology derived from their acute sense of the oppressive and systemic effects of class in British society and the struggles of the 1960s against class inequality and oppression. Studies of subcultures in Britain sought for new agents of social change when it appeared that sectors of the working class were being integrated into the existing system and conservative ideologies and parties. Their attempts to reconstruct Marxism were influenced as well by 1960s struggles and political movements. The turn towards feminism, often conflictual, was influenced by the feminist movement, while the turn towards race as a significant factor of study was fuelled by the anti-racist struggles of the day. The move in British cultural studies towards focus on education was related to political concern with the continuing bourgeois hegemony despite the struggles of the 1960s. The right turn in British politics with Thatcher's victory led in the late 1970s to concern with understanding the authoritarian populism of the new conservative hegemony.

Developments in the past decade of British cultural studies have been responses in part to struggles by a multiplicity of different groups which have produced new methods and voices within cultural studies (such as a variety of new feminisms, gay and lesbian studies, critical multiculturalism, critical pedagogy and critical media literacy. Thus, the focus of British cultural studies at any given moment was determined by the struggles in the present political conjuncture and their major work was conceived as political interventions. Their studies of ideology, domination and resistance, and the politics of culture directed cultural studies towards analysing cultural artefacts, practices and institutions within existing networks of power and of showing how culture provided both tools and forces of domination and resources for resistance and struggle. This political focus intensified emphasis on the effects of culture and audience use of cultural artefacts, which provided an extremely productive focus on audiences and reception, topics that had been neglected in most previous text-based approaches to culture.[8] Yet recent developments in the field of cultural studies have arguably vitiated and depoliticized the project.

Cultural populism and postmodernism

In the 1980s, there was a turn within British cultural studies and beyond to celebrations of the popular, the pleasure of consumption, and affirmation of a postmodern global culture of multiplicity and difference which led many in cultural studies to uncritical celebration of 'popular culture'. However, just as the term 'mass culture' is ideologically loaded and overly derogatory, so too is the term 'popular culture' overly positive (see the discussion in Kellner, 1995a). In its usage by John Fiske (1989a, 1989b) and other contemporary practitioners of cultural studies, the term 'popular culture' suggests that mass-mediated culture arises from the people, covering over that it is a top-down form of culture that often precludes participation. The discourse of the 'popular' has long been utilized in Latin America and elsewhere to describe art produced by and for the people themselves as an oppositional sphere to mainstream or hegemonic culture. Thus, in Latin America and elsewhere, 'popular forces' describe groups struggling against domination and oppression, while 'popular culture' describes culture of, by and for the people, in which they produce and participate in cultural practices that articulate their experience and aspirations.

The concept of 'popular culture' also presents a celebratory gloss associated with the Popular Culture Association, which often engages in uncritical affirmations of all that is 'popular'. Since this term is associated in the United States with individuals and groups that often eschew critical, theoretically informed and political approaches to culture, it is risky to use this term, though Fiske has tried to provide the term 'popular culture' with an inflection consistent with the socially critical approach of cultural studies. In an interview in 1991, Fiske defines the 'popular' as that which audiences make of and do with the commodities of the culture industries. He argues that progressives should appropriate the term 'popular', wresting it from conservatives and liberals, using it as part of an arsenal of concepts in a cultural politics of opposition and resistance (discussion in Austin, Texas, September 1990). Fiske (1989b) has even written that 'there can be no popular dominant culture', thus excluding the 'popular' from domination and manipulation in principle.

More debate is needed as to whether using the term 'popular culture' in any form risks blunting the critical edge of cultural studies, and whether it is thus simply better to avoid terms like 'mass culture' and 'popular culture'. A possible move within cultural studies would therefore simply be to take culture itself as the field of one's studies without divisions into the high and the low, the popular and the elite – though, of course, these distinctions can be strategically deployed in certain contexts. Thus, I believe that instead of using ideological labels like 'mass' and 'popular', I think it is preferable to talk of 'media culture' (Kellner, 1995a) and to develop a cultural studies cutting across the full range of culture.

Moreover, especially as it has developed in the United States, many current configurations of cultural studies are too one-sided producing new bifurcations of the field and, in part, occluding the field of communications proper, by focusing too intently on cultural texts and audience reception. In his study of Madonna, for instance, Fiske writes:

> A cultural analysis, then, will reveal both the way the dominant ideology is structured into the text and into the reading subject, and those textual features that enable negotiated, resisting, or oppositional readings to be made. Cultural analysis reaches a satisfactory conclusion when the ethnographic studies of the historically and socially located meanings that *are* made are related to the semiotic analysis of the text. (1989a: 98)

This focus on text/audience, however, leaves out many mediations that should be part of the cultural studies and a sociology of culture, including analyses of how texts are produced within the context of the political economy and system of production of culture, as well as how audiences are produced by a variety of social institutions, practices, ideologies and the uses of different media (see Kellner, 1995a).

Thus, focusing on texts and audiences to the exclusion of analysis of the social relations and institutions in which texts are produced and consumed truncates cultural studies, as does analysis of reception that fails to indicate how audiences are produced through their social relations and how to some extent culture itself helps produce audiences and their reception of texts. Fiske's claim, for instance, that a cultural studies analysis of Madonna merely needs to analyse her texts and the ways that her audiences use the texts overlooks the social construction of 'Madonna', her audiences and the ways that her marketing strategies, use of new media technologies, and resonance to her sociohistorical moment all account for important dimensions of the 'Madonna phenomenon'.

Madonna herself first appeared in the moment of Reaganism and embodied the materialistic and consumer-oriented ethos of the 1980s ('Material Girl'). She also appeared at a time of dramatic image proliferation, associated with MTV, fashion fever and intense marketing of products. Madonna was one of the first MTV music video superstars who consciously crafted images to attract a mass audience. She used top production personnel to produce her videos and music and brilliant marketing strategies to incorporate ever larger audiences. Her early music videos were aimed at teenage girls (the Madonna 'wanna-be's), but she also incorporated black, Hispanic and minority audiences with her images of interracial sex and a multicultural 'family' in her concerts. She appealed as well to gay and lesbian audiences, and eventually to feminist and academic audiences, as her videos became more complex and political ('Like a Prayer', 'Express Yourself', 'Vogue', and so on).

Madonna also had at her disposal one of the top publicity firms in the business and probably no performer in the past decade has had more publicity or was more in the public eye. Thus, Madonna's popularity was in large part a function of her marketing and public relations strategies, and her production of music videos and images that appealed to diverse audiences was a function of new technologies of music video and the ascendancy of MTV, with which she was immediately associated. The meanings and effects of her artefacts can best be discerned within the context of their production and reception, which involves discussion of MTV, the music industry, concerts, marketing and the production of images. Understanding Madonna's popularity also requires focus on audiences, not just as individuals, but as members of specific groups, such as teenage girls, who were empowered in their struggles for individual identity by Madonna, or gays, who were also empowered by her incorporation of alternative images of sexuality within popular mainstream cultural artefacts. Yet appraising the politics and effects of Madonna also requires analysis of how her work might merely reproduce a consumer culture that defines identity in terms of images and consumption.

Fetishism of the audience and the popular

Indeed, in many versions of contemporary cultural studies, the focus on the audience and reception is too one-sided. Hence, there is the danger of the fetishism of the audience in the recent emphasis on the importance of reception and audience construction of meanings.[9] On the whole, there has been a large-scale shift in emphasis during the past decade within cultural studies from focus on text and the context of its production to emphasis on the audience and reception, in some cases producing a new dogmatism whereby the audience, or reader, alone produces meaning. The texts, society and system of production and reception disappear in the solipsistic ecstasy of the textual producer, in which there is no text outside of reading – resulting in a parody of Derrida's *bon mot* that there is nothing outside of the text.

Furthermore, there has been a fetishism of resistance in some versions of cultural studies. There is a tendency within the cultural studies tradition of reception research to dichotomize between dominant and oppositional readings. Hall's distinctions between 'dominant', 'negotiated', and 'oppositional' readings (1980b) is flattened in Fiske's work to a dichotomy between the dominant and the oppositional. 'Dominant' readings are those in which audiences appropriate texts in line with the interests of the dominant culture and the ideological intentions of a text, as when audiences feel pleasure in the restoration of male power, law and order, and social stability at the end of a film like *Die Hard*, after the hero and representatives of authority eliminate the 'terrorists' who had taken over a high-rise corporate headquarters. An 'oppositional' reading, by contrast, celebrates the resistance to this reading in audience appropriation of a text; for example, Fiske (1993) observes resistance to dominant readings when homeless individuals in a shelter cheered the destruction of police and authority figures, during repeated viewings of a video-tape of *Die Hard*.

There is, however, a tendency in cultural studies to celebrate resistance *per se* without distinguishing between types and forms of resistance (a similar problem resides with indiscriminate celebration of audience pleasure in certain reception studies). Thus resistance to social authority by the homeless evidenced in their viewing of *Die Hard* could serve to strengthen brutal masculinist behaviour and encourage manifestations of physical violence to solve social problems. Violence, however, as Sartre, Fanon and Marcuse, among others, have argued, can be either emancipatory, directed at forces of oppression, or reactionary, directed at popular forces struggling against oppression. Many feminists, in turn, see all violence as forms of brute masculinist behaviour and many people involved in peace studies see it as a problematical form of conflict resolution. Moreover, unqualified valorization of audience resistance to preferred meanings as good *per se* can lead to populist celebrations of the text and audience pleasure in its use of cultural artefacts. This approach, taken to an extreme, would lose its critical perspective and would lead to a populist positive gloss on audience experience of whatever is being studied. Such studies also might lose sight of the manipulative and conservative effects of certain types of mass-mediated culture and thus serve the interests of the cultural industries as they are presently constituted.

While emphasis on the audience and reception was an excellent correction to the limitations of purely textual analysis, I believe that in recent years cultural studies has overemphasized reception and textual analysis, while underemphasizing the production of culture and its political economy.[10] While earlier the Birmingham groups regularly focused attention on media institutions and practices, and the relations between media forms and broader social forms and ideologies, this emphasis has waned in recent years, to the detriment of much current work in cultural studies, I would argue. For instance, in his classical programmatic article 'Encoding/Decoding' Stuart Hall began his analysis by using Marx's *Grundrisse* as a model to trace the articulations of 'a continuous circuit', encompassing 'production–distribution–production' (1980b: 128ff.). He concretizes this model with focus on how media institutions produce messages, how they circulate and how audiences use or decode the messages to produce meaning.

Moreover, in a 1983 talk published in 1985/1986, Richard Johnson provides a model of cultural studies similar to Hall's earlier model, based on a diagram of the circuits of production, textuality and reception, similar to the circuits of capital stressed by Marx (see his diagram on p. 47). Although Johnson emphasizes the importance of analysis of production in cultural studies and criticizes *Screen* for abandoning the perspective of production in favour of more idealist and textualist approaches (pp. 63ff.), much work in cultural studies has replicated this neglect. One could indeed argue that most recent cultural studies have tended to neglect analyses of the circuits of political economy and production in favour of text and audience-based analyses.

Indeed, the fetishism of the popular in contemporary cultural studies overlooks the role of marketing and public relations strategies in helping to produce the popular. The 'popular' is not just created by audiences alone as Fiske would have it, but is negotiated between audiences and cultural producers with the mediation of cultural industry hype, public relations and critical media discourses. In other words, part of the popular is produced by advertising, public relations, critics' praises or generating of controversies, and general media discussion which tells audiences that they *must* see this film, watch this television show, listen to this music, be familiar with this celebrity to be with it, to be in the know. I discussed the role of marketing strategies, public relations, critical hype and media discourses in producing the Madonna phenomenon above, and will note here how the Michael Jackson phenomenon is at least in part a product of the hype surrounding him and his successful image manipulations and public relations strategies.

Indeed, after years of superstardom promoted by MTV specials, a tremendous amount of media promotion and successful advertising campaigns and marketing of his product and image, it appeared that Michael Jackson's reputation might be destroyed when there were recurrent accusations of sexual molestation of children. But after settling financially with the family of a young boy who had claimed that Jackson had sexually abused him, Jackson undertook a desperate attempt at an image refurbishing campaign. He married Lisa Marie Presley, Elvis' daughter, thus positioning him as a husband, a father (of Lisa Marie's children by a previous marriage) and as in the lineage of pop music royalty, as a successor to the throne held by King Elvis. With the 1995 release of *HisStory*, a multi-record collection of his greatest hits and current work,

Jackson undertook a massive publicity campaign with Sony records supported with a $30 million budget. The record did not match his earlier sales, but at least brought Jackson back into the limelight as it was accompanied by an unparalleled media blitz in the summer of 1995 with ABC Television dedicating entire special programmes to Jackson and his wife, and to Jackson on-line with his fans in a live Internet 'dialogue'. Not to be outdone, MTV devoted an entire week's prime time programming to Jackson which presented him as the King of Pop. But Jackson's separation from Presley in 1996 produced a new round of negative media commentary and provided yet another challenge to the Jackson publicity machine to once more reconstitute and refurbish his image. Those who live by the media can also die by it.

Analysing the marketing and production of stardom and popularity thus demonstrates how the popular is a negotiated interaction between the culture industries and audiences. Obviously, for a celebrity or product to be popular they must resonate to audience experiences and fantasies, but the culture industries pay people incredible amounts of money to research precisely what will sell and then aggressively market this product. Breaking with a fetish of the popular can help reveal how the popular is a construct and could also help to demystify the arguably false idols of media culture and to produce more critical audience perception. Analysing the business dimension of media culture can thus help produce critical consciousness as well as better understanding of its production and distribution. Such a dimension, I have been arguing, enhances cultural studies and contributes to developing a critical media pedagogy that supplements analysis of how to read media texts and how to study audience use of them.

The fetishism of the popular also induces dominant trends in British and North American cultural studies to the neglect of high culture and the engagement of modernist and avant-garde movements such as distinguished the work of the Frankfurt School, whose analyses ranged from the most esoteric modernist art to the most banal artefacts of media culture. It appears that in its anxiety to legitimate study of the popular and to engage the artefacts of media culture, cultural studies has turned away from so-called high or elite culture in favour of the popular. But such a turn sacrifices the possible insights into all forms of culture and replicates the bifurcation of the field of culture into a 'popular' and 'elite' (which merely inverts the positive/negative valorizations of the older high/low distinction). More importantly, it disconnects cultural studies from attempts to develop oppositional forms of culture of the sort associated with the 'historical avant-garde' (Bürger, 1984). Avant-garde movements like Expressionism, Surrealism and Dada wanted to develop art that would revolutionize society, that would provide alternatives to hegemonic forms of culture.

The oppositional and emancipatory potential of avant-garde art movements was a primary focus of the Frankfurt School, especially Adorno, and it is unfortunate that British and North American cultural studies have largely neglected engaging avant-garde art forms and movements. This is connected with a failure of many versions of cultural studies and the sociology of culture to develop a radical cultural and media politics, such as is found in the works of Brecht and Walter Benjamin, concerned with cultural politics and the development of alternative oppositional cultures.

Towards a multiperspectival cultural studies

To conclude: I am proposing that cultural studies and a sociology of culture develop a multiperspectival approach, which includes investigation of a wide range of artefacts interrogating relationships within the three dimensions of:

1   the production and political economy of culture;
2   textual analysis and critique of its artefacts; and
3   study of audience reception and the uses of media/cultural products.[11]

This proposal involves suggesting, first, that cultural studies itself be multiperspectival, getting at culture from the perspectives of political economy and production, text analysis and audience reception.[12] I would also propose that textual analysis and audience reception studies utilize a multiplicity of perspectives, or critical methods, when engaging in textual analysis, and in delineating the multiplicity or subject positions, or perspectives, through which audiences appropriate culture. Moreover, I would argue that the results of such studies need to be interpreted and contextualized within critical social theory to delineate adequately their meanings and effects.

One can obviously not deploy the full range of methods and perspectives that I have discussed in each specific project that one undertakes, and the nature of particular projects will determine what perspectives are most productive. But one should none the less see the dimensions of political economy, textual analysis and audience research as complementing each other rather than as constituting separate domains. I am not, therefore, making the impossible suggestion that one adopt this comprehensive multiperspectival approach every time one sets out to do cultural studies or a piece of communications research. Obviously, intensely focusing on political economy, on audience reception, or on close textual reading and criticism alone can be very valuable and yield important insights. But exclusively and constantly focusing on one of these dimensions to the exclusion of others can be destructive for a sociology of culture or cultural studies that aims at developing comprehensive and inclusive approaches to culture and society, that interrogates culture in all of its dimensions.

Such a transdisciplinary project involves a synthesis of the Frankfurt School, British cultural studies, postmodern theory and other new approaches, combining empirical research, theory and critique. A new cultural studies would reject the distinction between high and low culture and would study a wide range of cultural artefacts. It would use the concept of an active audience and valorize resistance, but also explore manipulation and more passive reception. An activist cultural studies would follow earlier trends of British cultural studies with detailed focus on oppositional subcultures and alternatives to mainstream culture, but would also devise strategies of alternative media and an activist cultural politics. It would combine the Frankfurt School focus on political economy, on media manipulation, and on the ways that culture reproduces domination, with scrutiny of the emancipatory potential of a wide range of cultural artefacts ranging from modernism and the avant-garde to critical and subversive moments in media culture.

A critical sociology of culture and cultural studies would also draw upon feminist approaches and a range of multicultural theories to analyse fully the functions of gender, class, race, ethnicity, nationality, sexual preferences, and so on which are so important in constituting cultural texts and their effects, as well as fundamentally constitutive of audiences who appropriate and use texts. British cultural studies progressively adopted a feminist dimension, paid greater attention to race, ethnicity and nationality, and focused on sexuality, as the various discourses of race, gender, sex, nationality and so on circulated in response to social struggles and movements. Indeed, it is of crucial importance for a sociology of culture and cultural studies continually to appropriate the latest theoretical discourses and to modify its assumptions, programme and discourses in response to critiques of its previous work, the emergence of new theories that can be used to strengthen one's future work and new social movements which produce new critical political discourses. Both the Frankfurt School and British cultural studies continually modified their work in response to new theoretical and historical developments and in a period of rapid social-historical change and the proliferation of ever new theories, engagement with theory and history is of fundamental importance for all disciplines.

But a new cultural studies would also productively engage postmodern theory. We are currently living in a new image culture in which new technologies are changing every dimension of life from the economy to personal identity. In a postmodern media and computer culture, new critical strategies are needed to read narratives, to interpret the conjunctions of sight and sound, words and images, that are producing new cultural spaces, forms and experiences. This project also involves exploration of the new cyber-space and modes of identities, interaction and production that are taking place in the rapidly exploding computer culture, as well as exploring the new public spaces where new forms of political debate and struggle are evolving (Kellner, 1995b). Finally, a future-oriented sociology of culture should look closely at the development of the media and computer industries, the mergers and synergies taking place, and the new synthesis of information and entertainment, computer and media culture that are being planned and already implemented. A new techno-culture is our life world and fate, and we need to be able to chart and map it accordingly to survive the dramatic changes currently taking place and the even more transformative novelties of the rapidly approaching future.

Notes

1 Of course, there are still cultural conservatives who hold on to the idealist concept of culture advocated by Arnold, but they tend to be isolated in literature or art departments, while among the general academic milieu and fields of social theory the broader notion of culture – which includes practices of everyday life and a wide range of artefacts – is dominant.

2 On the Frankfurt School theory of the cultural industries, see Horkheimer and Adorno, [1947] 1972; the anthology edited by Rosenberg and White, 1957; the reader edited by Bronner and Kellner, 1989; the discussions of the history of the Frankfurt School in Jay, 1971 and in Wiggershaus, 1994; and the discussion of the Frankfurt School combination of social theory and cultural criticism in Kellner, 1989a.

3 I have analysed some of these effects from a reconstructed critical theory perspective in analyses of Hollywood film with Michael Ryan (Kellner and Ryan, 1988), two books on American television (Kellner, 1990, 1992), and a series of media cultural studies (collected in Kellner, 1995a and Best and Kellner, 1997).

4 There were, to be sure, some exceptions and qualifications to this 'classical' model: Adorno would occasionally note a critical or utopian moment within mass culture and the possibility of audience reception against the grain; see the examples in Kellner, 1989a. But although one can find moments that put in question the more bifurcated division between high and low culture and the model of mass culture as consisting of nothing except ideology and modes of manipulation which incorporate individuals into the existing society and culture, generally, the Frankfurt School model is overly reductive and monolithic, and thus needs radical reconstruction – which I have attempted to do in work over the past two decades.

5 The field of communications was bifurcated into a division, described by Lazarsfeld (1941) in an issue edited by the Frankfurt School on mass communications, between the critical school, associated with the Institute for Social Research, contrasted to administrative research, which Lazarsfeld defined as research carried out within the parameters of established media and social institutions and which would provide material that was of use to these institutions – research with which Lazarsfeld himself would be identified. Hence, it was the Frankfurt School that inaugurated critical communications research and I am suggesting that a return to a reconstructed version of the original model would be useful for media and cultural studies today.

6 In the 1930s model of critical theory, theory was supposed to be an instrument of political practice. Yet the formulation of the theory of the culture industries by Horkheimer and Adorno ([1947] 1972) in the 1940s was part of their turn toward a more pessimistic phase in which they eschewed concrete politics and generally located resistance within critical individuals, like themselves, rather than within social groups, movements or oppositional practices. Thus, the Frankfurt School ultimately is weak on the formulation of oppositional practices and counterhegemonic cultural strategies.

7 For standard accounts of this phase of British cultural studies, see Agger, 1992; Fiske, 1986; Grossberg, 1989; Hall, 1980b; Johnson, 1985/6; McGuigan, 1992; O'Connor, 1989; Turner, 1990. For readers documenting the positions of British cultural studies, see the articles collected in Grossberg et al., 1992 and During, 1993.

8 'Textualism' was especially one-sided in North American 'new criticism' and other literary practices which for some decades in the post-Second World War conjuncture defined the dominant approach to cultural artefacts. The British cultural studies focus on audience and reception, however, was anticipated by the Frankfurt School: Walter Benjamin focused on the importance of reception studies as early as the 1930s, while Adorno, Lowenthal and others in the Frankfurt School carried out reception studies in the same era. See the discussion in Kellner 1989a: 121ff. Apart from some exceptions, however, the Frankfurt School tended to conceive of the audience as primarily passive, thus the Birmingham emphasis on the active audience is a genuine advance, though, as I am arguing, there have been some exaggerations on this issue and qualifications to the notion of the active audience are now needed.

9 Some examples of an audience-centred cultural studies include Ang, 1985; Brunsdon and Morley, 1978; Fiske, 1989a, 1989b; Radaway, 1983.

10 Most North American cultural studies and other varieties of cultural studies which have been influenced by postmodern theory likewise neglect production and political economy. I am not sure whether this is the influence of Baudrillard's pronouncements on 'the end of political economy' ([1976] 1993), or just laziness and ignorance of the domain of political economy, or a certain softness in practitioners of cultural studies who are uncomfortable with the 'hard' domains of production and economics.

11 I set out this multiperspectival approach in an earlier article and book on the Gulf war as a cultural and media event (Kellner, 1991, 1992), and illustrate the approach in studies of the Vietnam war and its cultural texts, Hollywood film in the age of Reagan, MTV, TV entertainment like *Miami Vice*, advertising, Madonna, cyberpunk fiction and other topics in Kellner, 1995a. Thus, I am here merely signalling the metatheory that I have worked out and illustrated elsewhere.

12 Curiously, Raymond Williams (1981) equates precisely this multiperspectival approach in his textbook on the sociology of culture to a mainstream 'observational sociology' perspective, though I am suggesting more critical and sophisticated approaches to production, textual analysis and audience reception. Interestingly, Williams privileges an institution and production approach in his sociology of culture, whereas British and North American cultural studies have neglected these dimensions for increasing focus on audiences and reception.

Bibliography

Adorno, T.W. (1981) *In Search of Wagner*. London: Verso Books.

Adorno, T.W. (1991) *Notes on Literature. Volume One*. New York: Columbia University Press.

Adorno, T.W. (1992) *Notes on Literature. Volume Two*. New York: Columbia University Press.

Agger, B. (1992) *Cultural Studies*. London: Falmer Press.

Ang, I. (1985) *Watching Dallas*. New York: Methuen.

Antonio, R.J. and Kellner, D. (1992) *Metatheorizing Historical Rupture*. London: Sage.

Arnold, M. (1963) *Culture and Anarchy*. Cambridge: Cambridge University Press.

Baudrillard, J. ([1976] 1993) *Symbolic Exchange and Death*. London: Sage.

Benjamin, W. (1969) *Illuminations*. New York: Schocken Books.

Best, S. and Kellner, D. (1991) *Postmodern Theory: Critical Interrogations*. London/New York: Macmillan/Guilford Press.

Best, S. and Kellner, D. (1997) *The Postmodern Turn*. New York: Guilford Press.

Bronner, S. and Kellner, D. (1989) *Critical Theory and Society. A Reader*. New York: Routledge.

Brunsdon, C. and Morley, D. (1978) *Everyday Television: 'Nationwide'*. London: British Film Institute.

Bürger, P. (1984) *Theory of the Avant-Garde*. Minneapolis: University of Minnesota Press.

Centre for Contemporary Cultural Studies (1980) *On Ideology*. London: Hutchinson.

de Certeau, M. (1984) *The Practice of Everyday Life*. Berkeley, CA: University of California Press.

During, S. (1993) *The Cultural Studies Reader*. London and New York: Routledge.

Eliot, T.S. (1949) *Christianity and Culture*. New York: Harcourt, Brace & World.

Fiske, J. (1986) 'British cultural studies and television', in R.C. Allen (ed.), *Channels of Discourse*. Chapel Hill: University of North Carolina Press. pp. 254–89.

Fiske, J. (1987) *Television Culture*. New York and London: Routledge.

Fiske, J. (1989a) *Reading the Popular*. Boston, MA: Unwin Hyman.

Fiske, J. (1989b) *Understanding Popular Culture*. Boston, MA: Unwin Hyman.

Fiske, J. (1993) *Power Plays, Power Works*. New York and London: Verso.

Grossberg, L. (1989) 'The formations of cultural studies: an American in Birmingham', *Strategies*, 22: 114–49.

Grossberg, L., Nelson, C. and Treichler, P. (1992) *Cultural Studies*. New York: Routledge.

Hall, S. (1980a) 'Cultural studies and the centre: some problematics and problems', in S. Hall et al., *Culture, Media, Language*. London: Hutchinson. pp. 15–47.

Hall, S. (1980b) 'Encoding/decoding', in S. Hall et al., *Culture, Media, Language*. London: Hutchinson. pp. 128–38.

Hall, S. (1987) 'On postmodernism and articulation: an interview', *Journal of Communication Inquiry*, 10(2): 45–60.

Hall, S., Hobson, D., Lowe, A. and Willis, P. (1980) *Culture, Media, Language*. London: Hutchinson.

Horkheimer, M. and Adorno, T.W. ([1947] 1972) *Dialectic of Enlightenment*. New York: Herder and Herder.

Jay, M. (1971) *The Dialectical Imagination*. Boston: Little, Brown & Co.

Johnson, R. (1985/86) 'What is cultural studies anyway?', *Social Text*, 16: 38–80.

Kellner, D. (1978) 'Ideology, Marxism, and advanced capitalism', *Socialist Review*, 42 (Nov–Dec): 37–65.

Kellner, D. (1979) 'TV, ideology, and emancipatory popular culture', *Socialist Review*, 45 (May–June): 13–53.

Kellner, D. (1982) 'Kulturindustrie und Massenkommunikation. Die Kritische Theorie und ihre Folgen', in Wolfgang Bonss and Axel Honneth (eds), *Sozialforschung als Kritik*. Frankfurt: Suhrkamp.

Kellner, D. (1989a) *Critical Theory, Marxism, and Modernity*. Cambridge/Baltimore, MD: Polity Press/ Johns Hopkins University Press.

Kellner, D. (1989b) *Jean Baudrillard: From Marxism to Postmodernism and Beyond*. Cambridge/Palo Alto, CA: Polity Press/Stanford University Press.

Kellner, D. (1990) *Television and the Crisis of Democracy*. Boulder, CO: Westview Press.

Kellner, D. (1991) 'Toward a multiperspectival cultural studies', *Centennial Review*, XXVI (1): 5–41.

Kellner, D. (1992) *The Persian Gulf TV War*. Boulder, CO: Westview Press.

Kellner, D. (1995a) *Media Culture. Identity, Politics, and Culture between the Modern and the Postmodern*. London and New York: Routledge.

Kellner, D. (1995b) 'Intellectuals and new technologies', *Media, Culture, and Society*, 17: 427–48.

Kellner, D. and Ryan, M. (1988) *Camera Politica: The Politics and Ideology of Contemporary Hollywood Film*. Bloomington, IN: Indiana University Press.

Lazarsfeld, P. (1941) 'Remarks on administrative and critical communications research', *Studies in Philosophy and Social Science*, IX: 2–16.

Marcuse, H. (1968) *Negations*. Boston, MA: Beacon Press.

McGuigan, J. (1992) *Cultural Populism*. London and New York: Routledge.

Morley, D. (1986) *Family Television*. London: Comedia.

O'Connor, A. (1989) 'The problems of American cultural studies', *Critical Studies in Mass Communication*, December: 405–13.

Radaway, J. (1983) *Reading the Romance*. Chapel Hill, NC: University of North Carolina Press.

Rosenberg, B. and White, D. (eds) (1957) *Mass Culture*. Glencoe, IL: The Free Press.

Turner, G. (1990) *British Cultural Studies: An Introduction*. New York: Unwin Hyman.

Wiggershaus, R. (1994) *The Frankfurt School*. Cambridge, MA: MIT Press.

Williams, R. (1981) *The Sociology of Culture*. New York: Schocken Books.

8 Sex after 'Sexuality': From Sexology to Post-Structuralism

Arlene Stein

During the last half of this century, as Western societies experienced profound and unsettling changes in sexual and gender relations, the sexual realm has become increasingly contested, commercialized and commodified (Freedman and D'Emilio, 1988). The heterosexual couple is still viewed as the building block of social life and social policy, yet the forces holding it together have never been more tenuous. Conservative groupings in the United States and to a lesser extent Britain have successfully capitalized on this growing anxiety by attempting to legislate their own definitions of 'proper' sexuality for all. One need only to look at the current range of public discourse – teen pregnancy, sex education, pornography, abortion and, most explosively of late, AIDS, to support the claim that sex is on the front-line of politics, and is an increasingly important terrain of social relations (Foucault, 1978; Rubin, 1984).

Writing 20 years ago, Ken Plummer suggested that sexuality is 'surrounded by such a veil of emotion, dogma, ignorance and blind prejudice that informed debate and humane help remain scarce, while personal suffering and public confusion remain abundant' (1975: 124). The complex of intimate desires, behaviours, cultural attitudes and identities that has come to be called 'sexuality' fails to receive the sort of reasoned political and intellectual debate it deserves (Stein and Plummer, 1994). But during the past 20 years, some of this 'veil of emotion, dogma, ignorance and blind prejudice' has been removed, at least in scholarly circles, where sexuality has become an increasingly viable area of social research.

The earliest research viewed sexuality in terms of the biological and psychological capacities of individuals existing prior to social life. Rooted in the scientific efforts of nineteenth century sexology, sex was viewed as an overpowering instinctual drive, a 'basic biological mandate' which must be firmly controlled by the cultural and social matrix (Weeks, 1985). In this view, sexual desires and behavioural patterns are powerful, natural and unchanging.

Beginning in the 1960s, sociologists suggested that sex is 'socially constructed'. While sexuality may be grounded in biological drives, these drives are extremely plastic. Humans are driven by their biological constitution to seek sexual release and nourishment, but their 'biological constitution does not tell [them] where they should seek sexual release and what they should eat' (Berger and Luckmann, 1966: 181). Studies suggested that sexuality is shaped by social and cultural meanings and situational encounters and has no natural, ineluctable foundation; it may be subject to sociocultural moulding to a degree surpassed by few other forms of human behaviour (Gagnon and Simon, 1973).

In the current period, the most influential theorizing comes from the late Michel Foucault and his post-structuralist followers, who extend the work of social constructionist theory, conceptualizing sexuality in terms of power, pleasure and practices. Like the interactionists, these theorists suggest that 'the real' is itself an effect, the product of a positivist epistemology. Historically, certain social groups – namely religious, and now medical experts – have possessed disproportionate power to define the meaning(s) of sexuality. Sexuality cannot be separated or understood apart from them.

In the following, I will briefly trace the history of sexual theory, focusing upon three moments: sexology and psychoanalysis; sociological social constructionism; and post-structuralist discourse analysis. Each of these moments marks a reordering of the meaning of sexuality; taken together, they signify a growing reflexivity with respect to sexuality.

Drive theory: sexology, biologism and psychoanalysis

Sex research began in Europe during the latter part of the last century, at a time when medicine was undergoing rapid professionalization, in part the historical product of a long process of 'disenchantment' in which religious authority was overturned in favour of the scientific. Sexologists believed that they could explain the properties of the complex of sexuality by reference to an inner truth or essence and they set out to discover this truth in biology, to devise a 'science of sex' which would reveal a single, basic, uniform pattern ordained by nature itself (Weeks, 1985).

The 'modernization of sex', its transformation into a field for rational rather than moral enquiry, was evidenced by the work of such researchers as Richard Krafft-Ebing, who conducted a series of detailed case studies, categorizing the vast array of sexual variations, from acquired sexual inversion to zoophilia. His elaborate taxonomy of natural sexual 'variations' was conceived against the notion that these were immoral deviations. Sexuality, sexologists believed, inhered in anatomy and physiology, not in values and emotions (Robinson, 1976). The sexual drive was a biological, unchanging force, given at birth.

Drawing a strict separation between the researcher as 'subject' and sex as 'object' of study, such positivistic explanations failed to consider that humans, unlike animals, have the capacity for self-reflection, and that this capacity plays a powerful role in shaping the expression of seemingly physical drives. This was taken up by Sigmund Freud, who devised a more complex and sophisticated psychodynamic understanding of the operation of 'normal' sexuality and its relation to the whole person. Rather than focus on the species, the body or the syndrome, as did sexology, Freud revealed the operations of sexuality through the protracted, intersubjective relationship between analyst and patient. He went beyond positivism to acknowledge the volatile, psychic origins of adult sexuality.

Freud is perhaps best known for his theory of childhood sexuality. Libido, the psychic energy associated with the sexual drive which impels the individual towards erotic activity, is already at work in the infant, he suggests (1905), influencing behaviour and clamouring for gratification. Before the Oedipal phase, the sexuality of the child is labile and relatively unstructured – as Freud put it, 'polymorphously perverse'. In the drama of the Oedipal crisis, the child struggles with incestuous desires for the mother and father, to an eventual identification with the parent of the same sex. This proceeds along a course determined broadly by constitutional factors which are common to all, but which can 'accidentally' vary considerably from person to person. Homosexuality, for example, is the product of a developmental failure in which the child fails to resolve his/her Oedipal complex and identify with the same sex parent.

While he acknowledged that the sexual instinct is made up of component parts, comprised of a direction (some specific aim to accomplish) and an object (the instrument by which the aim is to be fulfilled) that need not vary together, Freud retained a telos of 'normal' development, arguing that when the instinct diverges in terms of aim and object, exists without an object, or is displaced, such sexual fixations result in perversion (Freud, 1905). However much he may have relativized the notion of 'perversions', believing in an essential 'bisexuality', and seeing 'perversion' or 'abnormality' as value-neutral terms, his telos of normal development pathologized deviations from gendered, heterosexual genital sexuality.

For Freud, sexual drives require restraint in order for society to function properly. Sex is a fixed quantity, 'a motor force in culture and an innate force with which culture must contend' (Person, 1987: 38). The instinctual aims of the infant are incompatible with the requirements of civilization; the developmental process which forms subjectivity necessarily entails a great deal of sexual repression and sublimation of desires. This repression helps to shape the individual but it also leads to various perversions and neuroses which 'form part of the normally accepted constitution' (Freud, 1905: 33–4). It is the particular way in which sexual drives are channelled and regulated, rooted in the structure within which the child's love-life is confined, the Oedipal triangle, that gives rise, in Freud's case histories, to 'hysterical misery'.

Sexual desire is deeply structured by infantile experience and internal conflicts not fully resolved, and repressions of instincts in early life. Sexual repression is incorporated into the very structure of the psyche, and is instrumental in forming the mature ego (Chodorow, 1985). It is not something which is imposed upon the adult, from which she/he can be liberated. But the internalization of sexual norms is typically incomplete: unresolved sexual problems and/or unrealized sexual wishes often seek expression in sublimated form, and this sublimation of sexual energies, Freud believed, is the impulse behind creative endeavour and a necessary means of stabilizing the institutions of civilization.

A bitter controversy rages to this day in search of the 'true' Freud, due in large part to his own ambivalence and ambiguities in his writing. The debate centres on the extent to which Freud emphasized psychological versus neuropsychological factors in explicating human behaviour – whether he saw his central task as the search for meaning, seeking clues to the unconscious, or whether he was primarily interested in mechanical and physical analogues: energies, forces, cathexes (Rabow et al., 1987). Klein argued that Freud worked simultaneously with two distinct conceptions of sexuality. The 'clinical theory' focuses upon 'the values and meanings associated with sensual experiences in the motivational history of a person from birth to adulthood', emphasizing psychological factors (1976: 51). The 'metapsychological theory' sees sexuality as an 'energetic force that seeks discharge'.

Whether sexual motives should be seen as inherently social and inter-subjective (a striving to bond), or whether they should be viewed more as instinctual, biologically rooted forces (a striving to relieve sexual tension) is at times unclear. While the clinical, or psychological theory, suggests the existence of an unconscious psychic realm which is relatively autonomous from both biology and society, the metapsychological, or drive-discharge theory is rooted in the biologism of Freud's sexological contemporaries. Metapsychological variants of Freudian theory construct an opposition between human connectedness and human nature, privilege primal aggressive and libidinal drives over love and relationality, and contain an implicit assumption that people are originally antisocial (Chodorow, 1985).

Clinical theory, on the other hand, acknowledges that the sexual realm is not a thing-in-itself, the essence of selfhood which is somehow inscribed on to the individual at birth, but is deeply rooted in intrapsychic fantasies stemming from the individual's infantile sexuality, formed in relation to parental intervention (Freud, 1905). It recognizes the importance of subjectivity and meaning in the shaping of human sexual experience, and is continuous with object-relations theory, an attempt to purge psychoanalysis of its drive orientation (Person, 1987). Yet metapsychological variants have achieved the 'spurious status' of being seen as *the* Freudian theory of sexuality (Klein, 1976).

In the final analysis, Freud extended the meaning of the word 'sex' beyond the sexological emphasis on physical outlet, suggesting that it included all the activities and love that originated in the primitive sexual drives, as well as impulses expressing themselves in ways no longer evidently sexual (Freud, 1920). But even as he expands the meaning of the word 'sexual', the drive model obscures the importance of later develop-ment and adult experience, understates the impact of the social milieu that shapes those experiences, and retains a telos of normal sexual development.

The drive model posited a universal theory of human nature which claimed that 'infancy is transhistorical . . . any human infant has much more in common with all other human infants in all times and places than with the older humans of its own time and place' (Horowitz, 1987: 71).

Therein lie the primary strengths and weaknesses of psychoanalytic theory for understanding sexuality: it puts forth a powerful universal theory of sexual development but is unable adequately to account for sexual diversity or social change. It renders nature partly social, moving beyond the biological determinism of sexology to begin to understand how desire is constituted intersubjectively. By isolating the existence of an unconscious psychic realm autonomous from both biology and society, psychoanalysis moved beyond the simplistic biologism of sexology. Yet its value for analysing sexuality is limited by a drive theory which sees sexuality as a shaper of society, rather than the other way around.

Social constructionism: scripts, identities and cultures

In the 1960s, biological and psychological essentialism was challenged by social constructionism. The notion of determinate, essential sexualities that are given at birth or in early childhood, consistent over time and relatively stable, gave way to a belief that sexuality is fluid, unstable and subject to choice and change. In late modernity, all aspects of social activity are susceptible to chronic revision in light of new information or knowledge (Giddens, 1991). All existence is contingent and is a problem, a project to be worked on. The self becomes a 'reflexive project'. We talk about 'finding ourselves', 'healing ourselves', 'constructing identities' and so forth. Never before have self-identities, and social institutions, been seen as so much subject to conscious, reflexive action. Increasingly, this is true of sexuality as well, according to social constructionists (Giddens, 1992).

The drive model of sexuality which informed sex research was first called into question by the research of Alfred Kinsey. In the 1950s, Kinsey and his associates conducted a series of surveys of the sexual behaviour of middle class Americans, correlating such activities as masturbation, homosexuality and premarital sex with age, class and gender variables. The massive amount of interview data collected revealed the enormous diversity of behaviour within the United States, evidencing a great disparity with the accepted social norm of procreative, heterosexual intercourse. Having uncovered a much greater incidence of homosexual activity, particularly among men, than was popularly believed to exist, the 'Kinsey Scale' placed homosexuality and heterosexuality on a continuum (Kinsey et al., 1948).

Kinsey helped to relativize sexual behaviour and debunk notions of pathology, calling into question rigid sexual norms and laying the foundation for a more liberal sex research. But his research drew preliminary links between sex and social structure at the expense of understanding the connections between sexuality and the self, and failed to get beyond the notion that sexual activity was anything more than a 'summation of orgasms' (Brake, 1982: 23). It was up to symbolic interactionists to examine sexual *meanings*. After having been associated with the Kinsey Institute, Gagnon and Simon (1973) applied a symbolic interactionist approach to studies of sexuality. Incorporating elements from interpretative and behaviourist viewpoints, they suggested that sexuality reflects one's relationship to the world, breaking with drive theory to claim that all sexuality is 'socially constructed'.

When applied to the field of sexuality, the central task of symbolic interactionism was to describe and theorize the processes by which sexual meanings are negotiated through interaction. Against the Freudian model, they argued that sexual behaviour is not somehow fixed in early childhood through the machinations of the Oedipal complex; sexual 'conduct' emerges with adolescence and is, for the most part, discontinuous with early childhood. Sex is not a drive; it has no existence outside of society but is itself a product of social forces, shaped through daily overt influences, part of a life-long learning process (Gagnon and Simon, 1973). Ken Plummer ([1975] 1980) compared the essentialist and constructionist views thus:

> Where the clinician highlights man's physiology, interactionism stresses his consciousness and symbol-manipulating ability: 'drives' become subservient to 'meanings'. Where the clinician highlights fairly permanent sexual structures awaiting 'release', the interactionist analyses the often precarious, always emergent task of constructing and modifying sexual meanings: determinism becomes subservient to man's intentionality and points of choice. Where the clinician views sexuality as an independent variable – one shaped through conjoint action – the social context becomes central for comprehending sexuality as it is commonly experienced in everyday life. ([1975] 1980: 131)

Modern societies tend to bestow an exaggerated importance to sexuality; sexual behaviour is, for the most part, a simple, everyday occurrence constructed from social motives and settings which are variable. Individuals are active agents who negotiate sexual conduct through social interaction. Interactionists shifted the focus from the determining power of social norms to the more interactive developmental and situational circumstances. Sexual behaviour is not a matter of socialization into sexual roles within the family; it is the product of a much more interactive process, embodied in the notion of 'sexual scripts' (Gagnon and Simon, 1973).

Every individual has a motivation to seek out sexual gratification, and it is through socialization that the person learns some or all of the scenarios that are available through which to achieve this, they claimed. A *cultural scenario* is a set of beliefs that specify in general terms the parameters of some social activity, designating the roles involved in the activity, the times and places appropriate for the activity, and the kinds and sequences of activities that are acceptable. A scenario provides general behavioural guidelines, with which an actor matches his/her preferences, and when specific actors interact following these guidelines, their behaviour constitutes a *script*. While certain sexual scripts – heterosexual intercourse, for example – remain dominant in the contemporary era individuals are not shaped by cultural scenarios, or social roles, in any simple fashion: the social world 'requires that we bargain with life for our identities' since 'contemporary societies provide fewer bases for external imposition of continuities' (Gagnon and Simon, 1987: 371). These ideas proved very fruitful for studies of homosexuality and other forms of sexual 'deviance'.

The first wave of constructionist studies of homosexuality was conducted by US labelling theorists and UK 'new deviancy theorists', young radical scholars who rejected the orthodoxies of criminology and traditional deviance study and challenged the very categories of deviance, locating 'deviance', not deviants, within frameworks of power.[1] They analysed the ways in which desires are expressed, sexually and non-sexually, in situationally varied everyday behaviour, the product of earlier experiences and social learning. Against the Freudian view that homosexuality is the product of an individual developmental failure, constructionists suggested that homosexuality was 'socially constructed'. Social stigma masks the fact there is no essential difference between heterosexuals and homosexuals. The differences between those two groups are the effect of cultural categories, specifically the emergence of a 'homosexual role' (McIntosh, 1968). The variability of sexual behaviour across cultures, as evidenced by numerous anthropological studies, calls into question the notion of a discrete group of people called homosexuals, sharing certain common characteristics (Herdt, 1981; Ortner and Whitehead, 1981).

The social science literature on lesbianism after 1960 reflects this shift in understanding: lesbianism ceased to be a sexual or social disease and became, according to Krieger (1982), 'a lifestyle choice linked with a sense of personal identity', a product of multiple influences rather than traceable to a single cause. Indeed, aetiology, or explanations of causes, of homosexuality, ceased to dominate the discussion, replaced by studies of behaviours and perceptions of experience, focusing less on how lesbians differ from the norm to how they are similar to other women. Such studies viewed the homosexual in a social context – in relationships, institutions, communities and a larger society – rather than in isolated individual terms or in relation to a family of origin. They considered homosexuality to be a matter of total personal identity rather than primarily a sexual condition, subject to choice, and as changeable in definition rather than something that is given.

In the broadest sense, there was a shift from 'thinking about lesbianism in terms of deviance, narrowness, simple causation, isolated occurrence, and fixed nature to thinking of it in terms of normality, diversity, multiple influence, social context, choice and change' (Krieger, 1982: 227). Much the same could be said for male homosexuality (Bell and Weinberg, 1979). Reified conceptions of homosexuality as pathology were debunked and deconstructed, setting the stage for a conception of 'homosexual' as 'adjective rather than noun' (Risman and Schwartz, 1988).[2]

Social constructionism was also enthusiastically embraced by feminists, who broadened the definition of sexuality to include non-genital intimate relations and theorized the relationship between power and intimate relations. The 'exchange of women' – compulsory heterosexuality – they suggested, was the bedrock of the sex/gender system (Rubin, 1975); male domination is the central dialectic which orders the 'sex/gender system' (Kitzinger, 1987; MacKinnon, 1987). Some feminists utilized object relations psychoanalytic theory, replacing Freud's notion of primary narcissism with a primary rationality, embodied in the pre-Oedipal relationship of mother and child. In a patriarchal society, dominant conceptions of sex, constructed by men, tend to be individualistic and drive-oriented (Chodorow, 1985). The primary aim of the 'sex drive', object relations theorists suggested, is object seeking rather than pleasure seeking. Adult sexuality is less a single physical event, as in Freudian drive theory, than an interpersonal achievement (Fairbairn, 1952; Greenberg and Mitchell, 1983). For women, the relational aspects of sexuality are key; lesbian relationships, some suggested, are less concerned with sexual expression than with intimate partnership (Rich, 1980).[3]

More recently, social constructionist theory has been central to much research on sexual behaviour and AIDS transmission, a pressing area of current interest, and perhaps the largest category of social scientific writing on homosexuality in the past 10 years. HIV transmission does not tend to respect sexual categories and hetero–homosexual boundaries; though they may engage in homosexual practices at times, contrary to popular stereotypes, many people at risk for HIV infection do not possess gay identities. Social constructionist approaches, which question the naturalness of sexual categories and acknowledge the disjuncture between identities, behaviours and desires, lend themselves well to research in this area (Connell and Kippax, 1990).

In summary, social constructionism brought to studies of sexuality a deep scepticism about the fixity of 'normal' sexuality, and an appreciation for the diversity of sexual patterns historically, cross-culturally and situationally. Rather than see society as shaped by sexuality, they saw sexuality as shaped by society. They problematized the binary relationship between homosexuality and heterosexuality, suggesting that the labels are fictions and a means of social control. The radical theories of this tradition described, and embodied, the growing reflexivity of sexual arrangements, and anticipated a number of ideas which emerged in the 1980s and 1990s in the form of post-structuralist discourse theory.

Discourse theory: power, pleasures and practices

Not only are the forms of regulation of sexual behaviour and the separate elements of a sexual script social constructions, but so too is the notion of sexuality itself, according to discourse theorists. 'Sexuality must not be thought of as a kind of "natural given" which power tries to hold in check, or as an obscure domain which knowledge gradually tries to uncover. It is the name that can be given to a historical construct.' So wrote Michel Foucault (1978: 152), who extended the work of symbolic interactionists and labelling theorists, conceptualizing sexuality in terms of power, pleasure and practices.

Foucault's larger intellectual project was to show how institutional discourses, expressed through expert 'regimes of truth', come to construct subjectivity. Sexuality is not some pre-existing instinct, biological force or transhistorical psychoanalytical category, the truth or essence of our being, held somehow in check through the operation of social norms. Rather, sexuality is constructed through the very operation of these norms. During the Victorian era, as the result of a 'discursive explosion', sexuality became a mainstay of individual identity, heterosexual monogamy came to function as a norm, and sexual deviants came to see themselves as distinct persons, possessing particular 'natures' and stigmatized identities. Sexology and psychoanalysis, disciplines whose object it was to examine and uncover the 'truth' of sex and to explain 'unnatural' sexualities, made sexuality a key component of the modern self through processes of 'individualization' and 'normalization' (1978: 58).

Foucault breaks with the positivist tradition; sex is not a natural, universal entity which can be isolated and 'discovered'. Like the inter-actionists, he argues that 'the real' is itself an effect, the discursive product of a positivist epistemology. Historically, certain social groups – namely religious, and now medical experts – have possessed disproportionate power to define these cultural meanings. Sexuality cannot be separated or understood apart from them. In the end, the only objects of study (or of belief or of consciousness or politics) are not objective realities but epis-temological categories.

One might suppose that he is posing a vision quite compatible with the sociological notion of social control. But for Foucault, there is no pre-existing natural sexual instinct that is repressed by social forces; power is diffuse and productive rather than repressive. It operates relationally, with the full participation of the individuals upon which it impacts, by colonizing a 'microphysics' of powers that operate locally according to their own logic. While power may have originated in the experts, it has since taken on a life of its own, centred in a multiplicity of freeflowing discourses which circulate through time and inscribe themselves upon individuals.

In the face of this diffuse type of power Foucault believes that we can no longer point to any one locus of power, or central institution, such as the family, which can somehow be overthrown, or reformed, thus liberating sexuality. The most we can hope for is that individuals could engage in a critical transgression of social norms, by 'deconstructing' sexual identities, and playing with 'bodies and pleasures' (1978). The hope is that the tremendous role that sexuality plays in society would lessen, and we would move towards a vision of social life as the pure, but diffuse, deployment of power, freed of systems of social norms and roles. This is not a vision of sexual liberation in the sense of Marcuse ([1955] 1969) or Reich ([1945] 1969).

Foucault's theories have been taken up by various theorists, particularly those who are concerned with homosexuality. In naming homosexuality, medical and psychiatric discourses unified the disparate groupings of individuals who possess 'deviant' desires, or engage in homosexual acts. Once individuals are subjected to the power of institutional definitions of sexuality, Foucault tells us, they come to see themselves through these definitions. This is the starting point for a loosely linked body of literature which has come to be known as 'queer theory'. Against essentializing definitions of the lesbian and gay population, queer theory, at least ideally, embraces the indeterminacy of the gay category and suggests 'the difficulty in defining the population whose interests are at stake in queer politics' (Warner, 1991: 16).

Clues as to what queer theory looks like can be glimpsed through some of its (emerging) canonical works, which come mainly from philosophy, literature and cultural studies. Judith Butler (1990) describes the 'unwritten and written codes of heterosexualized gender systems'. Drawing upon the queer practices of drag, cross-dressing and butch-femme, she develops a conception of gender as performance, and of gender parodies as subversive acts. Through readings of modern literature, Eve Sedgwick (1990) describes new ways of knowing and not knowing based on secrecy and outings, arguing that such knowledges constitute a medium of domination that is not reducible to other forms of domination, and that finds its paradigmatic case in the homosexual and the closet. Andrew Parker (1991) re-reads Marx's *Eighteenth Brumaire*, calling our attention to the homosexual dynamics of the collaboration between Marx and Engels and arguing that we need a 'sex-inflected analysis of class formations', an understanding of how sexuality is constitutive of class categories.

In texts like these we see the following hallmarks of queer theory:

1   a conceptualization of sexuality which sees sexual power embodied in different levels of social life, expressed discursively and enforced through boundaries and binary divides;
2   the problematization of sexual and gender categories, and of identities in general. Identities are always on uncertain ground, entailing displacements of identification and knowing;
3   a rejection of civil rights strategies in favour of a politics of carnival, transgression and parody which leads to deconstruction, decentring, revisionist readings, and an anti-assimilationist politics;
4   a willingness to interrogate areas which normally would not be seen as the terrain of sexuality, and to conduct queer readings of ostensibly heterosexual or nonsexualized texts (Stein and Plummer, 1994).

'The sexual order overlaps with a wide range of institutions and social ideologies,' writes Michael Warner (1991: 5), so that 'to challenge the sexual order is sooner or later to encounter those institutions as problems'. The homosexual/heterosexual divide developed in the nineteenth century comes to be a strategy for deconstructing and rereading texts previously assembled through heterosexuality. Much as feminists began treating gender as a primary lens for understanding problems that did not initially look gender-specific, queer theorists analyse nationalism, popular culture icons such as Madonna and Barbie, and just about everything under the sun.

After 'queer theory' it has become difficult to speak of sexual identity, culture, politics, or even sexuality in singular terms. Homosexuality has become 'decentred'. There are many homosexualities: many gay identities, many subcultures, many forms of politics, and even many sexualities, and sometimes the differences among them are as great as those which separate the gay and straight worlds. One could say that these arguments were predated by sociological social constructionism. Problematizing taken-for-granted linguistic codes and categories, symbolic interactionists had an 'elective affinity' with some versions of postmodernism (Denzin, 1986).

Critics of Foucault suggest that he presents a vision fundamentally at odds with many of the premises of modernist sociology (Lash, 1985). Using his work, it becomes difficult to develop a conception of causality central to much sociological enquiry. Correspondence theories of truth are challenged; causal models which analyse structural inequalities that flow from the cultural, social, historical, political, or symbolic realms are problematized (Denzin, 1986). Foucault may fail to provide an understanding of either the grassroots reality that is the object of discourses of power/knowledge, or a real sense of how that control might be resisted; the matter of how power is actually constituted is left rather vague. His attention to texts rather than actual sexual behaviour may lead one to mistake transformations of representations for transformations of conduct (Gagnon and Simon, 1987: 368).

Scientific discourse may indeed have reconstituted sexual practices and identities, fundamentally altering modern subjectivity, as Foucault has argued. But individuals, one could argue, are not simply plastic and directionless; they possess a fundamental core of identity, shaped through early experiences within the family, that resists total administration. Witness, for example, the enormous contributions of the lesbian/gay movements of the 1960s and 1970s, which have made homosexuality a viable option for many women and men. Lacking an appreciation for the dialectical relationship between identities as self-expressions and identities as ascriptive impositions, Foucault may fail to replace it with one that understands the relationship between sexuality and social structure in anything but repressive terms.

Foucault presents a reflexive critique of positivist knowledge, rejecting the notion of drives, and universalistic, totalizing theories such as psychoanalysis. Freud's notion that the family provides the bedrock upon which all individual desire is patterned is no longer applicable, if it ever was; a complex, diffuse array of sexual discourses shape individual subjectivity and sexual identity. Foucault extends the work of social constructionist theories of sexuality, but by suggesting that there is no longer a viable subject which is able to resist the defining power of sexual discourses, he may understate the possibility of constructing sexual arrangements to suit human needs.

Conclusion

We began with a look at how sexology, and at times Freudian theory, embodied a positivism in which techniques and procedures of the social sciences were seen as a means of uncovering laws that could predict and control sexual behaviour. Basic to this conception was the dichotomy of subject and object – the belief that the researcher, as subject, can stand back from the object (sexual behaviour) and study it 'objectively', separating out subject and object, culture and nature, the non-material world of ideas, attitudes, beliefs and the world of physical things.

Essentialist approaches assume an 'undialectical conception of the relationship between what people do and what they think' (Berger and Luckmann, 1966: 91). In response, interpretative sociologists opened up the possibility that institutions and roles may place limits on human behaviour, but such structures are subject to transformation by human action. Individuals shape sexual behaviour through social learning and daily situational interaction. There is no natural sexual impulse which must be repressed in order for society to function smoothly. Here we see the social roots of sexuality, rather than the sexual roots of society. Recent 'queer theory' continues these concerns, locating sexual deviance and transgression at the centre of sexual arrangements, and theorizing the discursive basis of sexualities. Queer theory, and post-structuralist theories of sexuality in general, mark a growing reflexivity. The more we know about sexuality, it seems, the more contested it has become.

However, while social constructionist theory has offered a viable challenge to the biological and psychological determinism of drive theory, questions remain. The 'oversocialized' model (Wrong, 1961) implicit in much social constructionism may skirt the question of how desire comes to be constituted within the individual. Why do people choose to adopt some sexual scripts over others? Why, for example, do some people become homosexual, while others do not? Whether sexuality is as fluid or freely chosen as much of the 'constructionist' literature has supposed is debatable. Notions of the fluidity and malleability of sexuality are often at odds with the experience of many homosexuals (and heterosexuals) who view their sexuality as an unchanging, core characteristic (Epstein, [1987] 1992). Social constructionist theory may fail to explain how deeply needs and desires are related to the development of the self. Missing is a nuanced theory of determination which could account for the persistence of heterosexual hegemony on the individual level.

What is needed is research that links the micro and macro levels, which theorizes the interweaving of personal life and social structure without collapsing towards voluntarism or overdeterminism on one side (as does much sociology) or biological or psychological reductionism (as does sexology and psychoanalysis). In a recent approach that overcomes some of these problems, Gagnon and Simon (1987) have revised their work to suggest that sexual scripts exist at three analytically distinct levels: cultural scenarios (social norms), interpersonal scripts (where social norms and individual desire meet) and intrapsychic scripts (individual desire).

Combining the insights of psychoanalysis, symbolic interactionism and discourse analysis, one could argue that all cultural scenarios which make sexual practices likely or possible are embedded, to some extent, in culture. By virtue of their early experiences, individuals develop certain desires, fantasies and predilections. Through their exposure to the mass media, popular culture, peer groups and other sources, and subsequent inter-actions, these desires shift and solidify into interpersonal scripts. At times, individuals come together to create social movements and subcultures which embody new cultural scenarios, and create new interpersonal scripts (Plummer, 1995). This multi-level model is one avenue for thinking about future research directions in the field of sexuality, a task made all the more important by its growing politicization.

Notes

1 See, for example, Stan Cohen, 'Footsteps in the sand' (1974).

2 There has, however, been a recent resurgence of essentialist research on homosexuality, marked by new biologism. LeVay (1993), for example, has tried to establish a relationship between sexual object choice and brain structure, arguing that it provides the basis for civil rights for homosexuals.

3 The problem with using feminist theory to investigate sexuality is that feminist theorists have been concerned primarily with gender, not sexual dynamics, and tend to conflate the two (Rubin, 1984). Certainly there are important links between sexuality and gender identity; we experience sexuality in a gendered way. For a recent effort to understand the 'sexual' from a feminist perspective in a more nuanced way, see Chodorow, 1994.

References

Bell, A. and Weinberg, M. (1979) *Homosexualities: A Study of Diversity Among Men and Women.* New York: Simon & Schuster.

Berger, P. and Luckmann, T. (1966) *The Social Construction of Reality.* New York: Anchor Books.

Brake, M. (ed.) (1982) *Human Sexual Relations.* New York: Pantheon.

Butler, J. (1990) *Gender Trouble: Feminism and the Subversion of Identity.* New York: Routledge.

Chodorow, N. (1985) 'Beyond drive theory: object relations and the limits of radical individualism', *Theory and Society,* 14: 271–319.

Chodorow, N. (1994) *Femininities, Masculinities, Sexualities: Freud and Beyond.* Lexington, KY: University Press of Kentucky.

Cohen, S. (1974) 'Footsteps in the sand', in M. McIntosh and P. Rock (ed.), *Deviance and Control*. London: Tavistock.

Connell, R.W. and Kippax, X. (1990) 'Sexuality in the AIDS crisis: patterns of sexual practice and pleasure in a sample of Australian gay and bisexual men', *Journal of Sex Research*, 27(2): 167–98.

Denzin, N. (1986) 'Postmodern Social Theory', *Sociological Theory*, 4: 194–205.

Epstein, S. ([1987] 1992) 'Gay politics, ethnic identity: the limits of social constructionism', in E. Stein (ed.), *Forms of Desire*. New York: Routledge. pp. 239–93.

Fairbairn, W.R.D. (1952) *An Object Relations Theory of Personality*. New York: Basic Books.

Foucault, M. (1978) *The History of Sexuality*, vol. 1. New York: Random House.

Freedman, E. and D'Emilio, J. (1988) *Intimate Matters: A History of Sexuality in America*. New York: Harper & Row.

Freud, S. (1905) *Three Essays on the Theory of Sexuality*. New York: Basic Books.

Freud, S. (1920) 'The psychogenesis of a case of homosexuality in a woman', in *The Standard Edition of the Complete Psychological Works of Sigmund Freud*. London: Hogaxler Press and the Institute of Psychoanalysis. Vol. 18, pp. 147–72.

Gagnon, J.H. and Simon, W. (1973) *Sexual Conduct: The Social Sources of Human Sexuality*. Chicago: Aldine.

Gagnon, J.H. and Simon, W. (1987) 'A sexual scripts approach', in J. Geer and W. O'Donohue, *Theories of Human Sexuality*. New York: Plenum. pp. 363–83.

Giddens, A. (1991) *Modernity and Self-Identity*. Stanford, CA: Stanford University Press.

Giddens, A. (1992) *The Transformation of Intimacy*. Stanford, CA: Stanford University.

Greenberg, J. and Mitchell, S. (1983) *Object Relations in Psychoanalytic Theory*. Cambridge, MA: Harvard University Press.

Henslin, J. (ed.) (1971) *Studies in the Sociology of Sex*. New York: Appleton–Century–Croft.

Herdt, G. (1981) *Guardians of the Flutes: Idioms of Masculinity*. New York: McGraw-Hill.

Horowitz, G. (1987) 'The Foucaultian impasse: no sex, no self, no revolution', *Political Theory*, 15: 61–80.

Kinsey, A., Pomeroy, W.B. and Martin, C.E. (1948) *Sexual Behavior in the Human Male*. Philadelphia: W.B. Saunders.

Kitzinger, C. (1987) *The Social Construction of Lesbianism*. Newbury Park, CA: Sage.

Klein, G. (1976) 'Freud's two theories of sexuality', *Psychological Issues*, 9: 14–70.

Krieger, S. (1982) 'Lesbian identity and community: recent social science literature', *SIGNS*, 8: 223–40.

Lash, S. (1985) 'Postmodernity and desire', *Theory and Society*, 14: 1–33.

LeVay, S. (1993) *The Sexual Brain*. Cambridge, MA: MIT.

MacKinnon, C. (1987) 'A feminist/political approach: pleasure under patriarchy', in J. Geer and W. O'Donohue, *Theories of Human Sexuality*. New York: Plenum. pp. 65–90.

Marcuse, H. ([1955] 1969) *Eros and Civilization*. London: Sphere Books.

McIntosh, M. (1968) 'The homosexual role', *Social Problems*, 16: 182–92.

Ortner, S. and Whitehead, E. (eds) (1981) *Sexual Meanings: The Cultural Construction of Gender and Sexuality*. Cambridge: Cambridge University Press.

Parker, A. (1991) 'Unthinking sex: Marx, Engels and the scene of writing', *Social Text*, 29(11): 28–45.

Person, E. Spector (1987) 'A psychodynamic approach', in J. Geer and W. O'Donohue, *Theories of Human Sexuality*. New York: Plenum.

Plummer, K. ([1975] 1980) 'Sexual stigma: an interactionist account', in R. Bocock, R. Hamilton, K. Thompson and A. Waton (eds), *An Introduction to Sociology*. Fontana.

Plummer, K. (1982) 'Symbolic interactionism and sexual conduct: an emergent perspective', in M. Brake (ed.), *Human Sexual Relations*. New York: Pantheon.

Plummer, K. (1995) *Telling Sexual Stories: Power, Change and Social Worlds*. New York: Routledge.

Rabow, J., Platt, G. and Goldman, M. (1987) *Advances in Psychoanalytic Sociology*. Malabar: Krieger.

Reich, W. ([1945] 1969) *The Sexual Revolution: Toward a Self Governing Character Structure*. New York: Farrar, Straus.

Rich, A. (1980) 'Compulsory heterosexuality and lesbian existence', *SIGNS*, 5: 631–61.

Risman, B. and Schwartz, P. (1988) 'Sociological research on male and female homosexuality', *Annual Review of Sociology*, 14: 125–47.

Robinson, P. (1976) *The Modernization of Sex*. New York: Harper & Row.

Rubin, G. (1975) 'The traffic in women', in R. Reiter (ed.), *Toward an Anthropology of Women*. New York: Monthly Review.

Rubin, G. (1984) 'Thinking sex: notes for a radical theory of the politics of sexuality', in C. Vance (ed.), *Pleasure and Danger*. Boston, MA: Routledge.

Sagarin, E. (1971) 'Sex research and sociology', in J. Henslin (ed.), *Studies in the Sociology of Sex*. New York: Appleton–Century–Croft.

Sedgwick, E. Kosofsky (1990) *Epistemology of the Closet*. Berkeley, CA: University of California.

Simon, W. and Gagnon, J. (1986) 'Sexual scripts: permanence and change', *Archives of Sexual Behavior*, April.

Stein, A. (1989a) 'Three models of sexuality: drives, identities and practices', *Sociological Theory*, 7(1): 1–13.

Stein, A. and Plummer, K. (1994) 'I can't even think straight: queer theory and the missing sexual revolution in sociology', *Sociological Theory*, 12(2): 178–87.

Warner, M. (1991) 'Fear of a queer planet', *Social Text*, 29: 3–17.

Weeks, J. (1985) *Sexuality and its Discontents*. London: Routledge.

Wrong, D. (1961) 'The oversocialized conception of man in modern sociology', *American Sociological Review*, 26.

AFFECTIVITY

9 Somatology: Sociology and the Visceral

Sean Watson and Peter Jowers

Contemporary social and political theory fails to explain the visceral and pervasive violence so common in human affairs. Neither can it comprehend any great sacrifice, love or solidarity which denies any 'rational maximization' of advantage. How do we begin to explain the genocides, slaughter, mutilation and fear which so disfigure humanity? Rwanda, Chechnya, Bosnia, East Timor and Iraq are only recent examples. Merely to list them is to do them another theoretical 'violence' (Lyotard, 1988). Only by attempting to understand such matters might a less paranoid style of politics be effected. The writers we discuss have sought both to comprehend and to intervene in specific 'bodily' forms of political action through their writing.

To examine the visceral is to be concerned with 'affect', those feelings and emotions derived from the body. To seek an understanding of the potential human violence coiled within discourses, practices and institutions entails attempts to theorize the flux of bodily desires. Simultaneously we need to remain reflexively alert and understand the desire to produce theory. Theory derived from some version of rational choice models and/or semiotics falls silent when faced with what Derrida has called 'the gap between thought, language and desire' (1992: 184).

We explore:

1 the contrast between certain 'modern' and 'postmodern' authors' theorization of affect;
2 tensions between their varied accounts of ego formation and its links to paranoia;
3 the way in which they all share a concern with the sublime or idiosyncratic; and
4 the links they discover between the breakdown of semiosis and affective perturbation.

First we take the work of Adorno and Horkheimer as exemplifying a modernist/humanist approach to these issues. Then we juxtapose the work of several writers: Gilles Deleuze and Felix Guattari, William Burroughs, J.F. Lyotard and Slavoj Zizek. We show how this latter group of post-modern and posthumanist thinkers proffer roughly comparable attempts to embody in their writing the desiring 'other-side' of signification. They are 'neomaterialists', a concept which must be strictly distinguished from any form of historical materialism. Sharing an interest in the political importance of understanding the workings of desire, they explore its intersection with signification, practices and institutions. They seek to distinguish between benign and malignant forms of desiring bodies. Posthumanists, they produce profoundly new experiences and understandings of the fluid links between the body, mind and material world.

Their strange vocabularies, imagery, neologisms and concepts seem forbidding, often violent and inhuman. Their writing evokes anxiety by violating normal expectations of taste and comprehensibility. It is traversed with strange disturbing hybridities, bizarre assertions and alien locutions. We show that they share a creative and vibrant zest which is directly targeted at the frozen, proto-totalitarian, life-denying social and political 'realities' of our age. Seemingly inhuman, their work is profoundly ethical. We wish to 'translate' between their often rapidly mutating vocabularies to reveal how they overlap and diverge. We assess their importance for a genuine sociology of 'multiplicity', rather than 'difference', where minorities might proliferate.

First, however, we would like to outline some of the themes central to the modern theorists of collective affect.

The moderns: on reflection and the ego

Theodor Adorno and Max Horkheimer's *Dialectic of Enlightenment* ([1944] 1992) is without doubt the most ambitious 'modernist' attempt to theorize the affective core of instrumental rationality, science, modern politics, the culture industry and human destructiveness in the modern age. The analysis reaches its most powerful with the discussion of paranoid hostility and destructiveness as the basis of anti-Semitism.

Human beings are claimed to have biological drives. Primary amongst these is the urge to mimic, or merge with, 'circumambient nature'.[1] However, human self-alienation from nature is deemed necessary if ego formation and individuation is to take place. The history of the human species is one of self-alienation and repression of instinct. Adorno and Horkheimer imply that this is revealed in the structure of mythology.

The species is not comfortable with itself. Certain social groups come to stand in as reminders of repressed longings; reminders of an idyllic, irrecoverable, happiness. Thus they become the focus for deep resentment and worse. Crucially, what makes these groups reminders of the repressed is that they are 'felt' to be different at some very deep, bodily level. This is revealed in things like their bodily gestures, their smell, their habits of dress, their music. These characteristics all somehow subtly, but very deeply, jar against the norm. They are 'idiosyncratic'.

Thus the presence of the Other in our midst somehow threatens to awaken forbidden desires. This in turn poses a threat to the integrity of the psyche itself, which is dependent for its existence on such renunciation. The threatened psyche is incapable of controlling its inner turmoil, nor can it purge itself of its repressed desires. Instead, these desires are projected outwards together with controlling, purging and destructive behaviour.

Thus we dispel our anxiety and gain perverse pleasure from dominating, controlling and purging our social surroundings – attacking our repressed desires in their projected form. Instrumental rationality, modern science, bureaucracy and capitalist economic behaviour, the elements of Weber's modern nightmare, appear in a new light. They are the inevitable conse-quence of an insatiable desire for controlling activity. At the pinnacle of this nightmare of twisted affective responses is Fascism, whose totali-tarianism lies fundamentally in the fact that 'it seeks to make the rebellion of suppressed nature against domination directly useful to domination' (Adorno and Horkheimer, [1944] 1992: 184). In other words, Fascism is a political phenomenon whose affective motor is the sublimated form of the very instincts which it suppresses. It is interesting that Slavoj Zizek, one of the postmodernists we shall be discussing, makes the very same point, but in a postmodern vocabulary.

> The Jew is the means, for Fascism, of taking into account, of representing its own impossibility: in its positive presence, it is only the embodiment of the ultimate impossibility of the totalitarian project – of its immanent limit. This is why it is insufficient to designate the totalitarian project as impossible, utopian, wanting to establish a totally transparent and homogenous society – the problem is that in a way, totalitarian ideology knows it, recognises it in advance: in the figure of the 'Jew' it includes this knowledge in its edifice. (1989: 127)

Where Adorno and Horkheimer locate the source of projected destruc-tiveness in repressed instincts, Zizek locates the same destructiveness in 'lack', or 'constitutive impossibility' at the heart of symbolic processes. Fascism can never attain symbolic closure (purity), indeed were it to do so then it would reach a point of affective stasis, thus robbing it of its dynamism.

Also very striking are the parallels between Adorno and Horkheimer's analysis of scientific rationality as paranoid in character, with Jacques Lacan's analysis of 'paranoid knowledge' (Lacan is, of course, Zizek's key theoretical point of departure). Again the argument is virtually identical in structure (Lacan, 1977: 17). Indeed, in Lacan's early work the paradigm is still highly biological rather than linguistic, making the line of argument look uncannily similar to Adorno and Horkheimer's.[2]

Adorno and Horkheimer claim that the paranoid and destructive tendencies have been peculiarly intense in this century. The explanation for this lies in the political-economy of advanced monopoly capitalism. The economic behaviour which is itself a consequence of the structure of the modern psyche is erosive of that self-same psyche (we shall find a similar account in Deleuze and Guattari's postmodern version of events). Current conditions are tending to erode the inner life of human beings, removing whole dimensions of reflective capacity, grinding subjectivity down to what Marcuse famously called 'one dimensionality'. This erosion of individuation, of ego boundaries, of our powers of self understanding, makes us less able than ever to tolerate internal ambivalence, and more likely than ever blindly to project our anxieties. In their view, weak egos make for 'authoritarian personalities', blind hatred, prejudice, suspicion, conspiracy fantasies and the urge to dominate and control or destroy. Their solution is to strengthen reflective consciousness, make stronger egos, more 'centred' subjectivity, more individuation. Strong egos are tolerant egos in this version of events.

This solution is highly characteristic of modernist/humanist analysis and therefore is a crucial point of divergence from the postmodernists such as Deleuze and Guattari. For them, as we shall see, the propping up of Oedipalized subjectivity is itself a concession to the paranoid forces of modernity. The only way out of the impasse is complete psychic fragmentation.

Schematically we can put it like this. For the postmodernist (as we shall see) fragmentation, dislocation and schizophrenic fluidity of the psyche lies in opposition to paranoid tendencies which seek coherence, rigidity, closure, homogeneity, purity and order. As such 'schizo' conditions are perceived to be positive and desirable. For the modernist/humanists, in contrast, schizophrenic fragmentation is always closely allied to paranoid affect as the former inspires anxiety and even terror which can only be dealt with, in the last desperate instance, by paranoid psychic mechanisms, often translated into bodily rigidities.[3] This is why more solid, reflective, self-confident subjectivity is always desirable.

Put into the vocabulary of the 'Kleinian' tradition of psychoanalytic theory, this latter schema becomes the distinction between the 'paranoid-schizoid position' on the one hand and the 'depressive' position on the other. Strong recent contributions to social and political theory derived from this tradition have been made by Michael Rustin (1991), Paul Hoggett (1992a, 1992b) and John Bird (1994), for example. It is beyond the scope of this chapter to outline their arguments in any detail. What is striking about them, however, is that they do not suggest the possibility of a normalized psychic life entirely free of internal contradiction, tension and ambivalence (this is how the modernist/humanists are often characterized by the post-modernists). Instead they emphasize the development of a kind of psychic strength which makes it possible to bear ambivalence and contradiction. Instead of resorting to paranoid-schizoid strategies of 'splitting' the world into good and evil we, at an individual and collective level, are able to acknowledge and bear contradictory desires and qualities in ourselves and others. We become truly, affectively tolerant of ourselves and others. This inner strength is the key to less ordering, controlling, dominating behaviour. For the postmodernists however, the 'inner world' is always suspect.

Deleuze and Guattari: desire and the material sign

Following Spinoza and Nietzsche, Deleuze and Guattari write of a human body that is capable of being affected, of having feelings, passions and sensations. Affects are flows of chemical, electrical, thermal and kinetic energy, and flows between these energy states. The energy states of the material body are linked to those outside it; there are connective flows between the body, other bodies, objects, matter. Within the realm of the human a major element of these connected flows (sometimes called 'desiring-machines' or 'assemblages') are signs. Signs are material objects with exactly the same ontological status as all other elements in these matter/energy assemblages. They serve as special connectors, or channels grooving the body into habits of feeling. Our pleasure and pain arise within linguistically grooved material assemblages connecting our body to itself and other objects (such as this text) in relatively predictable patterns.

At the philosophical level there is an ontological realism and materialism but an epistemological relativism. Since the sign has exactly the same ontological status as the referent, it cannot be transcendent. Knowledge can never be 'of' the world, it can only be 'in' the world. Deleuze describes himself and his philosophical forebears as developing a 'philosophy of immanence', in contrast to the major tradition of transcendence and logocentrism.

Over a period of some 25 years Deleuze and Guattari have developed a radical social and political theory out of this tradition. What are the major premises, mechanisms and implications of their work?

Desire is always potentially creative energy (sometimes called 'desiring-production'). Lack/want/need, on the other hand, is something which is itself artificially created. The fusion of desire and lack at the heart of the modern subject is a product of a certain sociopolitical organization, in particular, the combination of the modern state and the Oedipalizing family.

Modern subjects are simply one kind of assemblage among many. Parts of the body are linked to other objects, signs, energy flows in endless systems of productive activity. The connections which can be made, the channels which can be formed are, in theory, infinite. The 'schizo' hero/ine of the Anti-Oedipus is the perfectly random connecter (Deleuze and Guattari, 1977). S/he randomly connects signs, energy flows, data, knowledge, fantasy, objects and bodies in new flows of desiring production. S/he is the most extreme version of the 'nomadic subject'. This is a subject defined not by its fixity of identity but by its endless migration across the networks of assemblages/desiring machines. In some ways to call it a subject at all is a misnomer: it could perhaps more accurately be called the anti-subject. By contrast what makes the subject, and indeed society, is the limiting of connectivity and nomadism, the closing down of certain possible avenues of desiring-production. This limiting of desiring-production they call 'anti-production'.

Their technical term for the affective material body is the 'body without organs' (BwO). The combination of the BwO, and its energies, with the limitless resources of linguistic and other cultural codes is the key to the special kind of creativity and mutation which human beings are potentially capable of. The creative sign-body, engaged in nomadic 'lines of flight' across the codes, they call the 'full BwO'. The BwO can, however, be frozen into stasis; it can be grooved by repetitive, habituated, compulsive channels. Not only does such channelling of bodily energy lock the body into stasis but it makes it into the host of an affective parasitism. In particular, in modern society, it produces a sense of lack/need/want at the heart of the subject. This static, ordered body, at the limit, is the 'empty BwO'.

Deleuze and Guattari identify distinctive forms regulating desiring connectivity. Each of these is associated with a particular type of parasitism. At the centre is always a supreme fetishized object, the 'socius'. In relatively nomadic societies of 'supple segmentarity' the socius is the body of the earth. In more rigid despotic societies it is the body of the despot. In capitalism it is the body of capital itself. Below any 'socius' is a whole hierarchical system of fetishized material objects and signs which act as switching stations in channels of affective energy. These objects and signs are collectively known as 'miraculated bodies'. They have a charismatic aura which is actually a product of the object's key function in the assemblage but is misrecognized as an inherent quality of the object itself. Life energy appears to flow from these objects (religious relics, works of art, buildings, national flags, symbols of monarchy, the body of the monarch, great institutions of government, political leaders, symbols of race etc.). Such objects and their manipulation are the stuff of political action and mass culture. Modern man/woman with this socially produced gulf at the centre of subjectivity is offered the shining objects of revenge, order, commodities, nationhood, and so on, in return for passion. Power always aims at fixing the ways in which body/matter/desire/sign connections can be made in this way. The social is a dynamic of material desire.

Language begins as actual marks on the body and on the earth – tattoos, scarification, the marking of sacred sites and so on (the source of this argument in the writings of Durkheim, Mauss and Bataille is evident). These marks are, from the beginning, elements of assemblages connected to, and channelling energy through, the body. Then something comes from the outside. Conquest and despotism arrive. A process of 'overcoding' takes place. This is effectuated by the invention of administrative bureaucracy and writing proper.

Signs float away from the body of the earth. Thus begins the illusion of transcendence. Deleuze and Guattari have consistently argued that power in part comes with the ability to organize or compose systems of signification. Despotism 'deterritorializes'. It shatters the fluid 'worlds' of those it colonizes. It throws them from the body of the earth, from their self-generated local systems of meaning. It then reorganizes them into a system of meaning pivoting upon a 'transcendental signifier' which acts as the organizing pole around which meanings, taxonomies and 're-territorializing' occur.

Signs in reality remain artefacts, but now channel affect to focus on the despot. S/he glows with the charismatic energy produced by his/her particular material assemblages. Writing, bureaucracy and the state follow. Systems of representation are made stable, and recording, surveillance and normalization gradually begin to proliferate.

As capitalism emerges within despotic society such mechanisms of anti-production proliferate all the faster. The capitalist market is fundamentally schizophrenic – combining anything with anything into assemblages that can realize profit. Thus it 'deterritorializes'. The stability of signification of despotic societies is potentially lost as signifiers migrate across assemblages taking on ever different significance. The family and the elements of the state are retained within capitalism as agencies for recoding or, as Deleuze and Guattari put it, 'reterritorialization'. Capitalism oscillates between schizophrenia and paranoia, the latter effectively being terror of the disintegration of the subject and of the heterogeneity of possible assemblages, turned to an impulse to recode, rigidify, limit, homogenize, normalize etc. We can (and they do) read Foucault's story of the massive proliferation of discipline, normalization and surveillance as the concrete manifestations of this paranoid pole of the dynamics of capitalism.

Deleuze and Guattari speak of nomadism, creative 'lines of flight', deterritorialization. Their politics is famously a micro-politics of creative hybridization. It is also a refusal of revolutionary politics in the old mould. They do not seek to come from the 'outside' to become 'inside' – to become majority and ultimately totality. Rather, they seek always to 'become minor' – to make minorities. They are acutely aware (although perhaps not acutely enough) that within the context of this accelerating deterritorialization, and proliferation of minorities, the dark force of paranoia is ever present.

In *A Thousand Plateaus* they write of a 'war machine' which is a mechanism for exploding the frozen desire circuits of the paranoid state/ family mechanisms (Deleuze and Guattari, 1987) – an explosively creative nomadic connector. What would such a 'war machine' look like? Here we turn to William Burroughs.

William Burroughs: anti-literature

William Burroughs' awe-inspiring imaginative fecundity stems from his implacable, austere determination to explode the very rules through which we conceive of reality. His is a determined smashing of the codes of control, a 'cultural bomb'.

A concern with complexity as evolutionary openness, the affirmation of becoming, is a constant refrain within Burroughs' work and informs his insistence upon endless metamorphic possibilities where flesh, desire, the inorganic, the spiritual and politico-cultural elements are endlessly recombined in ever more bizarre forms. This returns thought to matter within us. At its base, thinking is material.

For Burroughs the sense of closure has driven his work from its outset. For Burroughs the sense of being controlled is palpable, visceral and immediate. The manner in which he has tried both to articulate and deal with this horror has mutated endlessly. His most regularly used metaphor for the physicality of social control is the stasis of junk addiction – locked metabolically into static repetitive parasitic patterns of affect, ultimately tending towards a suspension of affect altogether. Dried out, dead husks of bodies, zombies, make endless appearances in Burroughs' work. These, of course, are what Deleuze and Guattari would call 'empty BwOs'. The psycho-cultural equivalents of junk addiction are linguistically embedded 'archetypes'. These are directly comparable with Deleuze and Guattari's 'territorializations'.

Ultimately Burroughs is convinced that something deeply unhealthy lies somewhere at the heart of language's archetypical possession of the body. There are endlessly repeated images of aliens, monstrous creatures and imposter gods (Judeo-Christian gods) deriving their immortality from a revolting parasitism. 'He needs our energy to escape because he has none of his own. Who but an asshole wants to see people grovelling in front of him?' he says of the Judeo-Christian God imposter – the alien. When listing the characteristics and objectives of the aliens he says 'Their most potent tool of manipulation is the word. The inner voice' (Burroughs, [1983] 1989: 92). This could be a line straight out of Nietzsche, Foucault or Deleuze and Guattari.

Burroughs' technical innovations, primarily through writing, informed by these beliefs have sought to resist the ugly spirit and its traps of 'word sludge', 'blind prose', 'word and image locks' and the many other ever shifting terms he uses for this sense of entrapment in signs.

Burroughs also, much earlier than any others in our view, realized the futility of conceiving discourses merely textually. By this we mean that by the late 1950s, using collaborators he pushed way past conceiving of closure as merely textual, as the effects of words. His experiments with sound, with tapes, film and – later – out into video, performance, rap and so on mark an understanding of ever altering technologies and the manner in which they can effect control or be turned against their progenitors. As such Burroughs is in line with the avant-garde of this century and continues their inheritance. It is useless to write of an intertext here. Rather as Nicholas Zurbrugg (1984) has pithily argued, we should be thinking of an 'intermedia' or an 'intercontext', and Burroughs was the one who charted this territory way back in the late 1950s and 1960s, long before the current fad and hype of multimedia: 'What I'm talking about . . . is bringing the revolution into the 20th century, which includes above all, the use of the mass media. That's where the real battle will be fought.'[4]

We are haunted by an image of Burroughs working in an empty room save for three radios tuned to different frequencies of static. For it is in and through the random that the avant-garde of this century have sought one way of breaking the codes that deceive and virally structure us. Randomness. A gun splattering cans of paint into patterns. As he wrote in the catalogue of his exhibition at Cleto Polcina in Rome, May 1989:

> The tonal universe is the every day cause and effect universe, which is predictable because it is pre-recorded. The nagual is the unknown, the unpredictable, the uncontrollable. For the nagual [the term is Carlos Casteneda's] to gain access, the door of chance must be open. There must be a random factor: drips of paint down the canvas, setting the paint on fire, squirting the paint. Perhaps the most basic random factor is the shotgun blast, producing an explosion of colour into unpredictable, uncontrollable patterns and forms. Without this random factor, the painter can only copy the tonal universe, and his painting is as predictable as the universe he copies . . . He who would invoke the unpredictable must cultivate accidents and randomness . . . The bottom line is the creator. (Miles, 1993: 253–4)

This ultimately is how we must understand the perversity and horrors of Burroughs' writing then. It is a continuous attempt to evoke the nagual, the sublime. It is pure literature in the sense that Foucault demands as an antidote to the parasitic, disciplinary, codings of discourse. It is a writing of the 'other'. It is a 'line of flight' *par excellence* in Deleuze and Guattari's sense of a 'scrambling of the codes', a re-channelling of flows of desire, and a politics of rampant creativity. It is a writing of the 'inhuman' in the sense that Lyotard intends. An attempt to break the shackles of our slavery to post-Enlightenment identification with supposed standards of normal 'human' existence and the regimes of normalization that go with that identification, regimes that can ultimately end in extermination of the idiosyncratic, or the 'minor' as Deleuze and Guattari would put it. This violent shattering is not the only possible response, however. Here we turn to the work of J.F. Lyotard.

J.F. Lyotard: openness to the sublime

Lyotard's reflections upon the material, affective body and the sublime are linked. He distinguishes between 'inhumane' actions and the 'non-human', the latter conceived of as matter not assimilable to received forms of human experience. Sublime excess simultaneously always induces anxiety yet is also the material locus for creativity and resistance to signifying closure. He identifies a growing inhumanity in human relations. This is intensified by a techno-scientific instrumental rationality growing ever more powerful in its 'gain or efficiency' but where ethical considerations have become vestigial. Lyotard, like Deleuze and Guattari, and Burroughs, resists the closure of a specific conception of human subjectivity by opening frozen metaphysical borders demarcating between the human and non-human, between the mental and the material. He challenges essentialisms which abound in traditional discussions of human subjectivity. He insists upon the material quality of the mental. He prioritizes the non-human in order to resist the inhumane.

Lyotard's arguments are best understood by way of his discussion of three types of memory. The first produced through signification and then writing, 'opens a public space of meaning' by conserving signs of past events. Producing 'collective or shared memory' gives rise to 'stable energetic set-ups'. Such memory generates myth-based cultures as 'nebulae of clustered intersecting habits'.

The second form of memory takes a reflective turn. Commencing as philosophy it mutates into techno-science. These new genres of signification impose a particular shared conception of the relation of human subjectivity and material nature. These shared metaphysical assumptions result in quantum leaps in our power to use nature yet, simultaneously, questioning of human ends is progressively effaced. Any 'open reactivity . . . fades'. Materiality cannot be assimilated except when filtered by way of deeply sedimented metaphysical assumptions. The contemporary intensification of these tendencies via electronic communication media 'telegraphy', quantitatively intensifies regulated behaviour – 'performativity', 'gain', 'efficiency'. The result is qualitatively deepened forms of ethical inhumanity. The link to Deleuze and Guattari's concept of territorialization and Burroughs' archetypes is evident.

The third memory, 'passing', is a technique with no rule, or a negative rule, deregulation. A generativity with, if possible, no set-up other than the absence of set-up (Lyotard, 1992: 54). Logos, the previous form of memory, is turned against itself. 'The point is to pass beyond synthesis itself.' To experience the sublime is to be open to a materiality which 'has not been inscribed'. The first two forms of memory can only communicate the already known. Such 'information' can only be challenged when 'a scientific, artistic, or philosophical phrase is not susceptible to simple informational transmission'. Innovative signification is a material response to a material experience. Note that Lyotard distinguishes between creative science and techno-science.

Creative practice has the task of producing paradoxical phrases 'that have never been heard of before'. These should result in 'works that are necessarily strange'. To avoid a tyranny of telegraphic transparency – the fantasy of complete communicability – works should be produced 'which bring into question the rules constituting the work as such' (Lyotard, 1986/7: 212–14).

Lyotard's uniqueness is the manner in which he suggests an opening on to this other, very materially conceived sublime. Unlike the discursive violence of Deleuze and Guattari, and Burroughs, he urges a zen-like silence. He writes of a patient, quiet, open, receptive, gentle non-conceptual and felt synthesis of the 'occasion'. Sublimity is a gift only fleetingly granted when the ceaseless chatter of narcissistic auto-erotic projection and return is hushed. His debt to Heidegger and Levinas can only be hinted at here. The occasion will have been independent of 'the diachronic form of internal sense or . . . our way of remembering and anticipating'.

Lyotard's repeated discussion of the sublime in terms of receptivity, the line, tone, timbre, infancy, the 'yet to be encoded' etc. hint at the possibility of other more gentle, less violent tropic economies. How does this connect to our wider discussion of the body?

Lyotard writes of 'an immaterialist materialism'. Matter is vibrating energy. It is complexified within the mind via signs which are material 'transformers'. Derived from Bergson, this material conception of semiotic memory systems lies at the heart of his version of neomaterialism. Memory enables us to delay immediate stimulus/response reactions to alterations in our material environment. They place a gap or gulf or break between material 'input' and active 'human' response. This increases our 'material liberty' but at the cost of 'destabilization of the fit between the human subject and its environment'. Semiotic transformers are a 'supplement of complexity in the universe' (1992: 45–6). At its base thinking is a bodily process with both gains and losses. To break the pattern, territorialization, coding, archetypes, understanding – the terms are roughly comparable – is to alter the 'transformation' process. This is a bodily alteration – it can be visceral. Altereity is founded upon a material affectivity open to the other inhuman within us as materially embodied human subjects capable of 'suffering'. Suffering presumably stands in for the full as yet incomplete affective register. Openness and the capacity to suffer are twins. 'Thought must decide to be irresolute, to be patient, wanting not to want, not producing a meaning in place of what must be signified' (1992: 16).

Slavoj Zizek: the social organization of enjoyment

It should be evident that, despite their differences, this group of writers share common neomaterialist assumptions concerning the interaction of the body and the social. Despite our general sympathy with the projects, we feel some unease. This relates to Deleuze and Guattari's, and Burroughs', underestimation of the potentially destructive anxieties provoked by the 'minor', or idiosyncratic. Within contemporary post-structuralism there seems to be some disagreement regarding the precise conditions which provide the strength to attempt to be, and tolerate, the minor (this is also, of course, the point at which we left discussion of the modernist/humanist tradition).

Slavoj Zizek describes the mechanisms of capitalist libidinal economy in terms remarkably similar to those of Deleuze and Guattari:

> The elementary feature of capitalism consists in its inherent structural imbalance, its innermost antagonistic character: the constant crisis, the incessant revolutionizing of its conditions of existence. Capitalism has no 'normal' balanced state: its 'normal state' is the permanent production of an excess – the only way for it to survive is to expand. (Zizek, 1990: 59)

But where Deleuze and Guattari theorize and embrace the schizophrenic tendency inherent in this lack of 'balance', Zizek, using a Lacanian vocabulary, appears to be the major contemporary theorist of the paranoid backlash.

What holds a community together is not a shared set of values, but a 'shared relationship towards a Thing, towards Enjoyment incarnate'.[5] Interestingly the Thing turns out to be an empty tautology or a collection of fragments – the 'British way of life' – feasts, manners, gender relationships and so on. He notes that at the political level the Thing crops up not only as the underlying structure of the Right but also as a longing for pure community on the Left. As an Eastern European however, his centre of interest currently lies with the way in which the Thing inhabits the politics of nationalism – the 'nation Thing': 'A nation exists only as long as its specific enjoyment continues to be materialized in certain social practices' (Zizek, 1990: 53). The deconstructive emphasis on textual practices, he says, misses this 'real kernel of enjoyment' (Zizek, 1989: 124). This Thing 'is present', it 'appears' through the various elements of 'the way of life' of the community, and more specifically the nation. Ethnic communities, he argues, organize their enjoyment through national myths. Ethnic tensions are always to do with possession of the national Thing. The other is always accused of 'secret', 'perverse' and 'excessive' enjoyment: 'What really bothers us about the "Other" is the peculiar way it organizes its enjoyment: precisely the surplus, the "excess" that pertains to it – the smell of their food, their "noisy" songs and dances, their strange manners, their attitude to work' (Zizek, 1990: 54). (The similarity to Adorno's and Horkheimer's thesis is striking.)

Two arguments follow from this. First, groups organized around different structures of enjoyment will always categorically 'resist universalization'. This seems to put a firm end to Richard Rorty's ideal of a juridically formal, substantively empty, liberal democratic public space within which social diversity, hybridity and self creation, can flourish (Rorty, 1989). Or at least his diversity is limited to something like 'you can be as different from us as you like (at the superficial level) so long as you are the same as us (at the level of enjoyment)'.

This firm denial of such a possibility is seemingly reinforced by another step in Zizek's argument. He claims that antagonism to the Other is manifested in a conviction that the Other has somehow 'stolen' one's enjoyment. The Thing has been poisoned, spoilt, infected, eroded, cast aside and so on: 'Every nationality has built its own mythology narrating how other nations deprive it of the vital part of enjoyment the possession of which would allow it to live fully' (Zizek, 1990: 54). In a great hall of distorting mirrors the multitude of ethnic communities mutually define themselves in this manner. Ultimately the myth of 'stolen enjoyment' *is* the structure of enjoyment. Spiteful, paranoid, resentful, fearful and destructive fantasies are the structure of ethnic enjoyment. This vicious circle is set in motion by the motor of the super-ego. The hatred of the other's enjoyment is at heart a displaced 'hatred of our own excess enjoyment'. The final ultimate irony is that 'What we conceal by imputing to the Other the theft of enjoyment is the traumatic fact that we never possessed what was allegedly stolen from us: the lack ("castration") is original' (1990: 54). The ethnic community is pervaded by constitutive 'antagonisms' which are inherent to it, and which cannot help but drive paranoid, destructive impulses.

These are currently the stakes then in the libidinal economy of diversity. At one pole the ecstatic explosion of fluidity, anti-identity and the affective embrace of Nietzchean 'Becoming'. At the other pole the 'enjoyment' of identity, stasis, purity and annihilation of the Other, the idiosyncratic. Are the seemingly impossible position of the Burroughsian 'cultural bomb', or Deleuzian 'war machine' on the one hand, and the horror of ethnic cleansing on the other the only possible positions to take?

Conclusion

A current trend in the development of the Deleuzian paradigm seems to entail a shift away from the emphasis on the language-body interface towards an emphasis on neuroscience, and models drawn from recent developments in cybernetics, artificial intelligence and physics.[6] A socio-logical analysis of the background to this paradigm shift would provide an interesting study in its own right. In our view, however, it is a potentially worrying development.

Much contemporary Anglo-American sociology, and cultural studies, focuses only on the semiotics of the body, leaving completely untouched issues of affective intensity. We therefore sympathize with neomaterialist foregroundings of the bodily and the visceral. Nevertheless, along with postmodern notions of hybridity and creativity, we continue to value such humanist concepts as trust, tolerance and the capacity to live with ambivalence. Not all humanist discourse need necessarily be linked to the paranoid pole, stasis, closure or ego rigidity. We can easily derive a reading of Adorno and Horkheimer, for example, in which ego strength is not seen as brittle but rather as potentially supple, open, with the affective strength to hybridize, mutate and change. It is also possible to derive a reading of Deleuze and Guattari in which they have moved some way towards the modern humanists.

As amply demonstrated in their recent *What is Philosophy?* Deleuze and Guattari (1994) have always been deeply aware of the power of the concept in its relation to the body. They no doubt had this in mind when they drew away from the 'machinic' metaphors of *Anti-Oedipus* (1977), in favour of the 'nomads' and 'rhizomes' of *A Thousand Plateaus* (1987). Anti-humanists or not, something told them that a fundamental destructiveness lay in the former conceptualization. Indeed in many ways *The Anti-Oedipus* is a highly paranoid text; it certainly displays little tolerance or accom-modation of the perceived opposition. The agents of 're-territorialization' –

the disciplinary state, and 'daddy-mommy-me' – are unqualified evil. Neither does it appear to perceive any ambivalence in its advocacy of schizoid fragmentation and de-territorialization. Sophisticated readers might perceive in this a certain strategy, a hyperbolic statement of a case designed to open up a new perspective, rather than an analysis meant to be taken absolutely literally. In our view their intention in this early work was, as we have shown, to emphasize the affective and organizational polarity at work at the heart of the social process.

Contrast this, however, with their emphasis at the end of *What is Philosophy?* Here Deleuze and Guattari (1994: 201–9) discuss the relation of science, art and philosophy to chaos, the sublime, the idiosyncratic. They recognize the need for 'a little order to protect us from chaos'. They seek a minimum of order in varied semiotic forms, of resemblance, contiguity and causality which prevent our 'fantasy' from 'crossing the universe in an instant, producing winged horses and dragons breathing fire'. They claim there would not be chaos if there was not also a little order in things or states of affairs like 'an objective antichaos'. Some such regularity gives rise to opinions, a stability to our day-to-day lives. They claim that art, science and philosophy 'require more: they cast planes over the chaos'. These three discourses venture beyond doxa, into chaos and out again. They return from the land of the dead. They take off in creative lines of flight. They 'struggle against opinion which claims to protect us from chaos itself'. Chaos is no better than opinion, but art composes chaos in new sensations, philosophy generates new concepts and creative science 'takes a bit of chaos in a system of coordinates and forms a referenced chaos that becomes Nature'.

The neomaterialist philosophy they have developed does not, and should not, be taken to imply that sociology can be abandoned in favour of neuroscience and chaos theory. A much more fruitful line of development would be a conceptual exploration of areas of convergence with the 'modernist' theorists of ambivalence, in order to develop a neomaterialist, postmodern account of the conditions necessary for the collective tolerance of affective ambivalence and difference. This is the theme around which many of the key debates in sociology must lie if it is to be taken at all seriously in the next decade. Rapid social change, the erosion of the nation state, fluid communities and identities, ethnic rivalries, shrinking space, information explosion, shifting populations, the ongoing consequences of the end of communism – the affective body and the potential it provides for human destructiveness and/or joy must be at the heart of any postmodern sociology.

Notes

1 This is evidently a version of Freud's 'death drive'.

2 We can only speculate on the possible connections here, however Lacan's early papers in this area were written in the same period of the 1930s that Adorno and Horkheimer were

developing their ideas in this area. Walter Benjamin may prove to have been a decisive link between the Frankfurt School and the French surrealist circles from which French Post-Structuralists have clearly taken so much. For some indication of the involvement of Benjamin with Breton, Bataille, Blanchot, Caillois, Kojèv etc. see, for example, Hollier (ed.), 1988.

3 See also Julia Kristeva (1995).

4 From an interview in *Global Tapestry* cited in Miles (1993).

5 'Enjoyment' here has a specific Lacanian significance. It is a structuring of desire which is associated with the order of the 'Imaginary' in Lacan's schema. This is an order which is drawn towards repetition, stasis, fixity, the illusion of identity.

6 See, for example, the list of papers presented at the conference on Virtual Futures in the Philosophy Department of the University of Warwick in May 1995.

References

Adorno, T. and Horkheimer, M. ([1944] 1992) *Dialectic of Enlightenment*. London: Verso.

Bird, J. (1994) 'Bodies, boundaries and solidarities: a psychoanalytic account of racism and ethnic hatred', in J. Weeks (ed.), *The Lesser Evil and the Greater Good: The Theory and Politics of Social Diversity*. London: Rivers Oram.

Burroughs, W. ([1983] 1989) *The Place of Dead Roads*. London: Paladin.

Deleuze, G. and Guattari, F. (1977) *Anti Oedipus* (trans. R. Hurley et al.). New York: Viking.

Deleuze, G. and Guattari, F. (1987) *A Thousand Plateaus* (trans. B. Massumi). Minneapolis: University of Minnesota Press.

Deleuze, G. and Guattari, F. (1994) *What is Philosophy?* London: Verso.

Derrida, J. (1992) 'Given time: the time of the king', *Critical Enquiry*, 18 (Winter).

Hoggett, P. (1992a) *Partisans in an Uncertain World*. London: Free Association Books.

Hoggett, P. (1992b) 'A place for experience: a psychoanalytic perspective on boundary, identity and culture', *Environment and Planning D: Society and Space*, 10: 345–56.

Hollier, D. (ed.) (1988) *The College of Sociology, 1937–39*. Minneapolis: University of Minnesota Press.

Kristeva, J. (1955) *New Maladies of the Soul*. Columbia, NY: SUNY Press.

Lacan, J. (1977) 'Aggressivity in psychoanalysis', in *Ecrits*. London: Tavistock.

Lyotard, J.F. (1986/7) 'Rules and paradoxes and svelte appendix', *Cultural Critique*, Winter.

Lyotard, J.F. (1988) *The Differend: Phrases in Dispute*. Manchester: Manchester University Press.

Lyotard, J.F. (1992) *The Inhuman*. Cambridge: Polity Press.

Miles, B. (1993) *William Burroughs: El Hombre Invisible*. London: Virgin Books.

Rorty, R. (1989) *Contingency, Irony and Solidarity*. Cambridge: Cambridge University Press.

Rustin, M. (1991) *The Good Society and the Inner World*. London: Verso.

Zizek, S. (1989) *The Sublime Object of Ideology*. London: Verso.

Zizek, S. (1990) 'Eastern Europe's Republics of Gilead', *New Left Review*, 183: 50–62.

Zurbrugg, N. (1984) 'Burroughs, Barbes, and the limits of inter-textuality', *The Review of Contemporary Fiction*, 4(1): 86–106.

10 Body Amnesia – Comments on Corporeality

Thomas Osborne

> What is most surprising is rather the body; one never ceases to be amazed at the idea that the human body has become possible.
>
> Freidrich Nietzsche

> Health is life lived in the silence of the organs.
>
> Georges Canguilhem

> Sex is boring.
>
> Michel Foucault

If Nietzsche taught us nothing else, it was that forgetting has its uses. This is as true of the body as it is of anything else. What matters is not so much the body in itself, but the ways in which the body is forgotten – *body amnesia*.

Social theory and the body

It has been said that sociology – and maybe the other humanities – have forgotten the body and that it might help to remember it again: for instance, by making the body central to the renewal of sociology (Shilling, 1993; Turner, 1984). So the classical theorists pre-supposed the body, but did not analyse it as a subject in its own right – think of Marx on the reproduction of labour power, Weber on asceticism, Durkheim on suicide. Without disputing this contention, this chapter makes the case that the body is undoubtedly an arresting topic for the human sciences, but that the quest for a positive sociology of the body is unlikely to be particularly fruitful. *The* body is certainly not going to be the saviour of sociology; and notions like the habitus or the 'embodied subject' should not be expected to signal the end of hardy perennials like the structure/agency debate. Nevertheless, all this interest in the body is *itself* interesting. We need, instead of somehow 'founding' sociology on the question of the body, to take advantage of the disarray of sociology, its advertent lack of any territory proper to itself, to follow the varied problematizations of the body – for example, in relation to apparatuses of medical power.

It will not be particularly fruitful to start out from some preconceived idea or theory as to what the body is or is not: such things should be left to biologists, and others. Nor should we necessarily just speak of the body in the plural as if that would solve anything. For, as will be argued later, we do have good grounds for thinking that there is such a thing as the body, so that saying unequivocally that the body does not exist – that there are only bodies in the plural, or organs, or incorporations – is almost if not quite as misguided as saying that the body is everything. So it needs to be stressed at the outset that it is not a question here of undertaking anything too much resembling a postmodern approach to the body. Postmodernism often seems to privilege the body whilst making a big issue of fragmenting – and often, in effect, romanticizing – it. Baudrillard, for instance, has many interesting things to say about the body, but ultimately reduces it to a site of semiosis (Baudrillard, [1976] 1993: 101–21). Writing about strip-tease, for example, Baudrillard comments: 'The only good strip is the one that reflects the body in the mirror of gestures and follows this rigorous narcissistic abstraction: the gestural repertoire being the mobile equivalent of the panoply of signs and marks at work in situations such as erectile stagings of the body at every level of fashion, make-up and advertising' ([1976] 1993: 108). What seems to count for somebody like Baudrillard is the body as a surface or ground of signification. But there is more – or perhaps less – to the body than a postmodern semiotic. Not least, those collectivities we call bodies do seem to exist in space and time, to smell, hear and interact with other bodies, images, persons and things; and it is not surprising that attempts, like those of Michel Serres, to account for this kind of sensual corporeality have found themselves necessarily treading paths at some remove from orthodox academic discourse, with its repertoires of theories, descriptions and representations of what the body is (Serres, 1985, 1992: 192–3).

One suspects that if the body has become attractive, then this is because – for the postmoderns at least – having got rid of founding categories such as 'society', the body is a useful material upon which, perhaps surreptitiously, to ground their analyses. There is, moreover, something satisfyingly unintellectual about the body, something that is bound to appeal to intellectuals, especially those who are self-consciously perplexed with the status of their own intellectualism. However, being 'after' postmodernism in relation to the body is not necessarily a question of transcending or being smugly superior to postmodernism but rather of asking some more basic questions about the function of the thing we call the body in modern societies. In particular, we might take as our focus this very question of the forgetting of the body itself. This is what this chapter does. It argues – using some rather bluntly expressed examples to make its case – that it is something like a universal property of the collectivity that we call the body that it demands to be forgotten.

Strategic body amnesia

Those who would have a theory of the body often worry about its relation to the mind. But the problem is not whether to give priority to the mind or the body, but to find a way of not writing about either as if it were a subject. To avoid turning the mind into a subject, some people have turned to the body – only to turn the body into a subject in its turn. In fact, this approach only reproduces dualisms: one says that the body has priority, but then begins to speak of the body as if it were the mind or the mind as if it were the body. The only way out is to stop thinking about the body as a subject altogether, that is, to adopt a strategic body amnesia.

It is typical for accounts of corporeality to begin with a questioning of some of our apparent assumptions about the human body (Harré, 1991: 17–19; Turner, 1992: 33). Often, for instance, analyses point out that a renewed attention to the body is required because of the predominance of Cartesian assumptions concerning the links between mind and body. The Cartesian perspective makes of the body a passive material in contrast to the active potential of the human mind; the body becomes an object. Criticisms of such dualism are not novel, of course, and are certainly not the discovery of sociologists. Merleau-Ponty – who had a better understanding than most of the sophistication of Descartes' position – wrote famously against it in *The Structure of Behaviour* (cf. Jay, 1993: 298–328; Serres, 1985: 276). Yet this kind of analysis, which seeks to privilege the body, often does so at the expense of giving the body itself something like the subjective properties of the mind. When, for example, psychoanalytic theorists explain – taking the hysteric as their prototype – that the body is something that we think with, they run the risk not of subverting all dualisms or demolishing idealism once and for all, but simply of translating properties hitherto associated with mind and brain to the body itself. Hence the effect of these analyses: simultaneously to provide a certain frisson of counter-intuition with a marginal displacement – and duplication – of all the old epistemological problems associated with mind and body. And, in thus effectively turning the body into a subject, the very properties that had been initially valued in the body – its materiality, sensibility, pre-ideality – tend to lose their novelty and their distinctiveness. With such corporeal perspectives – to pursue a familiar sporting analogy – it is not even so much a question of moving the goalposts in order to change the very terms of the analysis; it is rather as if the corporeal perspective entails simply an exchange of the goalposts at one end of the pitch with those at the other.

This consideration already leads us in the direction of an advocacy of a certain amnesia with regard to the body. Perhaps we need to forget theories of the body itself, theories that seek out some fundamentalism of the body. All in all, the body is rather like one of those objects that you have to look away from in order to attain any clarity. As Mauss said, if we begin with a particular model of the body then we are unlikely to get very far: 'In any case, it is essential to move from the concrete to the abstract and not the other way around' (Mauss, [1934] 1979: 97). But if it is necessary to take a detour around the body – to begin, so to speak, by forgetting about it – then this is not at all to dismiss all known accounts of corporeality that have appeared hitherto. Rather, it is a matter of asking whether the very success of some of these accounts may itself be down to certain strategies of body amnesia that are inherent within them.

First, and briefly, there is what could be called the 'embodiment' approach. This is effective because whilst it seems to consider the body more or less directly, it is actually concerned with something secondary, that is, with the ways in which we experience the body. Harré, for instance, begins his book on the body precisely by making the point that he is not really talking about the body as such but about a psychology of embodiment. This is primarily a question of discourses and accounts. 'A corporeal psychology will be a collection of accounts of those discursive practices in which the fact of embodiment plays a central role, whether accomplished by the body itself or by body-centred talk' (Harré, 1991: 5). Harré, one might say, is concerned not with the body as such but with 'physical being', that is, with the body considered under the aspect of experience (whether or not the category of experience is itself justified in this context is, of course, another matter). Hence, his book is full of accounts of how we experience the body and of how the body gives rise to particular kinds of experience; body morphology, the grammar of body talk, corporeal boundaries, architectural anthropographics.

The second way of making a strategic detour from the body – or from specific theories or representations of the body – is what could be called the ethological approach. Deleuze glosses this in a piece devoted to Spinoza. 'Every reader of Spinoza knows that for him bodies and minds are not subjects but modes' (Deleuze, 1988: 123–4; cf. Rose, 1996: ch. 8). Ethology, in Deleuze's extension of the term, is not the study of the body in or for itself. Instead of starting at the very beginning with a fundamental principle, it starts in the middle, focusing upon the ways in which the body has a capacity for affecting and for being affected (Deleuze, 1988: 124). Ethology asks two questions (that are perhaps the same question): What can a body do? and What can be done to the body?

Marcel Mauss wrote some of the most celebrated pages on the first question. He did not write about the body as a kind of subject – for instance by 'theorizing' the body – but rather about the way in which the body could be used as an object of technique. In talking of techniques of the body, Mauss says: 'I mean the ways in which from society to society men know how to use their bodies' ([1934] 1979: 97). He is concerned with the plasticity of locomotion – swimming, digging, marching, walking. Mauss emphasizes that techniques have to be both effective and traditional; indeed, for Mauss, the cultural transmission of technique is fundamental to what distinguishes man from animals. Animals have bodies, but they do not have body techniques. For all its relativism, Mauss' essay assumes that a constant affect of the human body is to be amenable to transformation through the invention and persistent application of body techniques. The essence of the human body, if it has one, is its capacity for such transformation.

Michel Foucault writes of discipline in a similarly technicist language. He is concerned, however, much more than Mauss with the second issue, with what can be done to the body rather than what it can do – although one might say (contra the thrust of many of the criticisms of Foucault on this matter) that the possibility of the former is presupposed by the recognition of the latter. It is a feature of the thing we call the human body, Foucault thinks, that it can be tied to technologies of power that enhance the productivity of the body whilst simultaneously rendering it pliable and pacifiable. Unlike Mauss' techniques which are cultural and traditional, Foucault's technologies stem from a kind of 'unintentional' intentionality of power. Perhaps it is a feature of modernity that techniques of the body should have become subjected to wholesale *technologies*, that is, to more or less elaborated systems for producing particular affects in the body. Foucault, however, did not strive for anything like a theory of the body, and Shilling inadvertently complements Foucault when he says that the body is absent from his texts (Shilling, 1993: 80). Foucault's is more like an ethological account. It was assuredly not Foucault's point to argue that philosophy or social theory should take the body as its primary focus, but rather that one of the features of modern power is that it uses a thing like the body to think with and act upon.

This ethological approach, then, is not so much about making a representation of what the body is (of providing a theory of the body, or of asserting its irreducibility) but about logging the ways in which the body is a problem; and a problem in the positive sense – not just as an 'obstacle', but as a vehicle for thought and action. If, for example, the issue of sexuality has attained such a prominence in analyses of the body, this is not because sexuality is somehow more fundamental than anything else, but that it has a remarkable provenance as a problem (Gallagher and Laqueur, 1987; Hunter et al., 1993). There are many ways of analysing sexuality in terms of its problematization; and these go well beyond merely asserting that sexuality is something forever lodged within 'discourse'. Peter Brown, for instance, has logged a succession of ways of relating to the body, highlighting amongst many other things the distinct problematization of sexuality in the late Antique and early Christian worlds. 'Seen through the lens of the fully elaborated Christianity of the middle ages, the body image of second century persons seemed strangely blurred. A diffused sensuality flickered through it . . . Sexual desire itself was unproblematic: it was a predictable response to physical beauty; its satisfaction was accepted as an occasion that brought intense physical pleasure' (Brown, 1988: 30). Brown, however, is clearly not completely relativistic about perceptions of sexuality. For him the issue of sexuality is clearly a central aspect of body problematization whatever the age; although the specifics change, sexuality does seem more or less universal as a problem. But this is very different from arguing – as some kinds of psychoanalytic reductionism would have it – that either sexuality is the only issue that is important from the corporeal perspective, or even that sexuality itself is a constant force in history. The historicism of the ethological attitude should not be negotiable on this point (cf. Copjec, 1994; Minson, 1993).

Lastly, an essential corollary of the ethological attitude would be that the body never exists in what could be called a *discontinuous* state. Or at least, the thing we call the body always seeks a problematization that will bring it into continuity with other bodies. What requires investigation are the ways in which the various elements in the collectivity we call the human body are made to connect up to other bodies of various kinds. This is why, in spite of the perplexity, not to mention hilarity and irritation, which their texts tend to provoke, the work of people like Deleuze and Guattari needs to be taken seriously as a sustained attempt to find a language for thinking about the thing we call the body, whether human or not. To appreciate why this is so, one only needs to consider that the body is an indicator of extension or exteriority rather than interiority. Indeed, one of the central motivations for the contemporary 'turn' to the body is no doubt a certain resistance to the very notion – for what is perceived as its sentimentality, its mysticism, its humanism – of any straightforward idea of interiority. For those for whom there is no such thing as interiority, there is only a universal, if immanent, exteriority (which accounts for the attractions of varieties of Spinozism in various guises amongst those who are suspicious of the reductions of psychology). Such exteriorization both privileges and relativizes the body itself. If everything is to be understood upon the model of extension then the body itself – the human body, for example – can be given no ultimate explanatory privilege. Rather, what counts is the way that different exteriorities are tied together: the fusion of exteriorities; the mapping of the finite, discontinuous body on to the continuity of the exterior.

Corporeal fusion

A sociological study of body amnesia would be concerned to enquire into two kinds of force: the forces of fusion which promote the fusion of bodies, and the forces of disjunction which make the body discontinuous, which prevent or disrupt the fusion of bodies.

Bits and pieces of the thing we call the body – as some hastily assembled illustrations will now show – is something that always has to be, as it were, 'plugged in'; the more imperceptible the parts and workings of the thing we call the body, the more fused they are with the environment, then the better it is likely to be working. When the body is connected, the discontinuities of the body can be forgotten. There are many techniques for making such connections and fusions.

Network technique

Modern societies are governed in part upon the basis of the attributes of populations: longevity, mortality, pathology, productivity, morale. One key aspect of what has been called bio-power is a kind of infrastructural dimension that takes such issues as a central concern. Take, for example, the panoply of measures that have been directed at the body over the past two centuries under the guise of public health (de Swaan, 1992). Public health actually attends typically not directly to the body itself (which is rather difficult to seize upon directly) but to the external environment; it works on populations, air quality, probabilities, risk factors, but much more rarely on individual human bodies. The golden age of modern public health in the mid-nineteenth century entailed the draining of cities and the building of sewage systems and the proliferation of the private, domestic toilet. These infrastructural measures were means for bringing about – at the most profane level possible – a certain body amnesia. This is so obvious yet so sociologically important that it is surprising how little the provision of such measures has interested those concerned with the characteristics of modernity.

Sewage systems, for example, have several functions that allow us to forget about various body parts. At the most basic level, by carrying away human detritus, they are designed to prevent the causes of disease. Disease reminds us of our bodies, it brings our bodies back to themselves. Another function is yet more immediate: by avoiding the inconvenience of having to dispose of our bodily excrement, we avoid even having to *think* about our bodies all the time. Finally, there is a sort of transcendent function of such systems: toilets and the infrastructural systems that presuppose them are means for plugging our bodies into a wider, public, if subterranean, field of concerns. In fact, all our bodies are linked if not exactly to each other then to a series of networks that are common to us. Toilets take pipes from our bodies; our bodies become tied, so to speak, into a general economy of excrement. None of this necessarily has anything to do with psychological repression. It is not that our embarrassing bodily functions are neurotically shielded from us (cf. Schoenwald, 1973); it is that one of the affects of the collectivity we call the body is that it can be plugged in, and that when it is plugged in, it makes itself almost imperceptible as a discontinuous entity. To perceive the importance of all of this, one only has to consider the effect of a breakdown in the system. Of course, the infrastructure can break down, or we can find ourselves in an awkward absence from it. But also the body's own functions can themselves break down, making it impossible for our bodies to be meaningfully plugged into the system. Gillian Rose, in a painfully moving book, says that she wants to talk about shit. 'What having a colostomy makes you realize is that normally you bear hardly any relation to your excrement. It is expelled from the body from an invisible posterior organ and, with its characteristic solidity and odour, descends rapidly into water and oblivion' (Rose, 1995: 87–8). With a colostomy one can no longer forget the body; the body is brought into a painful discontinuity with its surroundings.

Time–space technique

Sociologists often link the character of modernity to greater mobility, a shrinkage of time–space relations. But what is perhaps most distinctive about modern corporeality is not so much that the body can be moved at ever greater speeds but that the body can remain sedentary whilst moving. In fact, many features of modern technology even when they allow us to move about at great speeds are all about enabling the body to stay still. Two symbols of this are the computer and the motor car. The computer enables us to work at home; if we are all networked, then our bodies can stay still. Again, it is a sort of body amnesia that is at stake; information is exchanged without our bodies being too much disturbed. The motor car takes us all over the place, but keeps us sedentary; we do not have to peddle or make too much of an effort. Whilst there is no point in being romantic about some essential or primordial 'nomadism' of the body, it might be worth pointing out that current so-called New Age protests focus upon just this question. New Age protest seeks to keep the body nomadic. New Age travellers and others are not keen on the motor car. They drive around in parodies of the luxury vehicle. The motor car makes the body move, but in a sedentary fashion – the body stays still. New Agers are happy about computers, but so long as they retain their nomadic functions; the net must remain anarchic, and so on. Finally, New Agers seek to return us to a kind of happy – and oddly de-sexualized – corporeality; what Maffesoli has called a new tribalism or dionysisme (Maffesoli, 1991, 1992: 148).

Psychic fusion technique

Everywhere the dream of the thing we call the body is to discard this sense of discontinuity. The body always wants to join up with other bodies. Theweleit, in a study of fascistic erotics (1986), writes about a kind of 'massification' of the human body. Here again the aim is to cause us to forget about the discontinuity of the body, but here body amnesia is reactionary and irrational. Theweleit shows us how, for the Nazi Freikorps, the individual body becomes submerged into the whole – a massified fighting machine, the army. Again, it is a bit like being plugged into an infrastructure, only here plugs and infrastructure are psychic. The body becomes a seam of flows and channels that harden and plug fast into ever-wider channels and flows. What must be resisted is the flood – here associated with women. None of this, in spite of Theweleit's terminology, has anything to do with psychoanalysis as such; what is at stake is rather a will to create a sturdy, erectile collective body resistant to disintegration and amorphousness.

Sociality technique

The collectivity we call the body is itself a rather cumbersome, or at least incredibly complex, medium of sociality. As Bruno Latour has argued, baboons bear their social relations almost entirely upon their bodies; their somatic resources are all important. 'They build the collective body with their own bodies alone, using no resources beyond these. This leads to the extreme complexity of their social skills, since they have no way of transforming a weak bond into a stronger one other than by using more social skills' (Latour, 1986a: 275). Human societies, and especially modern societies, strive to escape this reliance upon somatic resources. Here 'what counts in holding society together is mostly extrasomatic' (1986a: 276). Modern communications have allowed us to escape this logic. Latour's entire oeuvre serves to emphasize how modern communication is premised upon the construction of what he calls 'immutable mobiles' – non-corporeal tokens, graphs etc., which communicate for us and construct our forms of sociality without the direct usage or mediation of our bodies. Here perception is reduced so far as possible to the single corporeal dimension of what is visible immediately to the naked eye. Latour calls this 'graphism' (Latour, 1986b). All bodies perceive in the same way, and from the same point; the discontinuity, its specific location or contextual perspective, of the body is so far as possible eliminated. And if anthropologists are better at thinking about the body than are sociologists then this is because, as the Mary Douglas tradition has long been aware, so-called primitive societies do indeed seem to use the body much more directly as a bearer of social relations. Modern fashion – however important it may be for the imaginaries of modernity or postmodernity – is but a parody of the far more directly socialized significance of the body in 'anthropological' societies.

Corporeal disjunction

Then, secondly, there are the disconnections of the body: its corporeal discontinuity or disjunctions. A minimal anthropology might be in order here. If anything makes the collectivity we call the body somehow primordial it is not so much that we all possess a body, but that one of its fundamental attributes is that it can go wrong, or at least that we perceive that it can. Georges Canguilhem's definition of health, derived from the physician Leriche, entailed the notion of a silence of the organs (Canguilhem, 1989: 91). We are not healthy when we are aware of our bodies. Only sustained body amnesia is healthy. The problem is that the body cannot be forgotten so easily. Many images of such discontinuity are possible.

Pain

Physiologists and others have never quite got to the bottom of the functions of pain. It is a signalling system; it is the body's message that it is trying to harm or even kill you. Forgetting the philosophical and psychological treatises, amongst the greatest depictions of pain stands H.G. Wells' *The Island of Dr Moreau* (Wells, [1896] 1993). Dr Moreau, vivisector, manufactures Beast People in the House of Pain. Here are pains that are made all the more unbearable by their linkage to animality. But this poignancy is the opposite of anthropomorphic sentimentality; or rather, the force of Wells' descriptions stem only from a kind of reversal of such familiar sentimentality. It is not that we are made to feel the animal's pain as if it were human; rather, the torture resides in the fact that the animals are not just being dissected but are themselves being transformed into human beings. Wells' little book is full of ghastly tableaus that seem to come straight from a Bacon canvas. 'Then through an open doorway beyond, in the dim light of the shadow, I saw something bound painfully upon a framework, scarred, red and bandaged . . .' (Wells, [1896] 1993: 48). What could be better expressions of the discontinuity of the body than these grotesque Beast People that are by definition the unique products of acts of torture inflicted upon the body, and each of whom bears the distinguishing echo of a particular beast? 'Each of these creatures, despite its human form, its rag of clothing, and the rough humanity of its bodily form, had woven into it, into its movements, into the expression of its countenance, into its whole presence, some now irresistible suggestion of a hog, a swinish taint, the unmistakable mark of the beast' (Wells, [1896] 1993: 40).

Disability

What is disability if not the feeling – whether subjective or the product of the perceptions of others – that one cannot forget about one's body? If disabled people get angry it is not because they are bound by the demands of a new political correctness, nor simply that disability is something to be straightforwardly celebrated or affirmed. In fact, the affirmation of the disabled body is only an aspect of a more fundamental will to be able to forget about the body altogether. The affirmation of the disabled body is only expressive of a deeper demand – the right to bodily amnesia. But the disabled never seem to be allowed to forget about their bodies, perhaps above all because other people will not let them forget about them either – as Goffman showed, using the rubric of stigma (Goffman, 1975). A stigma is a sign, it is a memento, a corporeal reminder: it impedes forgetting. But there is more to disability than marks of perception. The 'problem' with disability is not, one suspects, primarily that the disabled person has a disabled body, that being disabled is awkward and difficult but – more fundamentally – that the disabled person has a body at all. The misfortune of the disabled is not that they signify – for themselves or others – corporeal dysfunction but that they recall embodiment as such. The disabled – and here one might add in other characterizations such as those surrounding 'womanhood' or femininity – are symbols not of disability itself but of the travails of embodiment, of having a thing called a body at all.

Corporeal affirmation

No doubt this thesis (which I have loosely derived from Canguilhem) – that there is something about the thing we call the body that makes us want to forget it – commits the triple sin of being unremarkable, boring and unfashionable. Is it not better to celebrate our bodies, to love the body, to participate in the current affirmations of the body? But, in fact, such affirmation only does a certain injustice to the body itself, for the simple reason that what usually goes under the rubric of celebrating the body is more often than not itself an endeavour to forget the body and its discontinuities. Consider very briefly three such kinds of apparent body affirmation.

Eroticism

Sexuality and eroticism have less to do with the body than we might think, and much to do with forgetting about it. Sexuality is important in relation to the body for the simple, and no doubt vulgar, reason that sexuality is about connections, the subversion of discontinuities. George Bataille preferred to talk about eroticism: 'assenting to life to the point of death' (Bataille, 1962: 11). This was not because sexual orgasm was analogous to a 'little death' but because Bataille associated death with 'continuity of being', and eroticism would be a way of seeking continuity of being in the realms of the living. One gets the impression that Bataille would have been rather bored by the postmodern or poststructuralist obsession with sexuality and sexual identity. Eroticism is much more simple, much more general a problem, and much more interesting than might be suggested by the obsession with the guilty, finite little secrets of sexuality.

Fitness

Fitness cults are also all about finding methodologies for forgetting about the body. Exercise can, no doubt, have several functions. There are two main kinds: obsessive and mundane. Obsessive exercise – for example, by producing an adrenalin rush – can seduce us into thinking that our bodies have transcended themselves: that our bodies have become, so to speak, *over*-bodies. The whole project of working obsessively upon the body – as in body-building cults or Eastern martial arts and body-relaxation techniques – is about making the body transcend itself; one dupes the body by working upon it so hard that it becomes something other than a mere body and hence forgets itself. On the other hand, mundane exercise – jogging, aerobics etc. – is only to play a slightly longer game with body amnesia. One goes through the tedious motions of working upon the body in the present instance in order to prolong its ability to forget itself, that is, to remain healthy and hence ultimately as amnesiac as possible about one's body. For most people, to go jogging is an unpleasant experience – hence the self-satisfying and virtuous feelings that can stem from it – for which the reward is a prolongation of the quiet of the body in the future; a future pay-off is the reward for a current deficit of body amnesia. But there is a paradox here, which stems from the problem of balancing the future pay-off with the current deficit. If one works just too hard upon the body, one can become obsessed with it and amnesia becomes impossible – instead one just becomes neurotic, hypochondriac or narcissistic in relation to the body.

Arts

It hardly requires the insight of a Panofsky or a Baxandall to recognize that the arts bear complicated relations with the question of the body. In some of their best corporeal moments, the arts can illuminate body amnesia itself. The arts can show us how body amnesia is more or less generic. They can show us the ways in which those collectivities we call our bodies are the most taken-for-granted thing that we have. The plastic and other arts have addressed this aspect of our bodies – that the body is made up of strange parts that we are apt to take for granted. Bataille and the surrealists, for example, were very interested in the big toe. Bataille wrote an article which is, on Hollier's account, one of the best descriptions of the subject. Bataille said: 'The big toe is the most human part of the human body' (quoted in Hollier, 1989: 78). The big toe is what allows us, after all, one of our defining characteristics as human beings; to stand up. Bataille was also keen on the mouth, about which he also wrote a celebrated article. It is a strange thing, the mouth, because it is not an organ at all but a cavity, a hole in the body. Francis Bacon took up this theme of the mouth in paint (cf. Ades, 1985: 14–16). Those who see in Bacon's work nothing but horror see these mouths as emblems of the human scream. But Bacon is quite clear that it is the mouth itself that interests him, not the scream as such. 'You know how the mouth changes shape. I've always been very moved by the movements of the mouth and teeth' (Sylvester, 1980: 48). But the arts can also serve to show how bodily amnesia is not just a fundamental human attribute, it is also a property of the body itself. The body tries to get free of *itself*. Countless writers and artists have depicted the attempts of the body to find release from the tiresome presence of itself; again, perhaps none has matched the visual dream of Bacon. According to Deleuze (in a truly great work of aesthetics), part of what Bacon was up to was the depiction of a variety of ways in which the body tries to escape from its own orifices (Deleuze, 1981: 16–17). It is not just 'us' that seek to be corporeal amnesiacs. Even the body is trying to get rid of itself!

Medicine and the disclosure of corporeality

Where have these hasty reflections got us? Certainly no nearer to anything like a positive sociology of the body. In fact, sociology has no privilege over the body. It means very little to say that there is something 'social' about the body. Doctors, anthropologists, biologists, nymphomaniacs and artists are all likely to know much more about the body than sociologists.

Especially doctors – but why should that be so? Medical sociology might do well – forgetting for a moment its misguided aspiration to be a kind of alternative branch of medicine itself – to pay more attention to that side of its vocation to be a sociology *of* medicine; that is, it might pursue the varied grammars of the body that are given to us through medicine and other therapeutic disciplines. This would be to make the sociology of medicine more akin to the tradition of philosophical anthropology than to that of the tired tradition of critical sociology (Turner, 1992). This would be not to criticize or refute the dominance of medicine, but to indicate the place of medical reasoning in our present; to indicate what it is that medicine brings to our self-conceptions and styles of existence (Rose, 1994). If medicine is interesting from the perspective of the body, it is not just because medicine controls, regulates or represses the body. Nor is it just a question of the endless and repetitive recovery of so-called 'lay' perceptions of the body. Medicine is interesting from the perspective of our corporeality because it fights against two things: discontinuity and – what is the same thing in the end – death.

If medicine is interesting, it is because it exists at the intersection of the body understood as a continuity and the body as discontinuity. Medicine seeks a restoration of corporeal continuities, even at the price of allowing less room for discretion in the scope of these continuities. Indeed, medicine shows us that the continuous body and the discontinuous body are not opposed to each other as binary terms. Matters are more complicated; the body needs to function in a discontinuous way precisely if it is to be connected up to wider bodies and apparatuses – and medicine takes as its necessary object precisely the reconstitution of the discontinuous powers of the body. But medicine is not a 'science' in any orthodox sense. Medicine deploys the procedures of science, but medicine itself is, so to speak, beyond science – medicine takes sides, medicine is partisan with regard to human life. This is not just to say, along with Canguilhem again, that medicine intervenes 'on the side of life' in opposition to other vital values such as disease. Rather, medicine intervenes specifically on behalf of the (human) organism, the body as a whole. Medicine is a generically perspectivist enterprise; the perspective it takes, what it values above all, is the individual body.

This is not as laughably self-evident as we might think. Take for instance – by way of a counter-thesis – the findings of symbiosis theory in biology. Human beings are, Lynn Margulis informs us, merely folds in nature (see Margulis and Sagan, 1991). Instead of an evolutionary narrative focusing on human development, she gives us a narrative of bacterial evolution, mutation and symbiosis. The human body is, in the context of evolution in general, a rather localized and chancey mixture of bacterial species. It is not a necessary unity, but, as Sagan expresses it, the subject of a particular set of incorporations: 'the body becomes a sort of ornately elaborated mosaic of microbes in various states of symbiosis. The distinct presences of these microbes become noticeable only when festering and illness throw normal populations and metabolite turnover out of equilibrium' (Sagan, 1992: 369).

What, then, is medicine but the discipline that seeks to advocate the maintenance of the local norms of the human body against the general tendencies of – in this example, microbial – evolution? Medicine takes the side of one, local kind of organized life against other forces of life that should threaten it. If the body is to forget itself, it must have a relation to the right kind of exterior to which it can be connected – and certain bacteria are not the best kind of allies of the body. A certain paranoia is often visible in medical sociology concerning the fragmentation that medicine imposes upon the body, but this should be, if anything, reversed. The very existence of medicine is predicated upon taking sides on behalf of the whole human body against the forces that would decompose it. This does not mean that medicine is misguided or – as Sagan seems to suggest (1992: 363) – that it has a necessarily naive view of the human body. It means, rather, that what constitutes the human body – its 'incorporations' – are never given once and for all. Medical sociologists would do well to involve themselves, then, not in constant advocacy of the 'patient's view' against the efforts of medicine, but in investigation of the historicity of ways in which medicine as a human art – for modern Western medicine itself is more or less specific and contingent – has sided with the human body.

Indeed, in a certain way, all this means that the body understood as a totality is an effect of medicine itself. If medicine is, as Canguilhem says, something like an anthropological universal, then this is not because there is some kind of universality inherent within *the* body. It is not the body that is primary but the *fact* of medicine; the very idea of the body, our very notion that there is a body to be cured, is the effect of the very universality of medicine itself, or at least of the universality of the fact that medicine is possible as a field of human activity. This, by the way, is not to re-hash the dubious 'constructionist' – or rather idealist – notion that medical discourse somehow 'produces' the body (Armstrong, 1983). It is rather, in a more abstract way, that medical activity – as a general dimension of human endeavour – is a field that forever discloses the fact that we have things that we might want to call bodies. The existence of medicine *provokes* the notion of the body. So if we have spoken at times in this chapter of *the* body, and if we have used the term body amnesia – as if there were indeed something to *be* forgotten – then this is only the unavoidable consequence not of medicine as this or that institution but of the very fact that medicine exists; for it is medicine – in all its historical variations – that discloses to us that there is a body to be cured, treated, cared for, protected, watched over. In this sense, medicine is the prototype of all technology, in that it is the practical art of uncovering error, mistakes, things that are amiss. It is, above all, the existence of medicine that teaches us the primacy of error, abnormality and pathology as the spur to thought, invention, problematization and action (Canguilhem, 1989, 1994).

How, then, are the human sciences to specify the originality of 'man'? Perhaps not through language, mind or any of the usual philosophical candidates, but maybe through the existence of medicine. Man, one might

say – and to realize that this is so, one only has to consider the nonsensi-
cality of the idea that animals 'have' bodies – is above all a medicalizing
animal.

And if there is always a certain ambivalence involved here, in our regard
for medicine, then this is because medicine is always both for and against
the human body. In attempting to preserve and renew the powers of the
human body, medicine has to decompose the body, to make of it a
discontinuity. It is precisely here that the success, or at least the specificity
of Western medicine, resides. Medicine is predicated upon the demand that
humans should be able to live out their lives in the silence of the organs, to
forget their bodies. But medicine is beset by an impossibility, a paradox:
that our main technology of body amnesia is condemned to be forever
reminding us of our bodies. On the one hand, it can only bring about body
amnesia by drawing massive and sustained attention to our bodies through
fitness campaigns, admitting us to hospital, inducing neuroses, iatrogeneses
and hypochondria – in short, by giving us cause to recollect the body. On
the other hand, medicine has to take as its focus and set as its object of
cure, the individual, discontinuous human body. Doctors are people who
have looked the discontinuous body squarely in the eye, their whole lives
are devoted to giving our bodies new – albeit usually lesser – continuities.
But medical technology is not, in this sense, reductive of the body. On the
contrary, transplants, kidney machines, drips – all the frightening para-
phernalia of medicalization – all serve to make new connections, to make
our bodies more continuous with an outside, even if they reduce the
boundaries of that outside. In this sense, medicine does not make absolute
discontinuities of us but local discontinuities. It seeks endlessly to ward off
that final, often horrific discontinuity that is death.

For it is death, of course, that is the ultimate stake in the whole medical
game – a fact which sociologists and others have been quite wrong and
misguided to bemoan. Medicine discloses the body, and bodies are what
die. If Bataille associated eroticism with death, that is, with the ultimate
experience of continuity, then, even so, the act of death, the moment of
death, is the moment of ultimate disjunction not continuity. It is our body
that has to die, and nothing else; and in that it is completely alone,
disconnected. Death is a relative concept, of course. Michel Foucault wrote
of a modernity that had constituted death as a thousand localized forms of
violence on the body, and of the medical gaze that it was an eye that had
seen death (Foucault, 1973; Hollier, 1987: 93–4). In this, Bichat tried to
multiply the moment of death, to transform its discontinuity into a series.
No doubt this was the condition for the emergence of a stable epistemological vantage point upon death, one which the new clinical medicine was
to exploit. Still, the basic element of death remained intact. Death is the
place where the body reaches its ultimate discontinuity, and that is what is
horrific about death, which – as opposed to merely *being* dead – is the
fundamental form of bodily discontinuity and the one thing that really
cannot be forgotten.

Acknowledgement

This chapter owes much to my friend Ivan Connor, 1964–95.

References

Ades, D. (1985) 'Web of images', in D. Ades and A. Forge, *Francis Bacon*. London: Thames and Hudson.
Armstrong, D. (1983) *Political Anatomy of the Body*. Cambridge: Cambridge University Press.
Bataille, G. (1962) *Eroticism*. London: Boyars.
Baudrillard, J. ([1976] 1993) *Symbolic Exchange and Death* (trans. Iain Hamilton Grant). London: Sage.
Brown, P. (1988) *The Body and Society: Men, Women and Sexual Renunciation in Early Christianity*. London: Faber.
Canguilhem, G. (1989) *The Normal and the Pathological* (trans. C.R. Fawcett). New York: Zone.
Canguilhem, G. (1994) *A Vital Rationalist* (ed. F. Delaporte). New York: Zone.
Copjec, J. (1994) *Read My Desire*. London: Verso.
Deleuze, G. (1981) *Francis Bacon. Logique de la Sensation*. Paris: Etudes de la Difference.
Deleuze, G. (1988) *Spinoza: Practical Philosophy* (trans. R. Hurley). New York: City Lights.
Foucault, M. (1973) *The Birth of the Clinic* (trans. A. Sheridan-Smith). London: Tavistock.
Gallagher, C. and Laqueur, T. (1987) *The Making of the Modern Body*. Berkeley, CA: University of California Press.
Goffman, I. (1975) *Stigma*. Harmondsworth: Penguin.
Harré, R. (1991) *Physical Being*. Oxford: Basil Blackwell.
Hollier, D. (1987) 'The word of God: "I am dead"', *October*, 44: 75–87.
Hollier, D. (1989) *Against Architecture: The Writings of Georges Bataille* (trans. B. Wing). Cambridge, MA: MIT Press.
Hunter, I., Saunders, D. and Williamson, D. (1993) *On Pornography*. London: Macmillan.
Jay, M. (1993) *Downcast Eyes: The Denigration of Vision in Twentieth-Century French Thought*. Berkeley, CA: University of California Press.
Latour, B. (1986a) 'The powers of association', in J. Law (ed.), *Power, Action and Belief*. London: Routledge.
Latour, B. (1986b) 'Visualisation and cognition; thinking with hands and eyes', in H. Kusklick (ed.), *Knowledge and Society*, Vol. 6. Greenwich, CT: JAI Press.
Maffesoli, M. (1991) *Le Temps des Tribus*. Paris: Livre de poche.
Maffesoli, M. (1992) *La Transfiguration du Politique*. Paris: Grasset.
Margulis, L. and Sagan, D. (1991) *Microcosmos: Four Billion Years of Microbial Evolution*. New York: Touchstone.
Mauss, M. ([1934] 1979) *Sociology and Psychology* (trans. B. Brewster). London: Macmillan.
Minson, J. (1993) *Questions of Conduct*. London: Macmillan.
Rose, G. (1995) *Love's Work*. London: Chatto and Windus.
Rose, N. (1994) 'Medicine, history and the present', in C. Jones and R. Porter (eds), *Reassessing Foucault*. London: Routledge.
Rose, N. (1996) *Inventing Ourselves*. Cambridge: Cambridge University Press.
Sagan, D. (1992) 'Metametazoa: biology and multiplicity', in J. Crary and S. Kwinter (eds), *Incorporations*. New York: Zone.
Schoenwald, R. (1973) 'Training urban man', in H.J. Dyos and M. Wolff (eds), *The Victorian City*, vol. 1. London: Routledge and Kegan Paul.
Serres, M. (1985) *Les cinq sens*. Paris: Grasset.
Serres, M. (1992) *Eclaircissements, entretiens avec Bruno Latour*. Paris: Bourin.
Shilling, C. (1993) *The Body and Social Theory*. London: Sage.
de Swaan, A. (1992) *In Care of the State*. Oxford: Basil Blackwell.

Sylvester, D. (1980) *Interviews with Francis Bacon, 1962–1979*. London: Thames and Hudson.

Theweleit, K. (1986) *Male Fantasies*, 2 vols. Oxford: Basil Blackwell.

Turner, B.S. (1984) *The Body and Society*. Oxford: Basil Blackwell.

Turner, B.S. (1992) *Regulating Bodies: Essays in Medical Sociology*. London: Routledge.

Wells, H.G. ([1896] 1993) *The Island of Dr Moreau*. London: Everyman.

11 Sociology after Society

Mitchell Dean

Talk to me, so you can see
What's going on

Marvin Gaye, 'What's Going On', 1971

Sociology as diagnostics

It would be better, perhaps, to approach the history of sociology as a recurrent set of engagements with a series of discontinuous presents rather than as the smooth arc of the development of a science of society. This would be to approach it as a series of attempts to speak frankly, if often with empirical study, historical erudition and theoretical elaboration, to, as the song says, 'what's going on'.

It is some years since Michel Foucault suggested that we are heirs to a dual legacy in Kant's notion of enlightenment (1986). This legacy comprises one form of critical thought concerned with the conditions of true knowledge, an 'analytic of truth'. It also comprises another concerned with who we are today and with the difference that marks our present. This is a critical 'ontology of ourselves and our present'. When we consider who might be placed on the latter side of this division – Feuerbach, the Young Hegelians, Marx, Comte, Baudelaire, Durkheim, Weber, Neitzsche, virtually all of feminism, Bataille, Benjamin, Arendt, German critical theory, the French history of sciences – it is remarkable how much of this could be called sociology. Sociology has had its fair share of those who have contributed to what Jürgen Habermas (1987: 52) has called a 'worldly philosophical literature' with no clear institutional location. Its proponents belong to the dismissed 'privadozents', journalists, private literary men and women, ethnologists, historical scientists and so on, that make up Habermas' dissidents of modernity.

There is something marginal and *parvenu* about sociology. Even its central figures are ambivalent about their relations to the discipline. Think of Max Weber. Sociology draws from the margins of philosophy, from Marx, from Nietzsche and from political philosophy. It knows very little of the secure identity of the long-established humanities. It hovers around but never definitely crosses the threshold of scientificity. Its preoccupation with its own conditions of existence, manifest in its relentless reflexivity, is notorious. It is never sure whether it is pro-modern or anti-modern, whether it is calling for a completion of modernity, or its rejection in favour of what is 'pre' or what is 'post'. It is never clear whether it is conservative or radical, although it is perhaps rarely liberal.

This labile character of sociology constitutes its strength and is also the basis for a possible defence. If sociology ceases to be viewed as a science of society, an analytic of truth concerning what can be said about a distinctive interconnected unity, then we can begin to grasp it as a different kind of thing altogether. If we place it on the side of a critical ontology, it becomes an investigation into the conditions of existence of what we take to be our present and how we have come to think about and act on ourselves and others (Dean, 1996). Given this, the notion of society needs not be definitive of sociology.

This is the possibility I entertain here. I want to suggest that sociology is less a mode of production of truth than a kind of truth-saying, a contemporary form of what the ancient world called *parrhesia* (Brown, 1992; Flynn, 1988). It is speaking that divides its audiences by its direct and frank engagement with its present. As a form of truth-telling, it is supremely uncontemporary, untimely, 'acting against time, and thus on time, for the sake of a time to come'. Sociology is hence a 'diagnostic' that investigates the limits and possibilities of how we have come to think about who we are and what we do, of how we act on ourselves and others, and the present in which we find, and indeed discover, ourselves (cf. Deleuze, 1992: 164–5).

I want here to exemplify and engage in, rather than argue for, this *parrhesia* and this diagnostic. I try to provide a perspective on the current sense that sociology has lost its object. This is the sense Jean Baudrillard (1983) dramatized as the 'end of the social' and which others have addressed in more sober tones (for example, those authors discussed by Smart, 1990). Against Baudrillard, I would suggest that the discipline of sociology is more than a correlate of 'the social'. Among other things, it is – or at least, has been – a key means for the codification of the hetero- geneous practices and forms of knowledge that constituted the social and for their investment with a particular ethos. In this respect, I start from the assumption that the fate of theoretical disciplines like sociology has become bound to the destiny of the singular ethos of the social welfare state.

More recently, this ethos has been called into question in liberal demo- cracies, by Left and Right, by both 'social movements' and authorities, across a range of locales, with a variety of technologies, and in relation to a multiplicity of problems. It has been suggested that these 'problematiza- tions' have led to a new general set of formulae of rule and authority called 'advanced liberalism' or 'neoliberalism' (Burchell, 1993; Rose, 1993). While these terms need not detain us here, there has certainly been a trans- formation in the governmental and political practices of liberal demo- cracies. These include a certain revalorization of freedom (the 'New Contractualism') and responsibility (the 'New Prudentialism'), the deploy- ment of the polysemous rationalities around risk and a host of new 'calculative technologies', and the related emergence of a new and poly-valent cultural and political pluralism. This has undoubted consequences for forms of knowledge such as sociology.

In advanced liberal democracies, we are ceasing to understand the task of governing as one of governing society. We are ceasing to act upon the unitary and ideal space of society mapped on to the body of a population coincident with the territorial claims of the national state. We now rarely seek to act upon the social cement that bonds the otherwise fractious realities of anomic egoism and clashing classes. We find that it is less necessary to defend society against internal dangers and external threats. At best we act on ourselves and others as active subjects with polymorphous identifications. We govern ourselves as members of communities, house-holds, families, sub-cultures, neighbourhoods and regions, as enterprising selves, informed consumers, participants, empowered victims and respon-sible users of services. At worst we find ourselves in the truly demonic world of ethnic and religious tribalism and purity, of nationalism, zeno-phobia and racism. We find ourselves within and seek to govern something no longer quite the rational association of sovereign individuals nor the idyllic bonds of community. We seek to govern what, with Maffesoli (1990), can be called 'aggregations': the mobile, multiple, constructed, overlapping, transitory and a-logical nodes of attraction and repulsion with which we identify.

This chapter is a diagnosis of this present and its consequences for the discipline of sociology. Its thesis is not so much that of the end of the social as the death of society. By this I mean that, in at least one important version, liberal political reason and practice of government has found, for the first time in two centuries, a way in which society can be bypassed. For sociology, I ask, is there life beyond this death?

The rise of the social and sociology

The 'social' is a specific vector of our forms of knowledge, intervention and practices, of our ways of thinking about and acting upon ourselves and others, so that we might become certain types of people, engaged in certain kinds of conduct, inhabiting certain types of 'lifeworlds'. It is a complex and mobile assemblage of irreducible elements. It constitutes both a more or less organized and codified regime of institutional practices and an irreal domain shot through with all types of theories, programmes, plans and policies.[1] It generates relatively systematic ways of doing things yet remains an ideality, a set of discontinuous thought spaces. Here I seek to demon-strate only something of the instability and fractures of this composite character.

There is no single history of the social. Its genealogy shows it to have many sources, and to be composed of various elements and relations. Its story can be retold from different perspectives. For our purposes, we could begin to tell the story of the emergence of the social at any number of points.

We could begin with the notion of the citizen and his obligations and rights in classical antiquity. Citizenship, overtly in Imperial Rome but even in the Greek city-states, is limited and exclusionary. It belongs to the class of male notables who ruled the city and who were expected, as an expression of their nobility, to bestow gifts and benefactions upon it and its people ('bread and circuses') (Veyne, 1990). Citizenship is here based on a necessary exclusion, and the obligation to give and the rights to receive were limited to certain classes of persons even in the city itself. To receive in the late Empire, one had to belong to the *demos* (the people). This meant that one must not only come from a citizen family but also be a member of a recognized civic group. There were marks on the seats of the theatres and stadia for each of these groups (Brown, 1992: 85). We might note here that twentieth-century attempts to ground social welfare in a universal notion of citizenship (e.g. Marshall, 1963) have never quite succeeded in overcoming its limited and exclusive form as, indeed, feminists, among others, have shown (Pateman, 1988). Indeed the identification of the community of citizens with the nation-state has led to perhaps more virulent and aggressive systems of exclusions.

We might think a better source of the social lies in the history of the Hebraic–Christian pastorate, with its implicit universalism of souls, and the birth of almsgiving in the marginal communities of the ancient world (Brown, 1987; Foucault, 1988). Certainly we should not underplay the centrality of the history of almsgiving, and later of philanthropy, to the formation of the social, to notions of the universal bonds between individuals within a community and of the solidarity of rich and poor. It is possible that some of the difficulties associated with the ideal of a welfare state and the codification of the social in terms of the universal rights of citizenship might lie in the unholy attempt to marry the pastoral universalism of souls with the political model of the city and citizenship (Foucault, 1988). We might also note that there is nothing in contemporary liberal democracies that parallels an ethical culture that establishes either the obligation of the ruler as nourisher of the city in ancient Rome or the obligation of the almsgiver as sinner and penitent before God in Christianity (Dean, 1994b).

We might also take up this story of the rise of the social with the emergence in seventeenth-century Europe of a secular political rationality in 'reason of state' and in notions of 'police'. This is also the moment of the correlative birth of disciplines such as statistics (derived from the German *staatswissenschaften*, or sciences of the state), political arithmetic, political œconomy and *polizeiwissenschaft* (which might be translated as 'police science' or, better, 'policy science' or 'policy studies'). 'Reason of state' might be described as a secular, even atheist art of the government of the state, the aim of which is to reinforce the state against other states and against its own internal weakness, the aim of *security*. 'Reason of state' integrates both internal and external elements. Externally, it is concerned with maintaining and augmenting the strength of the state in relation to other states, with the diplomatic and military techniques crystallized on a European scale in the Treaty of Westphalia of 1648 after the Thirty Years War (Foucault, 1991: 23). Internally, it is concerned with augmenting the elements and forces that constitute the strength of the state. This internal set of techniques and the rationality they embody is called *police*. Police is *not* a police force, but a condition to be achieved in a well-governed state or community and the diverse means and regulations for achieving that condition (Knemeyer, 1980). Some police regulations are municipal and urban; others are concerned with the minutiae of manners, morals and civility. The important point here is that the police science situates itself in relation to a new object of knowledge and objective of government – the 'population' and what Delamare called 'men's happiness' (Pasquino, 1978).

This moment is also the birth of a secular government of the poor, of a police of the poor, in which 'the poor' is formed as a unified object of knowledge, subject to poor laws, to specific and secular regulation and provision, quite distinct from, but drawing on, the history of almsgiving (Dean, 1991: 53–67). Police and reason of state constitute a new kind of pastoral care in which all human individuals matter, but only in so far as they contribute, either positively or negatively, through their membership of industrious or idle populations, through their prosperity or discontent, to the strength of the state. In German cameralism (Small, 1909) and English 'national mercantilism' (Weber, 1927: 347–51) we witness the emergence of a concern with the commonwealth or 'commonweal' or the 'wealth, strength and greatness' of the state. For the cameralists, Albion Small wrote (1909: viii), the object was 'to show how the welfare of the state might be secured' given that 'the key . . . was revenue to supply the needs of the state'. Such a concern is linked to the forming of the population in a series of techniques for the calculation and comparison of the performance of states ranging from the balance of trade to the census.

Finally, we might begin with the liberal interrogation of the utopian pretensions of the ideal of a perfectly well policed state. Liberalism questions the possibility of fully knowing or completely determining the realities over which political sovereignty is exercised. It is first of all a 'critique of state reason' (Gordon, 1991: 15), a doctrine of limitation and wise restraint and an attempt to educate sovereigns about the limits of their power to know and to govern. It thus questions the identity of state reason and governmental reason characteristic of the conjunction of reason of state and police within European absolutism. Liberalism should thus be approached less as a theory, ideology, juridical philosophy of individual freedom or a set of policies, than as a 'rationally reflected way of doing things which functions as a principle and methods for the rationalisation of governmental practices' (Burchell, 1993: 269; Foucault, 1989: 110). The liberal space of government is one of constant and informed review of state practices. Liberalism is a polymorphous and permanent critique: of previous forms of government from which it seeks to demarcate itself; of contemporary forms it seeks to reform, rationalize and exhaustively review; and of potential forms it opposes on the ground of limiting abuses (Foucault, 1989: 113). However, liberalism retains the concern for security, as in Bentham's discussion of the ends of legislation (Dean, 1991: 187f). The liberal problem of security, as formulated by Bentham and his followers, is continuous with the 'holding out of the state' addressed by reason of state, but is located in a rather different field of visibility. Liberalism discards the 'police conception of order as a visible grid of communication' and affirms in its place the 'necessarily opaque, dense autonomous processes' of population, of economy and civil society, processes that it is necessary to enframe in mechanisms of security (Foucault, 1989: 114; Gordon, 1991: 20). Such mechanisms of security need to guard against the dangers posed by various disequilibria and crises caused by the rates of growth of population and subsistence, by the necessary decline in the rate of profit, by the conflicts between landlords, manufacturers and labourers, and by the political space as structured by liberalism itself. In regard to the latter, the mechanisms of security need to guard against the effects of liberal political culture itself, those that Hume had called 'enthusiasm' and 'faction', the latter the 'dangerous vice' that the American Federalists will declaim as corrupting to government (Burchell, 1991: 129; Hindess, 1996).

This brings us to a key aspect of liberalism. Starting with classical political economy of Smith and Ricardo, with Adam Ferguson's *Essay on the History of Civil Society*, and Malthus' essay on population, the art of government seeks to operate through positive knowledges of the domains to be governed: the *economy*, driven by the self-interested exchanges of the market; the *population*, regulated by the rates of growth of population and subsistence; and civil *society*, the 'self-rending unity' (Gordon, 1991: 22) of forces of order and dissolution, of egoism and sympathy, of unanimity and faction. These spheres establish certain types of free subjects whose action is necessary to the ends of government: the subject of interest, the subject of desire, the subject of need and the subject of opinion. However, liberalism will find great difficulties adjusting the action of these subjects and integrating these with the political and juridical sphere of sovereignty and the subject of right. It will find great difficulties in moderating and stabilizing the agencies it depends upon. These tricky adjustments and corrections are made, however, not directly through the exercise of sovereignty and by law but indirectly through a new kind of authority, the authority of expertise.

The liberal art of government is reducible neither to the legal structures and institutions of state sovereignty nor to the discovery of the quasi-natural market economy nor to the new realities of civil society. Rather it consists of the development of a technical form of government that seeks to adjust the relation between the security of the state and its political-legal sovereignty and the multiplicity of economic exchanges, the growth of population and its subsistence, the sympathetic bonds of human intercourse, and the political culture of public opinion. The end of security, however, presupposes the liberty of the governed. If economic processes depend on the economic subject, the laws of population on the prudential subject and the bonds of civil society on the ties of custom, habit, occupation, family and clan, then government must operate through the liberty – or rather, the liberties – of the governed. The liberal art of government then presupposes the naturally self-governing individual following interests, representing needs, calculating desires and expressing opinions as a component in any programme that seeks to ensure the security of the state. One consequence of this is that the exercise of these capacities becomes understood as corrupting of politics or of good government or as a threat to the interests of the community, as Barry Hindess shows (1996).

The liberal economy of government then not only prepares the way for a government of society and the production of knowledge of it. It establishes it as a necessity. The knowledges of society – from social economy, social physics and social statistics to criminology, educational psychology, sociology and beyond to feminism – become the 'dialogical partners' (Weir, 1996) of liberalism's process of self-review and self-renewal. Liberalism pre-structures the space of legitimate dissent. Social economy and social statistics can show that the economy is only self-regulating within certain parameters, that it results in urban misery, is subject to business cycles creating unemployment, and so on (Procacci, 1991). Experts on population, public health and social hygiene show that certain individuals imprudently procreate, that certain families are deficient in relation to norms of hygiene, domestic economy and health, and in the upbringing and education of their children. Still others demonstrate that certain individuals and groups do not possess the wherewithal to act as responsible citizens, that they form dogmatic opinions, wild enthusiasms and factions, that some do not have the mental capacities to make informed decisions, and that others are beyond rehabilitation and possess an intrinsic criminality (Pasquino, 1991).

From the mid-nineteenth century we see the emergence of a whole range of problematizations *within* the overall economy of this liberal governmental and institutional regime that have a kind of loose kinship. These occur about such concerns and themes as:

1 The *social question*: the health, living and urban conditions of the labouring classes, the elimination of pauperism and other social, political and moral evils.
2 *Social promotion*: the upbringing, health, security, sexuality and education of children, the position of women as housewives and mothers, and the family as a vehicle for social and economic aspirations.
3 *Social defence*: the defence of society by 'neutralizing' and eliminating the 'dangerous classes', the incorrigible delinquent, the recidivist, *homo criminalis*, the residuum etc.

4   *Social security*: securing society in matters of the economic and military
    efficiency of national population and even the 'race'.
5   *Social insurance*: the security of the population in relation to age,
    sickness, infirmity, unemployment, injury.

These questions are undertaken by agencies and figures whose expertise
is established in relation to such problems. Witness the emergence of the
statistical societies and the sanitary reform movement, the general practitioner, the social worker, the professional police officer, the child psychologist, the career public servant and so on. They are elaborated within a
range of new institutional or recently reformed institutional spaces – public
schools, juvenile courts, government departments, police stations, unemployment exchanges, wage-fixing tribunals, borstals, baby health and family
planning clinics, and so on.

These problems, agencies and authorities possess neither a necessary
coherence nor unity. However, from the late nineteenth to mid-twentieth
centuries, a common vocabulary was formed that sought both a general
codification of these problems as issues entailing the whole of society and a
way of articulating them with core values and norms. This vocabulary
sought to discover the means of translating the particular, the personal and
the private into the general, the public and the social. It sought to locate
the law, and the juridical subject of right and responsibility, as but one
region within the wider, concrete and more fundamental evolution of
society. It gave rise to a range of disciplines that more or less successfully
established themselves within universities and research institutions. These
included public health, sociology, welfare economics, social administration,
social work and social policy. Such disciplines made it possible to
understand all these previous developments as part of a unified process that
would culminate in a specific diagram of the operation of national governments – the 'welfare state', which was more an ethos or an ethical ideal,
than a set of completed or established institutions.

By the mid-twentieth century, the 'social' as conceived by this welfarist
vocabulary was formed as a domain of knowledge and interventions
around two poles, each of which possessed a distinctive rationality and set
of techniques (cf. Rose, 1993).

1   *Society*. Through this vocabulary it was possible to act not simply on
    particular problems but through them on to the bonds of solidarity and
    forces of division in society in such a way as to enhance the welfare of
    that population and to increase national security and prosperity. It was
    also necessary to defend society against social dangers and pathologies.
    Sociology is the key knowledge here. Consider the relation between
    Emile Durkheim's notion of social solidarity and *solidarisme*, Leon
    Bourgeois' official doctrine of the Third Republic (Donzelot, 1991: 172).
    We might call this the *solidarizing* pole, with its privileged instrument,
    social insurance, and with its goal of overcoming the threats to the
    security of the state raised by the factions, conflicts, egoisms and

fractures of civil society. The development of workers' compensation, with its collectivization of risk and 'de-dramatization' of social conflicts, can be viewed as a signal case of governmental techniques of this kind (Ewald, 1991).

2   The *individual*. The individual is known in relation to his or her place within society. This takes the form of his or her difference or deviation from a statistically produced norm, or in his or her deviancy defined in relation to a set of dynamic and even 'floating' social norms (Donzelot, 1979). The individual is made into a case. His or her dangerousness to society is to be neutralized. He or she is to be managed, counselled, rehabilitated and returned to the social domain. He or she, however, is also a responsible citizen, a contributor to national prosperity through paid or unpaid work, who pays debts and has obligations to society, and actively participates as a worker, voter, juror, taxpayer, mother and so on. This, then, is the individualizing pole of the welfarist codification of the social, one that finds its privileged techniques in the practice of social work case-work.

The ideal of a welfare state was an assemblage of unstable and heterogeneous elements. The Keynesian feedback loop between the economic and the social is only the most obvious. It is the one that will be exploited by 'neoliberal' and 'monetarist' arguments concerning the inflationary political cycle of the welfare state and the ungovernability of liberal democracies. There is also the attempt to fuse the care of the population – inherited from the Christian universalism of souls by way of philanthropy – with notions of citizenship, an irrevocably exclusionary status, within the liberal regime of security. Yet again, there are the difficulties inherent in an art of government that seeks to operate through and adjust the competing demands of the social subject with its needs, the prudential subject of desires, the economic subject of interest, with the juridical subject of right. The social was always then a hybrid assemblage of unstable elements. It was this instability that constituted the heart of the theoretical object of sociology – one conceived as the problem of anomie or alienation, of anti-social egoism and desires, of pathological forms of the division of labour, of dysfunctionality, of class conflict, or the lack of mutuality between the sexes, and so on. It is perhaps not surprising that liberal government would find a point of renewal in its constitutive resources: the self-determining person and self-governing community, the reflection on the limits to government and the invention of 'practices of freedom'. In this task of political invention, the distinctive problematic of sociology has not so much been called into question as ignored.

Practices of freedom after society

Since the 1960s and 1970s, the ways in which we think about governing in liberal democracies have changed. These changes are linked to the regimes of governmental practices that are the ground and the object of this thought. No longer do we think of government as an activity undertaken by the national state acting as a unified body upon and in defence of a unitary domain, society. No longer is the purpose of government conceived as securing the welfare of the population from the 'cradle to the grave'.

It would be mistaken, however, to imagine that this marks 'the end of the social'. There are still social workers, social security systems and even a proliferation of social policy specialists and case-managers. There are communities and community services engaged in seeking social justice and new kinds of social retribution and defence. The social remains as a domain of knowledge, intervention, practices and institutions, even if it has been reconfigured. Part of the resulting 'figuration' (Elias), however, is what I shall call the 'death of society'. In using this phrase I wish to suggest how this new regime of government no longer presupposes a unitary authoritative apparatus that acts upon the totality of a population within a territory coincident with the jurisdiction of the national state or upon persons as socially responsible citizens or social dangers. In this regime, the conventional domain of sociology has been outflanked rather than out-argued.

We could trace all of this to a number of critiques of the welfare state that had their origins in the 1960s. First, there were what might be called 'social movement' critiques of the welfare state. The welfare state was understood as a mechanism of social control, as a form of paternalism, relying on uniform provision which is bureaucratic, hierarchical, sometimes coercive and oppressive, and often unresponsive to the needs and differences of individuals and communities. Feminism and Marxism gave this critique a theoretical cast in the 1970s. The welfare state was shown to reproduce not only capitalist social relations but patriarchal divisions of labour and forms of dependency.

There were, secondly, the critiques of professions and expertise. The professions were said to be systems of exclusion, de-legitimating local, folk and alternative forms of knowledge, and de-skilling the population of its existing capacities. Feminism pressed for a new way of approaching issues of women's health. Theoretically it showed how the medical profession objectified and disciplined women's bodies in a patriarchal manner, excluded women as healers, and achieved dominance over female occupations such as nursing. What is at stake here is not merely professional accountability but a radical appropriation of control over one's own body and an assertion of autonomy and rights of self-determination within the doctor–patient or, more generally, professional–client relation. The feminist criticism of the medical profession is perhaps simply an exemplar of the critique of the formation of needs within the welfare state. As Yeatman has shown (1994: 106–10), the critique of professional domination thus makes way for a 'politics of need formation'. This occurs when various clientele of the welfare state – for example, those with disabilities, users of mental health services, and their carers – reveal that the construction of need is 'irreducibly multiple', appropriate the language of self-determination, and claim 'user's rights'. One consequence of this is that a 'politics of voice and representation' seeks to displace a welfare state held to be paternalistic.

Thirdly, there is also a renewal of what might be termed 'the culture of the self' and the elaboration of a set of techniques and tactics on the basis of this renewal. We might begin with 'counter-cultural movements', the mass experimentation in drugs among the young, and the importation of 'Eastern' religions, cults, healing practices, yoga, meditation and martial arts, and follow a strange path that unites self-improvement, jogging, gyms, body-building and even certain management philosophies. We might think of this as a kind of re-birth, or simply a massification, of the culture of self-emancipation and self-actualization. These movements, whether cultural or political, also start to renew the ways in which it is possible to act on oneself. They elaborate a whole series of techniques for self-actualization that will prove polyvalent in their application: techniques of consciousness raising, empowerment, self-esteem, alternative pedagogy, even of non-sexist and non-racist language, and so on.

While all this might seem peripheral, there is a point of intersection with neoliberal or neoconservative critiques of the welfare state in the new valorization of the self-actualized subject. Where the political and cultural movements sought a utopian vision of the emancipated self, however, the neoliberal critiques of the welfare state sought to redeploy the 'free subject' as a technical instrument in the achievement of governmental purposes and objectives.

Contemporary liberal rule, then, re-discovers freedom as a technical modality, and is able to translate roughly at least some of the concerns of social and cultural movements into its own vocabulary and set of practical formulae for the review, rationalization and renewal of governmental practice. It is worth drawing a set of contrasts between contemporary liberal practices of freedom and classical liberal modalities of government.

First, we can mark a difference in the conception of freedom. Freedom is no longer the freedom of the 'system of natural liberty' of Adam Smith but freedom as 'artefact' of Hayek (Burchell, 1993: 271). Freedom is no longer a natural attribute of *homo œconomicus*, the subject of interest, but something to be contrived as the free, entrepreneurial conduct of economically rational individuals.

Secondly, there is a difference in the conception of institutional design. With the German post-war *ordoliberalen*, for example, the market appears not as a set of natural relations but as something produced within definite political, social, legal and institutional conditions. The market is an 'artificial game of competitive freedom' undertaken under the legal guarantees and limits established by an institutional and juridical officialdom (Gordon, 1991: 41).

Thirdly, it follows that 'interests' themselves are reconceived. They do not reside in the nature of economic individuals but are something to be worked on and reshaped according to the requisites of government and policy oriented toward establishing the regime of a market economy. According to the 'vital policy' (*Vitalpolitik*) advocated by Alexander von Rüstow, for example, all aspects of life are to be reshaped according to the ethos of the enterprise. The Chicago School of Economics is even more radical on this point: it radically inverts, as it reactivates, *homo œconomicus* by displacing the subject of interest with 'manipulable man', the individual whose behaviour can be reshaped and made predictable within an indefinite extension of market rationality. Here, the individual will learn that freedom consists in not simply regarding oneself as an enterprise but becoming an entrepreneur of oneself and all the innate and acquired skills, talents and capacities that comprise what Gary C. Becker called 'human capital' (Gordon, 1991: 43–4).

Finally, contemporary rule in liberal democracies seeks to reinvent the notion of choice. This is especially the case with rational choice theory, public choice theory, agency theory and the new institutional economics. Choice here is no longer the rational response to the calculation of one's natural interest but a calculable element within the optimizing behaviour of individuals as workers, consumers and clients. Choice can be manipulated and produced by working on the conditions under which it is to be exercised. However, it over-rides and outflanks all arguments concerning social determination. If one should object that the determination of conduct by the embedding of market rationality in all spheres is just as much a danger as the totalitarianism of the state (Dean, 1994a: 193), the neoliberal economist might respond, as indeed do first-year sociology students, that the difference lies in the former involving the matter of individual choice. Collective beliefs and desires exist only as they are mediated by individual choice (Yeatman, 1995).

Contemporary rule in liberal democracies is composite, plural and multiform. It is reducible to no one single set of philosophical principles or one definite political ideology and should not be identified with a set of apparatuses. It operates rather through a multiplicity of 'practices of freedom', of ways of structuring, shaping, predicting and making calculable, the operation of choice. It operates by seeking to implant diagrams of free subjects produced by the theoretical knowledges mentioned above.

The full force of the term 'free subject' should be apparent: this is a subject (of need, desire, rights, interests, but above all, of choice) whose freedom is a condition of subjection. Subjection and 'subjectification' are laid upon one another. Each is a condition of the other. At one moment, they might be made identical (e.g. in disciplinary practices). At others, they are separated and made relatively autonomous (e.g. in practices of the self, in the entering of a contract) so that their relation becomes obscure and indistinct. Practices of rule in today's liberal democracies are 'practices of freedom' in the sense that there they continually associate and dissociate subjection and subjectification, domination and the fabrication of subjectivities. On the one hand they contract, consult, negotiate, create partnerships, even empower and activate forms of agency, liberty and choice of individuals, professionals, households, neighbourhoods and communities. On the other, they set norms of best practice, standards, benchmarks, performance indicators and quality controls to monitor, measure and render calculable the performance of these various agencies.

There are several features of these new regimes of government that are important to emphasize here: risk and its polysemous rationalities; the deployment of technologies of agency and performance; strategies of professional regulation and the related cultural and political pluralism.

The rationalities of risk

There is a certain affinity between contemporary liberal styles of rule and the rationalities and technologies of risk (cf. Rose, 1996). Risk is a polyvalent and polysemous vocabulary and set of practices and it would be premature to reduce the different risk rationalities and technologies to one another. For the purposes of the present discussion one can distinguish at least three types of risk rationality, calculation and technology.[2] Each depends on the calculation of probabilities or likelihood that certain harmful or dangerous events might occur.

1   *Insurantial risk* or actuarial risk. This type of risk is technically the 'actual value of a possible damage in a determined unit of time', although behind this idea are the notions of equity and justice. Each contributor to a common fund can expect a 'proportional share' according to his or her risk, that is the means of calculating the weight of the damage (Ewald, 1991: 205–6). This type of risk calculation is linked to a kind of biopolitical concern with populations in which individuality is formed relative to statistical norms of risk. What is insured is the human being as a form of capital against whose loss (of life, ability, health, employment etc.) the insurer offers a guarantee. As a technology insurantial risk is a way of collectivizing risk across the insured population. While this type of risk calculation and technology has a long history, recent liberal styles of rule represent a retraction of socialized risk techniques characteristic of the welfare state and a partial transformation of socialized actuarialism into privatized actuarialism (O'Malley, 1992).

2   *Case-management risk*. This kind of risk again has a long history. It is linked to a clinical practice in which certain symptoms lead to the imputation of dangerousness, such as the likelihood of a mentally ill person committing a violent act (Castel, 1991). Here risk concerns the qualitative assessment of individuals and groups, especially families, as falling within 'at risk' categories. Risk techniques are closely allied to the use of case-management in social security, social work, policing and the sphere of criminal justice. Those judged 'at risk' of being a danger to the wider community are subject to a range of therapeutic (counselling, self-help groups, support groups), repressive-disciplinary (prisons,

detention centres) and pedagogic-disciplinary (training and retraining) practices in an effort either to eliminate them completely from communal spaces (for example, by various forms of confinement) or to lower the dangers posed by their risk of alcoholism, drug dependency, sexual diseases, criminal behaviour, long-term unemployment, welfare dependency and so on. Rather than being replaced by newer risk technologies, we have witnessed something of a proliferation of case-management approaches beyond the older delineation of social work and clinical medicine – for example, as a response to structural unemployment in Australia and other OECD countries (Dean, 1995) or to dependency and the 'welfare mom' in the USA (Fraser and Gordon, 1994). This rationality makes possible a binding of case-management with disciplinary and sovereign practices.

3 *Epidemiological risk.* Here the calculus of risk is again undertaken on the basis of a range of abstract factors and their correlation within populations. Epidemiological risk can be linked to insurantial risk (health insurance, for example) but has its own distinctive rationality and techniques, as Lorna Weir has shown (1996). What is subject to risk calculation is not the loss of capital but the health outcomes of populations. The latter are detected by risk diagnostic techniques (antenatal records) and population screening techniques (blood tests, with their 'false positives'). It is not so much a displacement of clinical assessment and diagnosis with risk assessment, as an invasion of the clinical situation by risk diagnosis, and its combination with the preventive, 'systematic pre-detection' of populations in risk screening (Castel, 1991).

The point of coupling of risk technologies with contemporary formulae of rule might be described, after O'Malley (1992) and Rose (1996), as the New Prudentialism. Here, we witness the 'multiple responsibilization' of individuals, families, households and communities, for their own risks – of physical and mental ill health, of unemployment, of poverty in old age, of poor educational performance, of becoming victims of crime. Competition between public schools, private health insurance and superannuation schemes, community policing and 'neighbourhood watch' schemes, and so on, are all so many instances of contriving practices of freedom in which the responsibilities for risk minimization become a feature of the choices that are made by individuals, households and communities, as consumers, clients and users of services.

The New Prudentialism differs from older, nineteenth-century forms of prudentialism in a number of ways (cf. Rose, 1996: 342). It first of all multiplies the domains to be monitored and prudently managed. Early nineteenth-century Malthusianism added procreative prudence and independence from poor relief to earlier injunctions to industry, frugality in domestic economy and sobriety (Dean, 1991). Today the active citizen must add the monitoring of their risks of physical and mental ill-health, of sexual disease, of dependency (on drugs, alcohol, nicotine, welfare, or in personal relationships), or being a victim of crime, of lack of adequate resources in retirement, of their own and their children's education, of low self-esteem, and so on. Further, what is calculated is not the dangerousness of certain activities (gambling, drinking, poor hygiene), places (the alehouse, ghettos) and populations (the dangerous classes) but the risks that traverse each and every member of the population and which it is their individual and collective duty to control. Dangerousness is a qualitative judgement based on observable symptoms or empirical occurrences. Risk is both qualitative and quantitative; it is indicated by observable symptoms or by an invisible abstract correlation of factors. It does not divide populations by a single division (the dangerous classes versus the labouring classes) so much as follow the warp and weft of risk within a population. There are only 'at risk' groups, high and low risk groups. Some spaces and neighbourhoods, times of day and night, are inherently risky. Some are more risky than others. Risk, in this sense, never completely evaporates. It can be minimized, localized and avoided, but never dissipated. There are, it is true, sub-populations to be targeted, but the entire population remains the primary locus of risk.

One might want to talk about a division between *active citizens* (capable of managing their own risk) and *targeted populations* (disadvantaged groups, the 'at risk', the high risk) who require intervention in the management of risks. The crucial thing, however, is to realize that these are liminal categories marking a fluid threshold rather than a strict divide. Moreover, the New Prudentialism suggests, if not a new, at least an additional role for professions as calculators, managers and 'tutors of risk factors', taking on educative, estimative and preventive functions (cf. Rose, 1994b). The calculations of risk are intertwined with two different types of technology. One is invoked from below. The other, as it were, employed from above.

The technologies of agency

These are technologies of government that seek to enhance or deploy our possibilities of agency. There are two broad types of technologies of agency. The first comprises the extra-juridical and quasi-juridical proliferation of contract evidenced in the 'contracting-out' of formerly public services to private and community agencies, the agreements made by unemployed persons, learning contracts of schoolchildren, performance contracts between ministers and senior public servants, enterprise agreements, and so on. This proliferation of contract has been termed the New Contractualism (Yeatman, 1995). One of the key features of the logic of contractualization is that once its ethos of negotiated inter-subjectivity is accepted, then all criticism becomes simply a means to re-tooling and expanding the logic of contract.

The technologies of agency also comprise what Barbara Cruikshank (1993, 1994) has called 'technologies of citizenship', the multiple techniques of self-esteem, of empowerment and of consultation and negotiation, that are used in activities as diverse as community development, social and environmental impact studies, health promotion campaigns, teaching at all levels, community policing, the combating of various kinds of dependency and so on. These technologies of citizenship engage us as active and free citizens, as members of self-managing communities and organizations, and as agents capable of taking control of our own risks. All this is only dimly grasped in sociologists' relentless talk about recovering agency and grounding commitments in a theory of the subject, and in the celebration of resistance and the idolization of new social movements. Technologies of agency also include the instruments of 'voice' and 'representation' by which the claims of user groups can enter into the negotiation over needs (Yeatman, 1994: 110). This is not to cancel out agency but to seek to show how it is produced, how it is inserted in a system of purposes, and how it might overrun the limits established for it by a particular programme or even the strategic purposes of a regime of government.

Two points can be made here. First, these technologies of agency often come into play when certain individuals, groups and communities become what I have called targeted populations, that is, populations that manifest high risk, or are composed of individuals deemed at risk. Victims of crime, smokers, abused children, gay men, intravenous drug users, the unemployed, indigenous people, and so on, are all subject to these technologies of agency, the object being to transform their status, to make them active citizens capable, as individuals, of managing their own risk. Secondly, the two types of technologies of agency can be combined, for example, in the government of the unemployed (Dean, 1995). The long-term unemployed enter into agreements to subject themselves to technologies of citizenship (such as counselling to improve self-esteem, training to increase labour-market skills, etc.).

The advantage of this particular assemblage over earlier techniques of empowerment is that the contract (often underwritten with sovereign sanctions, e.g. the cutting-off of allowances, low grades, etc.) acts as a kind of 'obligatory passage point' (Callon, 1986: 196) through which individuals are required to agree to a range of normalizing, therapeutic and training measures designed to empower them, enhance their self-esteem, optimize their skills and entrepreneurship, and so on.

The technologies of performance

We are also witnessing a swarming of what I would like to call technologies of performance. These are the plural technologies of government designed to penetrate the institutional enclosures of professionals fostered under the welfare state and to subsume substantive domains of know-how and expertise (of the doctor, the nurse, the social worker, the school principal, the professor) to new formal calculative regimes. Here, the devolution of budgets, the setting of performance indicators, 'benchmarking', the establishment of markets in expertise and service provisions, the 'corporatization' and 'privatization' of formerly public services, and the contracting-out of services, are all more or less technical means for locking the moral and political requirements of the shaping of conduct into the optimization of performance. These technologies of performance, then, are utilized from above, as indirect means of regulating agencies at a distance, of transforming professionals into 'calculating individuals' within 'calculable spaces', subject to particular 'calculative regimes', to use Peter Miller's language (1992). Of great importance here is the explosion of audit first noted and analysed by Michael Power (1994). These technologies of performance present themselves as techniques of restoring trust (that is, accountability, transparency, democratic control) in the activities of firms, service providers, public services and professionals. As such, they presuppose a culture of mistrust in professions and institutions which they themselves contribute to, produce and intensify.

Strategies for professional regulation

This distinction between technologies of agency and technologies of performance allows us to examine two different but related strategies for the regulation of the activities of professionals, service providers, technicians and experts. This first strategy is what Miller and Rose have called 'government at a distance' (1990; Rose and Miller, 1992). It allows performance to dominate over agency and is, in this sense, utilized from 'above'. By deploying the technologies of agency, in particular the contract, this strategy seeks to establish institutional spaces – government departments, community organizations, hospital wards, service deliverers – as self-managed local centres. On the other hand, these local centres are to be self-surveilled and made accountable by the new technologies of performance that establish them as centres of calculation and subsume the substantive domains of expertise to new forms of formal rationality. It is a strategy that seeks to make these local centres into independent centres of budgetary calculation, or 'budget units' or 'cost units'. The regulation of services and the management of budgets of such units is undertaken by the polymorphism of the audit and various kinds of accounting.

Professionals are also regulated by a strategy that is deployed from below as it were. Here the language of sovereignty and its instruments are used. This takes the form of the enshrinement of 'user rights' in the internal regulation of government departments and the service providers (whether private for profit, or non-profit 'third' sector) with which they contract (Yeatman, 1994: 107). Needs formation is no longer a matter of the scientifically informed production of truth by professionals employed under the welfare state; it is allowed to enter into a space of negotiated settlement conducted in the name of user rights. From below, the agency and voice of users and carers enters into contestation with professional practice and knowledge. From above, user rights become the criteria for the evaluation of performance of professionals and a technique by which authorities can be open to a rich source of innovation and critical information about changing demographics, markets and environments. Further, the law, and particularly the fear of litigation, is deployed in a way that dovetails into the new emphasis on the rights of the clients and users of services as active citizens (Rose, 1996: 350–1).

A pluralisms of aggregations

Finally, I want to draw attention to the way in which all of this has led to a new kind of cultural and political pluralism. The targeted populations, through technologies of agency, can be empowered by, or enter into partnership with, professionals, bureaucrats and services providers. With the help of the markets in services, agencies and expertise, they are enjoined to manage their own 'communities', e.g. as gay men, ethnic groups, drug users, users of mental health services, victims of abuse and domestic violence, perpetrators of the same, and victims of violent crime. In place of a unified welfare state, we have a series of fragmented and discontinuous agencies. These may be public, quasi-autonomous, 'for profit', or from the rapidly expanding community or 'third sector'. All of these are agencies and specialists for dealing with targeted groups. They employ technologies of agency to transform 'at risk' and 'high risk' groups into active citizens. These citizens are to become self-managing, to enter into political partici-pation, and to demand action from governments. The eliciting of the participation of the 'gay community' in the fight against HIV/AIDS is perhaps a signal instance (Bartos, 1995). So too might be the way the victim status and the 'refusal of victimhood' have become a necessary component of our practices surrounding crime and punishment.

Community is quite evidently a key term in what I have just described (Rose, 1996). However, it is crucial to recognize that it is one among many second-order constructions of contemporary pluralism. Community, as much as the autonomous citizen, is a resultant of detailed work of political construction. It is an attempt to normalize particular sets of relations and practices, to transform local and transitory identifications into stable identities, and to establish relatively continuous regimes of authority. It works on the much more open and fluid identifications that characterize contemporary forms of sociality we have termed 'aggregations' (Maffesoli, 1990, 1991).

Indeed, nothing illustrates the death of society and the political construc-tion of community and its agency better than the sphere of criminal justice. There has been an extraordinary political reinstatement of victims of crime. The criminal is no longer the victim of environment, social conditions, or heredity, to be punished and rehabilitated and returned to society after paying his or her 'debt'. We have seen a kind of metamorphosis of *homo criminalis* discovered a century earlier by criminology (Pasquino, 1991). Now, however, criminal behaviour is simply a manifestation of a level of risk that exists within populations. *Homo criminalis* is an element within each and all, to be removed and contained, to be eliminated and neutralized, even, if possible, *before* its manifestation in crime. The victim of crime, however, now takes centre-stage. These victims need counselling and help (for example, post-traumatic stress counselling). They have failed to manage their own risk as individuals, as households and as neighbourhoods (O'Malley, 1992). Thus they need to be empowered, form support groups, acquire a political voice, reclaim risky times and spaces (feminist 'reclaim the night' marches, for example, and the use of private security firms, surveillance cameras, secure housing developments, 'neighbourhood watch' and 'community policing' schemes). The agency of victims is then mobilized (via 'victim support bureaus' and 'victim impact statements') to demand harsher penalties through such measures as 'truth in sentencing', 'three strikes legislation', and even, in the USA particularly, capital punishment. Our practices of punishment are no longer in the service of a social restitution in which justice is decided and regulated by the executive and juridical arms of the state. Rather, they are a contest between a criminal manifesting danger and a (politically constructed and institutionally supported) community at risk demanding a new form of retribution and a new type of social defence. The 'state' can then present itself as a neutralized and neutralizing referee in this contest. At least in this case, if not in others (the fight against AIDS, for example), the 'refusal of victimhood' would seem central to the political mobilization of the status of victims.

We have thus been enjoined and come to think of ourselves as self-managing individuals and communities, enterprising persons, active citizens, and as agentive members of a whole range of what Durkheim would have called 'intermediate groups' – households, families, work teams, associations, user groups and communities, rather than as members of a social and political community coincident with the national state. Now, however, these groups no longer stand as a mediation between Society and the Individual but as the plurality of agents that are constructed so that they might be put into play in diverse strategies of government. Government, if one likes, has become more multiple, diffuse, facilitative and empowering. It is also, however, strangely more disciplinary, stringent and punitive. The national state takes on less a directive and distributive role, and more a co-ordinative, arbitratory and preventive one.

Sociology after society

There is a case to be made not so much for the 'end of the social' as for the 'death of society'. We must no doubt understand this proposition in an entirely nominalistic fashion. What is called into question is not the empirical existence of societies but the notion of society as a particular thought complex within contemporary liberal ways of governing. 'Society' in this sense unifies the epistemological field over which authority is to be exercised. The historical and intellectual correlative of this unified object of knowledge is the claim to the monopoly of legitimate authority by the national state. This type of knowledge of society naturalizes the ultimate unity of power relations and its anchorage in the state and thus allows a codification of diverse practices, rationalities, techniques and ends of governing within a common political vocabulary. The death of this notion of society does not signal the end of the social or even sociality; in fact, it is a condition of the rediscovery of the multiple, reversible and loosely aggregated forms of sociality analysed by Maffesoli (1990, 1991).

The thesis I would finally like to advance can be expressed in three parts. First, for advanced liberal rule, we are ceasing to understand and act on ourselves as members of society, in which society is the totality of inter- actions and relations among a population existing within the territorially defined jurisdiction of a national government. We have ceased to act upon the social bonds that cement us into a collective totality through the agency of a unified social service animated by the ethos of the welfare state. Rather we seek to act upon ourselves and others as self-actualizing individuals moving within and between loose aggregations, as persons existing in intersubjective but a-logical relations of mutual adjustment, as professionals and workers, as service providers and consumers, as members of households, neighbourhoods, communities and regions.

Secondly, all this is both a condition and a consequence of a trans- formation in our regimes of government. We witness the utilization of two distinctive, yet intertwined technologies of government: technologies of agency, which seek to enhance and improve our capacities for partici- pation, agreement, and action; and technologies of performance in which these capacities are made calculable and comparable, so that they might be optimized. These two technologies are a part of a strategy in which our moral and political conduct is put into play as elements within systems of governmental purposes. Together these technologies seek a new linkage between the regulation of conduct and the technical requirements of the optimization of performance.

Third, these technologies form components of the assemblage of current governmental practices together with the polysemous rationality of risk. This assemblage is a condition of and conditioned by a form of pluralism that acts upon our loose forms of identification and aggregation to con- struct certain types of durable entities (communities, households, regions etc.) which discover themselves as social and political actors in partnership with markets in services and expertise.

This argument seems to suggest that the ethos of the 'welfare state' has been displaced by the ethos of 'performance government'. With the first, a unitary apparatus sought to act through and upon 'the social' to secure 'society'. With the latter, multiple agencies seek to put our actions into play so that they might be acted upon, rendered calculable and comparable, and so that we might optimize our capacities for performance as various types of persons and aggregations. Here the 'social' and its agencies (social workers, nurses, counsellors, community bodies, government departments, educational authorities, even social movements and support groups etc.) become our partners and facilitators, as well as being tutors in the multiple forms of risk to making the most of our lives, our skills and our capacities. Security – a key element within the liberal regime – becomes a matter of constructing centres of agency and activity, of making them durable, and of implanting continuous relations of authority. These centres are then placed under the discreet and indirect surveillance of regulatory authorities in order to normalize, stabilize and optimize activities, identities and power relations.

What, then, can be the tasks of sociology after society? The first, most grand, but perhaps least satisfying, one is to contribute to the task of political invention. In this regard, I wonder if there is not the possibility to construct a political rationality on the basis of this new regime of govern- mental practices that can translate the particular problems, struggles and actions of these plural agents and groups into a broader domain. I think we can hear the rumbling of such a rationality in the ceaseless calls for going beyond Left and Right, for rejecting both market- and state-based solutions. A key task of the social sciences, then, is one in which we try to find a way to produce a vocabulary, a mode of governance and a system of financing that can ensure the self-provision of communities and their associations, so that they might act upon and for themselves in ways that they feel necessary. This is the project of associationalism or associative democracy (Hirst, 1994). A central problem with this project, however, is that the looseness, transitory character and permeability of many contemporary forms of sociality do not fit the model of rational, durable association.

More modestly, but more in keeping with the project of sociology exemplified here, there is the task of *naming* and the recovery of the power of naming. This more than anything seems to account for the success of those who are defining the edge of contemporary social analysis – from, for example, Ulrich Beck's 'risk society' and 'sub-politics' (1994) to Michel Maffesoli's 'postmodern sociality' (1990). I have sought to provide a set of names for more humble and mundane features of our present that might prove useful in locating where we are. Naming is a key function of sociology as a contemporary form of *parrhesia*. To know how to act, we must know 'what's going on'. Yet it is crucial that we develop a language with which to engage our present. As parrhesiast, the sociologist is obliged to speak to the present in a way that might divide, if later to bind and cure (Flynn, 1988: 104).

Naming, then, is a prerequisite for *diagnostics*, for a symptomatic ana- lysis of the current situation, for the type of critical relation to 'presentism' found in thinkers as otherwise diverse as Benjamin, Elias, Foucault and Maffesoli (Dean, 1994a). It identifies the dangers the present holds and how they might be confronted, the crises that might emerge and how they might be resolved. For instance, there is little doubt that the impulsion toward local and tribal aggregation is also at work in reactive nationalism and in the reactivation of various programmes of ethnic and religious purity. Further, technologies of performance problematize the foundations of trust in public and private institutions, professions and knowledge.

In regard to such a task, I would suggest that it is certainly not possible to imagine a return to the ethos of the welfare state. We have come too far for the transformation sketched here to be reversed, as though all of this was merely the 'welfare state in crisis'. It is possible, however, to imagine a widespread rejection of the ethos of performance. This is manifest in its most immediate form in non-compliance and non-participation and in the more subtle form of hyper-compliance. There are signs that the crisis of trust cannot be resolved by the very technologies of accountability that elicit it. Witness the phenomenon of the 'audit expectations gap' (Power, 1994) and the rediscovery of ethical training as a component of professional education. A more radical opposition is, however, perhaps possible. If the ideal of a performance society is all speed and energy, competition and calculability, 'full of sound and fury signifying nothing', then it might be our duty to re-invent an art of living that valorizes slowness, deliberation, calmness, the reflective and the meditative, subtle techniques for the painstaking and infinite task of cooperation, of the care of ourselves and others, arts of friendship and bonds of sociality, collegiality and con-viviality – what might be called the 'arts of difference' or perhaps even an 'ethics of the aesthetic' (Maffesoli, 1991).

Perhaps after all we are simply witnessing a 'return to Greece' in diverse aspects of our political and ethical culture after a century or so of the preponderance of Judaic–Christian motifs. If this is the case, we need to realize that we can draw more from Hellenistic culture than just the image of the polis.

Notes

1 I have adapted the notion of an 'irreal' domain at the heart of the real from Maffesoli (1991: 12) and from Rose (1994a). Nikolas Rose's exploratory thesis (1996) on the death of the social and birth of community was published while the present chapter was in press. I have not been able to engage fully with his argument here and have chosen only to mark points of intersection.

2 I have excluded the kind of risk associated with nuclear, chemical, genetic and ecological 'mega-hazards' analysed by U. Beck precisely because these risks undo the basis of the calcula-tion and government of risk – they are global, they cannot be prepared for, they cannot be de-limited in time and space, and they undermine our means of calculation (Beck, 1992: 102).

References

Bartos, M. (1995) 'The queer excess of public health policy'. Unpublished paper delivered at the Sexuality and Medicine Conference, Melbourne, 6–9 July 1995.

Baudrillard, J. (1983) *In the Shadow of the Silent Majorities . . . or the End of the Social.* New York: Semiotext(e).

Beck, U. (1992) 'From industrial society to the risk society: questions of survival, social structure and ecological enlightenment', *Theory, Culture and Society*, 9: 97–123.

Beck, U. (1994) 'The reinvention of politics: towards a theory of reflexive modernisation', in U. Beck, A. Giddens and S. Lash, *Reflexive Modernisation: Politics, Traditions and Aesthetics in the Modern Social Order.* Cambridge (ed.): Polity Press.

Brown, P. (1987) 'Late antiquity', in P. Veyne (ed.), *A History of Private Life*, vol. 1 *From Pagan Rome to Byzantium.* Cambridge, MA: Belknap Press.

Brown, P. (1992) *Power and Persuasion in Late Antiquity: Towards a Christian Empire.* Madison, WI: University of Wisconsin Press.

Burchell, G. (1991) 'Peculiar interests: civil society and governing "The System of Natural Liberty"', in G. Burchell, C. Gordon and P. Miller (eds), *The Foucault Effect: Studies in Governmentality.* Brighton: Harvester Wheatsheaf.

Burchell, G. (1993) 'Liberal government and techniques of the self', *Economy and Society*, 22(3): 267–82.

Callon, M. (1986) 'Some elements of a sociology of translation: domestication of the scallops and the fishermen of St Brieuc Bay', in J. Law (ed.), *Power, Action and Belief: A New Sociology of Knowledge.* London: Routledge and Kegan Paul.

Castel, R. (1991) 'From dangerousness to risk', in G. Burchell, C. Gordon and P. Miller (eds), *The Foucault Effect: Studies in Governmentality.* Brighton: Harvester Wheatsheaf.

Cruikshank, B. (1993) 'Revolutions within: self-government and self-esteem', *Economy and Society*, 22(3): 327–44.

Cruikshank, B. (1994) 'The will to empower: technologies of citizenship and the war on poverty', *Socialist Review*, 23(4): 29–55.

Dean, M. (1991) *The Constitution of Poverty: Towards a Genealogy of Liberal Governance.* London: Routledge.

Dean, M. (1994a) *Critical and Effective Histories: Foucault's Methods and Historical Sociology.* London: Routledge.

Dean, M. (1994b) 'The genealogy of the gift in antiquity', *Australian Journal of Anthropology*, 5(3): 320–9.

Dean, M. (1994c) '"A social structure of many souls": moral regulation, government and self-formation', *Canadian Journal of Sociology*, 19(2): 145–68.

Dean, M. (1995) 'Governing the unemployed self in an active society', *Economy and Society*, 24(4): 559–83.

Dean, M. (1996) 'Foucault, government, and the enfolding of authority', in A. Barry, T. Osborne and N. Rose (eds), *Foucault and Political Reason.* London: UCL Press.

Deleuze, G. (1992) 'What is a *dispositif*?', in T.J. Armstrong (ed.), *Michel Foucault: Philosopher.* London: Harvester Wheatsheaf.

Donzelot, J. (1979) *The Policing of Families.* New York: Pantheon.

Donzelot, J. (1991) 'The mobilisation of society', in G. Burchell, C. Gordon and P. Miller (eds), *The Foucault Effect: Studies in Governmentality.* Brighton: Harvester Wheatsheaf.

Ewald, F. (1991) 'Insurance and risk', in G. Burchell, C. Gordon and P. Miller (eds), *The Foucault Effect: Studies in Governmentality.* Brighton: Harvester Wheatsheaf.

Flynn, T. (1988) 'Foucault as *parrhesiast*: his last course at the *Collège de France*', in J. Bernauer and D. Rasmussen (eds), *The Final Foucault.* Cambridge, MA: MIT Press.

Foucault, M. (1986) 'Kant on revolution and enlightenment', *Economy and Society* 15(1): 88–96.

Foucault, M. (1988) 'Politics and reason', in *Politics, Philosophy, Culture* (ed. L.D. Kritzman). New York: Routledge.

Foucault, M. (1989) *Resumé des cours.* Paris: Juilliard.

Foucault, M. (1991) 'Governmentality', in G. Burchell, C. Gordon and P. Miller (eds), *The Foucault Effect: Studies in Governmentality.* Brighton: Harvester Wheatsheaf.

Fraser, N. and Gordon, L. (1994) 'A genealogy of dependency: tracing a keyword of the U.S. Welfare State', *Signs*, 19(2): 309–36.

Gordon, C. (1991) 'Governmental rationality: an introduction', in G. Burchell, C. Gordon and P. Miller (eds), *The Foucault Effect: Studies in Governmentality*. Brighton: Harvester Wheatsheaf.

Habermas, J. (1987) *The Philosophical Discourse of Modernity*. Cambridge, MA: MIT Press.

Hindess, B. (1996) 'Fears of intrusion: anti-political motifs in Western political discourse', in A. Schedler (ed.), *The Politics of Anti-Politics*. London: Macmillan.

Hirst, P. (1994) *Associative Democracy: New Forms of Economic and Social Governance*. Cambridge: Polity Press.

Knemeyer, F-L. (1980) 'Polizei', *Economy and Society*, 9(2): 172–96.

Maffesoli, M. (1990) 'Post-modern sociality', *Telos*, 85: 89–92.

Maffesoli, M. (1991) 'The ethic of aesthetics', *Theory, Culture and Society*, 8: 7–20.

Marshall, T.H. (1963) 'Citizenship and social class', in *Sociology at the Crossroads and Other Essays*. London: Heinemann.

Miller, P. (1992) 'Accounting and objectivity: the invention of calculating selves and calculable spaces', *Annals of Scholarship*, 9(1/2): 61–86.

Miller, P. and Rose, N. (1990) 'Governing economic life', *Economy and Society*, 19(1): 1–31.

O'Malley, P. (1992) 'Risk, power and crime prevention', *Economy and Society*, 21(3): 252–75.

Pasquino, P. (1978) 'Theatricum politicum: the genealogy of capital – police and the state of prosperity', *Ideology and Consciousness*, 4: 41–54.

Pasquino, P. (1991) 'Criminology: the birth of a special knowledge', in G. Burchell, C. Gordon and P. Miller (eds), *The Foucault Effect: Studies in Governmentality*. Brighton: Harvester Wheatsheaf.

Pateman, C. (1988) 'The patriarchal welfare state', in *The Disorder of Women*. Cambridge: Polity Press.

Power, M. (1994) 'The audit society', in A. Hopwood and P. Miller (eds), *Accounting as Social and Institutional Practice*. Cambridge: Cambridge University Press.

Procacci, G. (1991) 'Social economy and the government of poverty', in G. Burchell, C. Gordon and P. Miller (eds), *The Foucault Effect: Studies in Governmentality*. Brighton: Harvester Wheatsheaf.

Rose, N. (1993) 'Government, authority and expertise in advanced liberalism', *Economy and Society*, 22(3): 283–99.

Rose, N. (1994a) 'Authority and the genealogy of subjectivity', in P. Heelas, P. Morris and S. Lash (eds), *De-Traditionalization: Authority and Self in an Age of Cultural Uncertainty*. Oxford: Basil Blackwell.

Rose, N. (1994b) 'The death of the social', in *Radically Rethinking Regulation* workshop, compiled by Mariana Valverde, Centre of Criminology, University of Toronto.

Rose, N. (1996) 'The death of the social? Re-figuring the territory of government', *Economy and Society*, 25(3): 327–56.

Rose, N. and Miller, P. (1992) 'Political power beyond the state: problematics of government', *British Journal of Sociology*, 43(2): 173–205.

Small, A. (1909) *The Cameralists*. Chicago: University of Chicago Press.

Smart, B. (1990) 'On the disorder of things: sociology, postmodernity, and "end of the social"', *Sociology*, 24(3): 397–416.

Veyne, P. (1990) *Bread and Circuses: Political Pluralism and Historical Sociology*. London: Allen Lane.

Weber, M. (1927) *General Economic History*. London: Allen Lane.

Weir, L. (1996) 'Recent developments in the government of pregnancy', *Economy and Society*, 25(3): 373–92.

Yeatman, A. (1994) *Postmodern Revisionings of the Political*. New York: Routledge.

Yeatman, A. (1995) 'Interpreting contemporary contractualism', in J. Boston (ed.), *The State under Contract*. Wellington, New Zealand: Bridget Williams Books.